Mighty Minorities?

Minorities in Early Christianity – Positions and Strategies

Essays in honour of
Jacob Jervell
on his 70th birthday
21 May 1995

Edited by

David Hellholm • Halvor Moxnes
Turid Karlsen Seim

SCANDINAVIAN UNIVERSITY PRESS
Oslo - Copenhagen - Stockholm - Boston

Scandinavian University Press (Universitetsforlaget AS),
P.O. Box 2959 Tøyen, N-0608 Oslo, Norway
Fax +47 22 57 53 53

Stockholm office
SCUP, Scandinavian University Press
P.O. Box 3255, S-103 65 Stockholm, Sweden
Fax +46 8 20 99 82

Copenhagen office
Scandinavian University Press AS
P.O. Box 54, DK-1002 København K, Denmark
Fax +45 33 32 05 70

Boston office
Scandinavian University Press North America
875 Massachusetts Ave., Ste. 84, Cambridge MA 02139, USA
Fax +1 617 354 68 75

© Scandinavian University Press (Universitetsforlaget AS),
Oslo 1995

ISBN 82-00-22451-1

All rights reserved. No part of this publication may be reproduced, stored in a retrieval
system, or transmitted, in any form or by any means, electronic, mechanical,
photocopying, recording, or other-wise, without the prior permission
of Scandinavian University Press. Enquiries should be sent to the Rights Department,
Scandinavian University Press, Oslo, at the address above.

The Laser fonts Super Hebrew, Symbol Greek and Coptic LS used to print parts of this
work are available from Linguist's Software, Inc., P.O. Box 580 Edmonds,
WA 98020-0580, USA (1-206-775-1130).

Typeset by Progressus Cunsultant KB (Christer D. Hellholm)
Jacket design: Astrid Elisabeth Jørgensen
Printed on Munken Print by Engers Boktrykkeri A/S, Norway 1995

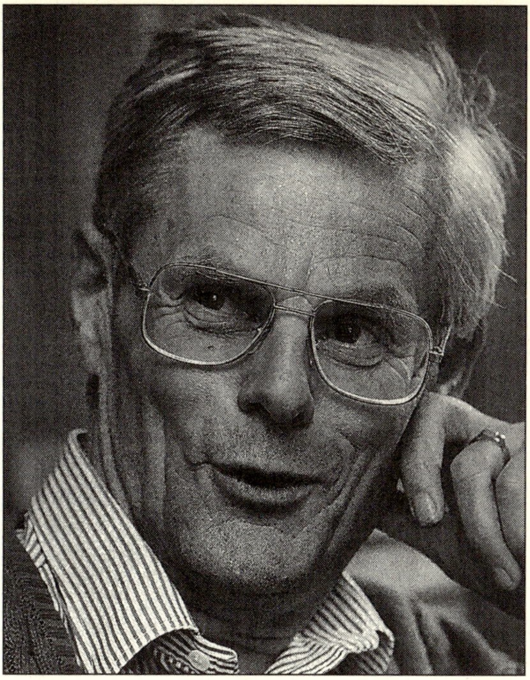

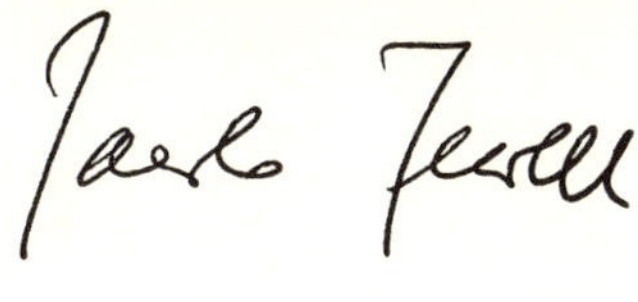

Preface

This collection of essays is dedicated to professor Jacob Jervell on the occasion of his 70th anniversary on 21 May 1995. With this collection we want to focus on Jacob Jervell's most significant contribution to New Testament scholarship: the rewriting of the history of earliest Christianity through a rereading of Acts. Jervell's main thesis is that the Jewish influence has been much more important and longlasting than earlier recognized. He bases his thesis particularly upon a new, careful reading of Acts. The first collection of essays pertaining to this question was published as *Luke and the People of God* (1972), followed by *The Unknown Paul. Essays on Luke-Acts and Early Christian History* (1984). The main substantiation of his thesis will be found in his large commentary on Acts, *Die Apostelgeschichte*, to be published shortly in German in the Meyer series. In English, there will be a shorter presentation in his *The Theology of the Acts of the Apostles* in the Cambridge New Testament Theology series (1995).

History of Early Christianity is only one of the areas within which Jacob Jervell has worked. He started with a major study of the use of Gen 1:26f. in Jewish, Gnostic and Pauline anthropology (*Imago Dei*, 1959), and has continued to write on Paul's theology over the years. He has also published books on the Historical Jesus and the theology of John's Gospel. As professor of New Testament at the Faculty of Theology in the University of Oslo from 1960 until 1988 he has been an enthusiastic and highly appreciated teacher of theological students.

Jacob Jervell's main challenge to New Testament scholarship is indicated by the title "Mighty Minorities?" that occurred for the first time in an article in *Studia Theologica* 34 (1980), the Nordic theological journal of which Jervell served as editor for many years. The contributions in this volume partly discuss Jervell's thesis, partly look at other aspects of minority groups within Early Christianity, or the first Christians as minorities within the larger Greco-Roman world.

David Hellholm • Halvor Moxnes • Turid Karlsen Seim

Table of Contents

Tabula Gratulatoria xi
Contributors xix
C. K. Barrett, What Minorities? 1
Adela Yarbro Collins, Mysteries in the Gospel of Mark 11
Lars Hartman, Humble and Confident. On the So-called
    Philosophers in Colossae 25
David Hellholm, The Mighty Minority of Gnostic Christians 41
Donald Juel, The Markan Community and the "Mighty Minority" . . . 67
Peter Lampe, An Early Christian Inscription in the Musei Capitolini . . 79
Edvin Larsson, How Mighty was the Mighty Minority? 93
Halvor Moxnes, "He saw that the city was full of idols" (Acts 17:16).
    Visualizing the World of the First Christians 107
Sigfred Pedersen, Israel als integrierter Teil der christlichen
    Hoffnung 133
Heikki Räisänen, The Clash Between Christian Styles of Life
    in the Book of Revelation 151
Turid Karlsen Seim, A Superior Minority? The Problem of Men's
    Headship in Ephesians 5 167
Gerd Theißen, Jünger als Gewalttäter (Mt 11,12f.; Lk 16,16).
    Der Stürmerspruch als Selbststigmatisierung einer
    Minorität 183
Stephen Wilson, The Apostate Minority 201
Svein Helge Birkeflet, Bibliography of Jacob Jervell's Scholarly
    Publications 213
Abbreviations 227
Index of passages 227

Tabula Gratulatoria

Agustín del Agua, Madrid
Lars Aejmelaeus, Helsingfors
Lars Alldén, Oslo
Kristian Alm, Hosle
Kirsten Elisabeth Almås, Trondheim
John Alsup, Austin, TX
Louise Alvik, Oslo
Tor Magnus Amble, Vikersund
Svein Andenæs, Oslo
Knut Andresen, Hamar
Ansgarskolen, Kristiansand
Øivind Berntzen Armann, Oslo
Ivar Asheim, Hosle
Tor Aurebekk, Kristiansand
Carl Jørgen Axelssen, Hamar
Michael Bachmann, Freiburg i Br.
Knut S. Bakken, Oslo
Turid Bakken, Oslo
Trond Bakkevig, Oslo
Baptistenes teologiske seminar, Stabekk
Baptistsamfundets teologiske seminarium, Tølløse
R. S. Barbour, Pitlochry
C. K. Barrett, Durham
Hans M. Barstad, Hokksund
Randi Bauer, Oslo

Pier Franco Beatrice, Padova
Hallvard Beck, Oslo
Ola Beisvåg, Oslo
Per Jarle Bekken, Oslo
Rolf Berg, Nesodden
Hans Dieter Betz, Chicago, IL
Johannes Beutler, S.J., Frankfurt am Main
Biblioteca del Seminario Arcivescovile di Milano
Per Bilde, Viby
Svein Helge Birkeflet, Oslo
Carl J. Bjerkelund, Oslo
Vemund Blomkvist, Oslo
Marie Rein Bore, Stavanger
Thor Bjarne Bore, Stavanger
Geir Sverre Braut, Stavanger
Vidar Aanund Brekke, Fyllingsdalen
Hans Bringeland, Bergen
Anne-Lise Brodtkorb, Høvik
Christian Brodtkorb, Høvik
Kristján Búason, Reykjavik
Bjørn Bue, Stavanger
Else-Marie Bue, Stavanger
Christoph Burchard, Heidelberg
Ulrich Busse, Duisburg
Kjell Olav Bø, Gerlingen

Kari Böckman, Trondheim
Peter Wilhelm Böckman,
  Trondheim
Jarl Bøhler, Bodø
Bodhild Baasland, Oslo
Ernst Baasland, Oslo
William S. Campbell, Birmingham
Donald A. Carson, Deerfield, IL
David Catchpole, Exeter
Britt Christoffersen, Oslo
Svein Aage Christoffersen, Oslo
Collège dominicain de philoso-
  phie et de théologie, Ottawa,
  ONT
Adela Yarbro Collins, Chicago, IL
John M. Court, Canterbury
Nils Alstrup Dahl, Oslo
Per Arne Dahl, Vikersund
Tor Edvin Dahl, Oslo
Anne Dalen, Skjetten
Ole Davidsen, Århus
Gunnar Danbolt, Bergen
Gerhard Dautzenberg, Giessen
Det Norske Bibelselskap, Oslo
Det praktisk-teologiske seminar,
  Oslo
Det teologiske fakultet,
  Universitetet i Oslo
Det teologiske fakultetsbibliotek,
  Universitetet i Oslo
Trond Skard Dokka, Oslo
Dominikanerinnene –
  Katarinahjemmet, Oslo
Dominikanerne, Oslo
Karl P. Donfried, Amherst, MA
Dennis C. Duling, Buffalo, NY
James D. G. Dunn, Durham

Gullaug Lereim Dybdahl,
  Trondheim
Ecole biblique et archéologique
  française, Jerusalem
Renate B. Eggen, Trondheim
Markus Bernt Eidsvig, Kloster-
  neuburg
Ingrid Lycke Ellingsen, Drammen
Terje Ellingsen, Drammen
E. Earle Ellis, Ft. Worth, TX
Hallgeir Elstad, Skedsmokorset
Siv Elstad, Skedsmokorset
Odd Erik Embretsen, Norbyhagen
Troels Engberg-Pedersen, Roskilde
Astrid Engen, Sandnes
Sverre Engen, Sandnes
Heidemarie Enger, Halden
Trond Enger, Halden
Eldon Jay Epp, Cleveland, OH
Anne Cecilie Eriksen, Moss
Claus Andreas Eriksen, Moss
Ellen Eriksen, Moss
Frode Eriksen, Moss
Hans Henrik Eriksen, Moss
Richard Eriksen, Skien
Craig A. Evans, Sumas, WA
Exegetiska institutionen vid Åbo
  Akademi, Åbo
Faculté autonome de théologie,
  Genève
Lone Fatum, København
Arne Fauske, Hundorp
Sonja Fauske, Hundorp
Arnfinn Fiskå, Stavanger
Arnhild Fjose, Nesodden
Leif Magne Flemmen, Sandefjord
Ole Jacob Flæten, Østre Gausdal

Tord Fornberg, Uppsala
Stein Eirik Foss, Bergen
Øyvind Foss, Stavanger
Jarl Fossum, Ann Arbor, MI
Jorun Fougner, Oslo
Ole Thorstein Fougner, Oslo
Daniel Fraikin, Kingston, ONT
Carin Selen Fribu, Gjøvik
Albert Fuchs, Linz
Kåre Fuglseth, Trondheim
Reginald H. Fuller, Richmond, VA
Berge Furre, Oslo
Ann-Marie Fæhn, Sandvika
Helge Fæhn, Sandvika
Geir Gallefoss, Landos
Carl Sitter Geving, Namsos
Heinz Giesen, Hennef
Michael Goulder, Birmingham
Lasse Gran, Lena
Leif Grane, København
David Granskou, Kimberley, ONT
Halvor Gregersen, Klavestad-
  haugen
Grenland familiekontor, Skien
Kjetil Hafstad, Fredrikstad
Anne Grete Hagen, Oslo
Per Halse, Hovdebygda
Karstein M. Hansen, Oslo
John S. Hanson, Silver Spring, MD
Christopher Hansteen, Skien
Inger-Lise Hansteen, Skien
Wolfgang Harnisch, Marburg
Lars Hartman, Uppsala
Jens Gabriel Hauge, Oslo
Martin Ravndal Hauge, Oslo
Frederick C. Hayes, O.F.M, East
  Aurora, NY

Gunnar Heiene, Oslo
Hans August Heier, Hølen
Geir Hellemo, Oslo
Ragnhild Hellemo, Oslo
Berit Hellholm, Hammarö
David Hellholm, Hammarö
Jan-Olav Henriksen, Ås
Per Jan Henriksen, Fredrikstad
Randi Henriksen, Fredrikstad
Dagny Herlofson, Arendal
Lai Herlofson, Arendal
James D. Hester, Redlands, CA
Georg Hille, Oslo
Egil Hjelde, Kristiansand
Turid Hoffart, Brumunddal
Paul Hoffmann, Bamberg
Karin-Helene Hognestad,
  Trondheim
Olav Hognestad, Trondheim
Cecilie Holdø, Moelv
Per Holdø, Moelv
Anders Mikal Holen, Stadsbygd
Ingunn Holen, Stadsbygd
Hans Jørgen Holm, Austmarka
Bengt Holmberg, Lund
Idar Magne Holme, Kristiansand
Stein Erik Horjen, Oslo
Pieter W. van der Horst, Utrecht
Morten Hansen Hunstad,
  Lierskogen
Reidar Hvalvik, Oslo
Leif Jørn Hvidsten, Hamar
Svein Hvile, Skårer
Hans Hübner, Göttingen
Johan B. Hygen, Oslo
Ragnhild Hygen, Oslo
Einar Ims, Billingstad

Institut des Sciences Bibliques,
  Lausanne
Tom Jacobs, S.J., Yogyakarta
Rolv Nøtvik Jakobsen, Trondheim
Roger Jensen, Oslo
Andrea Jervell, Jar
Anne Jervell, Jar
Stephan Jervell, Jar
Richard L. Jeske, Saratoga, CA
Robert Jewett, Evanston, IL
Hanne-Kirsti Joachimsen, Harstad
Kjell Joachimsen, Harstad
Erling Johansen, Spillum
Knut Erling Johansen, Snertingdal
Donald Juel, St. Paul, MN
Gunnar M. Karlsen, Oslo
Harry R. Kendall, Evanston, IL
Karl Kertelge, Münster
René Kieffer, Uppsala
Hanne Gebhardt Kleveland, Oslo
Knut A. Knudsen, Voss
Trygve Knutzen, Oslo
Robert A. Kraft, Philadelphia, PA
Karen Krogseth, Oslo
Otto Krogseth, Oslo
Carl W. Krohn-Hansen, Hamar
Gerd Krohn-Hansen, Hamar
Theo C. de Kruyf, Zeist
Hans Kvalbein, Sofiemyr
Robert W. Kvalvaag, Oslo
Ole Chr. M. Kvarme, Oslo
Viva Mørk Kvello, Longyearbyen
Rosemarie Köhn, Hamar
Sigurd Laland, Skien
Torstein Lalim, Drammen
Peter Lampe, Kiel
Ragnar Lange, Heimdal

Bente Bagger Larsen, Hjallerup
Jørgen Børglum Larsen, Hjallerup
Edvin Larsson, Uppsala
Michael Lattke, Brisbane
Aila Lauha, Helsinki
Risto Lauha, Helsinki
Paul Leer-Salvesen, Kristiansand
Oddbjørn Leirvik, Oslo
Ragnar Leivestad, Ås
Ole Petter Lerseth, Oslo
Inger Marie Lindboe, Hosle
Lars Gunnar Lingås, Oslo
Gunner Ljødal, Eidsvoll
Aasmund Ljønes, Slidre
W. R. G. Loader, Murdoch, WA
Kirsten Lunde, Asker
Aage Lunde, Asker
Hilde Lundquist, Spillum
Ulrich Luz, Bern
Leif Henrik Løkeberg, Levanger
Egil Lønmo, Vestmarka
Esther Sonderegger Lønmo,
  Vestmarka
Inge Lønning, Oslo
Kari Lønning, Oslo
Evald Lövestam, Lund
Maj Lövestam, Lund
Arne Løwe, Trondheim
Lars Mandrup, Århus
I. Howard Marshall, Aberdeen
J. Louis Martyn, Bethany, CT
Edgar V. McKnight, Greenville, SC
Wayne A. Meeks, Hamden, CT
Per-Arne Mehren, Askim
Kristin Stang Meløe, Moen
Helmut Merklein, Bonn
Anton Chr. Meyer, Landås

Magda Meyer, Landås
Oddvar M. Michaelsen, Landås
Caetano Minette de Tillesse, Fortaleza
Kari Sørheim Mjøs, Tromsdalen
Ole Danbolt Mjøs, Tromsdalen
Karin Moe, Valen
Vera Molland, Oslo
Elisabeth Eger Mollestad, Oslo
Kristian Vilhelm Mollestad, Oslo
Hugo Montgomery, Oslo
Ingun Montgomery, Oslo
C. F. D. Moule, Cambridge
Halvor Moxnes, Oslo
Robert Murray, S.J., London
Aage Müller-Nilssen, Oslo
Mogens Müller, København
Lars Helge Myrset, Stavanger
Sverre Møller, Trysil
Mark D. Nanos, Kansas City, MO
Inger Anne Naterstad, Oslo
Trygve Natvig, Bekkestua
Frans Neirynck, Leuven
Poul Nepper-Christensen, Århus
Anders Nielsen, Århus
Grethe Nielsen, Ottestad
Helge Kjær Nielsen, Aarhus
Kirsten Nielsen, Århus
Asbjørn Nilsen, Oslo
Knut Nilsen, Trondheim
Johannes Nissen, Århus
Bent Noack, Løgumkloster
Egil Stray Nordberg, Oslo
Kjellaug Anda Nordberg, Oslo
Lars-Erik Nordby, Fredrikstad
Per Anders Nordengen, Oslo
Kristin Molland Norderval, Oslo

Øyvind Norderval, Oslo
Norges kristelige studentforbund, Oslo
Norsk teologisk tidsskrift, Oslo
Birger Olsson, Lund
J. C. O'Neill, Edinburgh
Karen Onshuus, Flatåsen
Susan Oppegaard, Trondheim
Sven Oppegaard, Trondheim
Maja Osberg, Tønsberg
Sigurd Osberg, Tønsberg
Birger A. Pearson, Escalon, CA
Jon Helén Pedersen, Sogndal
Sigfred Pedersen, Århus
Richard I. Pervo, Evanston, IL
Aage Pilgaard, Århus
Hilleborg Poller, Oslo
Wiard Popkes, Hamburg
Præstehøjskolen, Løgumkloster
Ragnhild Radejko, Oslo
Trygve Ramberg, Oslo
Tarald Rasmussen, Oslo
Jon Even Redtrøen, Rygge
Kari Repstad, Kristiansand
Pål Repstad, Kristiansand
Martin Rese, Münster
John Reumann, Philadelphia, PA
Dagfinn Rian, Trondheim
Harald Riesenfeld, Uppsala
Morgan Rochstad, Oslo
Eugen Ruckstuhl, Luzern
Heikki Räisänen, Vantaa
Marit Rødningen, Haslemoen
Nils Aksel Røsæg, Eiksmarka
Øyvind Sagedal, Øyer
Jone Salomonsen, Oslo
Bjørn Gunnar Saltnes, Oslo

Arne Sand, Skedsmokorset
Kari Lise Brinch Sand, Skedsmokorset
Merete Sand, Alta
Signe Sandberg, Solheimsviken
Karl Gustav Sandelin, Åbo
Hildur Sander, Oslo
Jack T. Sanders, Eugene, OR
Karl Olav Sandnes, Oslo
Bjørn Helge Sandvei, Oslo
Bjørn Sandvik, Oslo
Sankt Andreas katolsk bibliotek, København
Akira Satake, Tokyo
Gerd Grønvold Saue, Ski
Erling Schau, Hamar
Jacques Schlosser, Strasbourg
David M. Scholer, Pasadena, CA
Jan Schumacher, Billingstad
Giuseppe Segalla, Padova
Turid Karlsen Seim, Oslo
Arvid I. Seines, Haslemoen
Claes Selim, Uppsala
Folker Siegert, Neuchâtel
Aud Sigurdsen, Oslo
Christina Sindre, Skarnes
Pål Sindre, Skarnes
Britt-Kirsten Skarpsno, Bekkestua
Oskar Skarsaune, Oslo
Gerd Skomsøy, Slependen
Børre Aa. Sneltorp, Krokelvdal
Graydon F. Snyder, Chicago, IL
Lisbeth Solberg, Oslo
Hans Kristian Solbu, Sakshaug
Yngve Solaas, Bekkestua
Ola Steinholt, Tromsø
Krister Stendahl, Cambridge, MA

Ingrid Stige, Skien
Tor Strandenæs, Stavanger
Peter Stuhlmacher, Tübingen
Gunnar Stålsett, Oslo
Sturla Stålsett, Oslo
Ove Kr. Sundberg, Fetsund
Jón Sveinbjørnsson, Reykjavik
Martin Synnes, Oslo
Terje Teksli, Hallingby
Teologiska institutionens bibliotek, Lund
Teologiska institutionens bibliotek, Uppsala
Mona Thelle, Oslo
Notto R. Thelle, Oslo
Gerd Theißen, Heidelberg
Dag Thorkildsen, Skjetten
Elling Tjønneland, Judaberg
Hanne Birgitte Sødal Tveito, Olso
Anne Tveter, Jar
Helene Tvinnereim, Landås
Ragnar Tvinnereim, Landås
Joseph B. Tyson, Dallas, TX
Bjørg Ulriksen, Åfjord
Einar A. Ulriksen, Åfjord
Universitetsbiblioteket, Oslo
Tor Vegge, Kristiansand
Kari Veiteberg, Trondheim
Per Voksø, Oslo
François Vouga, Bielefeld
Tor Øystein Vaaland, Hosle
Nikolaus Walter, Naumburg
Elin Wedege, Oslo
Nils-Petter Wedege, Oslo
Karl William Weyde, Oslo
Stephen Wilson, Ottawa, ONT
Mikael Winninge, Uppsala

Paul Erik Wirgenes, Oslo
N. T. Wright, Lichfield
Trygve Wyller, Fredrikstad
Walter Übelacker, Lund
Øivind Østang, Oslo
Arna Østnor, Oslo
Lars Østnor, Oslo
Jostein Ådna, Stavanger
Åpen kirkegruppe, Trondheim
Andreas Aarflot, Oslo
Hilde Marie Aarflot, Ås
Karna Aarflot, Oslo
Kirsti Aasen, Oslo
Reidar Aasgaard, Oslo

Contributors

C. K. Barrett
22 Rosemount
Plawsworth Road
Durham, DH1 5GA
England

Svein Helge Birkeflet
University of Oslo
Faculty Library
Faculty of Theology
P.O. Box 1023 Blindern
N–0315 Oslo
Norway

Adela Yarbro Collins
The Divinity School
Swift Hall
The University of Chicago
Chicago, IL 60637
USA

Lars Hartman
University of Uppsala
Department of Theology
P.O. Box 1604
S–751 46 Uppsala
Sweden

David Hellholm
University of Oslo
Institute for Biblical Studies
Faculty of Theology
P.O. Box 1023 Blindern
N–0315 Oslo
Norway

Donald Juel
Luther Seminary
2481 Como Avenue
St. Paul, MN 55108
USA

Peter Lampe
Theologische Fakultät
Christian-Albrechts-Universität
Leibniz-Straße N50a
D–24118 Kiel
Germany

Edvin Larsson
Tiundagatan 41
S–752 30 Uppsala
Sweden

Halvor Moxnes
University of Oslo
Institute for Biblical Studies
Faculty of Theology
P.O. Box 1023 Blindern
N–0315 Oslo
Norway

Stephen Wilson
Department of Religion
Carleton University
Ottawa, Ontario
Canada K1S 5B6

Sigfred Pedersen
University of Aarhus
Department of Biblical Studies
Faculty of Theology
DK–8000 Aarhus
Denmark

Heikki Räisänen
Department of Biblical Exegetics
P.O. Box 37
FIN–00014 University of Helsinki
Finland

Turid Karlsen Seim
University of Oslo
Institute for Biblical Studies
Faculty of Theology
P.O. Box 1023 Blindern
N–0315 Oslo
Norway

Gerd Theißen
Ruprecht-Karls-Universität
Wissenschaftlich-Theologisches
Seminar
Kisselgasse 1
D–69117 Heidelberg
Germany

What Minorities?

C. K. Barrett

It may seem paradoxical and indeed discourteous to accept, and to accept with great pleasure, the privilege of contributing to a number of *Studia Theologica* designed to honour one for whom I have the highest regard, and then to propose a brief study whose title sets a question mark against the theme not only of the Festschrift but of one of Professor Jervell's most notable essays, an essay from which every New Testament historian has much to learn. I have in fact more than one question in mind—and I shall be very happy if my questions provoke from Professor Jervell a vigorous reply that will make me think again.

My first question is one that may seem to be mere playing with words, though I think it is more than that. Is it possible in the period that we have in review—the first Christian century, let us say, especially A.D. 70-100—to identify minorities and majorities? It may be due to the relics of an original training in mathematics that I prefer to avoid such words as minority and majority when we have no numerical information. "We do not have exact figures for those years of Jewish and Gentile Christians."[1] The fact is that we do not have any figures at all, exact or approximate, for the period A.D. 70-100, of which Dr. Jervell is speaking in this sentence. Nor do we have exact figures for the earlier years. True, we have 3000 in Acts 2.41 and 5000 in Acts 4.4; but no one is likely to take these figures as exact, and Acts 6.7, with its πολὺς ὄχλος τῶν ἱερέων, contains no figures at all and is valueless from the numerical point of view—and perhaps from other points of view also. It may well be true (and this I presume is all that Dr. Jervell wishes to assert) that if the numbers of Jewish Christians and of Gentile Christians were plotted against years on the same piece of paper the curves would probably intersect at a point somewhere between A.D. 70 and 100; they would probably intersect a

---

1 J. Jervell, *The Unknown Paul* (Minneapolis, MN: Augsburg, 1984), 33, in the essay "The Mighty Minority".

number of times before the Gentile curve decisively took off and left the Jewish curve behind. This, however, would be an over-simplification. We should need a fresh sheet of paper for every centre of population; the rates of change would not everywhere be the same. This is not merely pernickety purism; it is one way of bringing out the fact that we know very little about the racial and social make-up of the earliest Christian churches. Even the interesting and important results of sociological study give us little that we can build on here. Recognition of our ignorance opens the way to further questions.

Indeed, one is tempted to throw a charge of paradox back at Professor Jervell. The theme of his essay on the Mighty Minority is that in the last decades of the century the influence of the Jewish Christians was out of all proportion to their numerical strength. He traces this influence in a series of fascinating studies. There is not only plain opposition to Paul, there is an effect upon Paul's own thinking: Paul's understanding of Israel and of Israel's destiny in Romans 9-11 is different from his earlier teaching. The influence persists and is to be traced in later books of the New Testament. Dr. Jervell sums up his argument:[2]

> The problem of the validity of the Mosaic torah and of Israel as the elected people of God dominates the apologetic in the controversies with the synagogue. We find this, inter alia, in the gospels of Matthew, Luke, and John. And precisely in the years from 70 to 100 we find a most lively discussion of the mission among Gentiles. Long ago the Gentile mission started and only after some years, especially between A.D. 70 and 100, do we find the discussion of how this mission can be understood theologically and justified. I can only see the *Sitz im Leben* for this lively discussion in what happened to the Jewish Christians after they had to live in Gentile surroundings, separated and isolated from their own people, still claiming to be Israel. Precisely in the years from A.D. 70 to 100 the Jewish influence in the church reaches its climax. This is not only due to the influx of Jewish thoughts and ideas, but also to literary influences. We can mention here the Letter to the Hebrews, the Apocalypse of John, and the first use of Jewish pseudepigrapha as Christian documents by the means of interpolation.

The paradox is clear: "Precisely in the years from A.D. 70 to l00 the Jewish influence in the church reaches its climax"—as the proportion of Jews to Gentiles decreases. It must be said at once that though paradoxical this is by no means impossible. Influence is not necessarily (though it

---

2 *Unknown Paul*, 39.

often is) proportionate to numerical strength. But ought we not at least to query the assumption (for assumption is what it appears to be) that this period of Jewish Christian influence is one in which Jewish Christians were in a diminishing minority? Perhaps we should question also the statement that Jewish Christians "had to live in Gentile surroundings". True, they no longer lived in Jerusalem.[3] But outside Jerusalem, outside Palestine, how greatly did their environment change? It is not easy to give a confident answer, and no doubt (if we had the evidence) every centre of population would call for a different answer. Where there is evidence, it seems that Jewish communities in Asia Minor led a stable existence, enjoying on the whole good relations with their Gentile neighbours. This has been demonstrated, for example, with regard to Sardis, where the fine and centrally situated synagogue survived till the seventh century.[4] This of course tells us nothing about the relation between Jewish Christians and Gentile Christians. There is no archaeological evidence for the existence of Christians in Sardis, but there is the literary evidence not only of Rev 3.1-6 but Melito's tract *On the Passover*. From the former little is to be deduced except on the basis of silence. The churches of Pergamum and Thyatira are warned against those who eat food sacrificed to idols and commit fornication. Those who do these things are presumably either Gentiles or Jews who have been infected by Gentile freedom; they do not observe the decree of Acts 15.29. There is no such complaint in the letter to Sardis. Melito's Homily however contains a vigorous attack on the Jews;[5] it was hardly written by a Jewish Christian, and does not suggest a mixed church with good relations between its Jewish and Gentile components. Much can happen in a hundred years.

Professor Jervell's discussion of the works he mentions in the passage quoted above are of great interest and for the most part convincing; the writings of the period A.D. 70-100 do show awareness of the problems that must have arisen in mixed, Jewish and Gentile, communities. We

---

3 Or at least not many of them did. For the continuation of Jewish practices in Jerusalem after A.D. 70, see K. W. Clark, "Worship in the Jerusalem Temple after A.D. 70", *NTS* 6 (1960), 269-80.
4 For a recent account see P. R. Trebilco, *Jewish Communities in Asia Minor*. SNTSMS 69 (Cambridge: Cambridge University Press 1991), 40-51, with his bibliography, especially A. T. Kraabel, *ANRW* 2.19.1 (Berlin/New York: de Gruyter 1979), 477-510. For Antioch see W. A. Meeks and R. L. Wilken, *Jews and Christians in Antioch*. SBL Sources 13 (Missoula, MT: Scholars Press 1978), especially p. 18.
5 See especially p. 72-99.

may take as perhaps the clearest examples Matthew and Acts. On Matthew: "We have in this gospel a clear antisynagogue sentiment *and* a preference for Jews".[6] Professor Jervell refers to 10.5f. ("Go nowhere among the Gentiles") and implies a reference to 28.19 as he makes the point that "the church behind the gospel in which it is said 'not a dot will pass from the law' (5.18), is a church for the Gentiles" (p. 47). In it Jews may live along with Gentiles because the old law is still valid, though it receives (in Matt 5-7) a new, true interpretation. It is "a mixed church with a mixed theology, in which the Jewish Christians played a dominant part" (p. 48).

A similarly pervasive influence is to be seen in Acts. Professor Jervell's two most important points refer to Luke's understanding of the church and to his portrait of Paul. "The church in Jerusalem lived in complete obedience to the law of Moses. The outcome was that the church in the beginning rejected any mission to the Gentiles, but God forced Peter to address the Gentiles and acknowledge them (Acts 10-11). The apostolic decree is in itself a manifestation of the law insofar as it expresses what the Mosaic torah (Leviticus 17-18) demands of Gentiles ..." (p. 40.) Most important is the Acts' picture of Paul, a law-observing Pharisee, "not the ex-Pharisee, because he remains a Pharisee after his conversion" (p. 41). This is correct observation (see Acts 23.6), but it is important to go a little further; for example in regard to Acts 21.21-24. Does this passage imply that "Paul teaches Jews and Jewish Christians in the diaspora to circumcise their children and observe the law"? (p. 41). It does not say so much; it goes no further than "Paul does not teach Jews and Jewish Christians not to circumcise their children and not to observe the law." He probably regarded such matters as adiaphora (Gal 6.15) and those who made a fuss about them as *weak*. This is probably the historical truth (if we may depend on Paul's letters) and may be what Luke intended; but it does not control the motivation behind Acts, in which Paul is on the whole represented as a law-abiding Jew. The Jewish Christians whose work Dr. Jervell sees in Acts represented him as conforming to their own position.[7]

There is much in this that is convincing and of the greatest value, and all must be grateful to Dr. Jervell (a mighty minority even on his own?) for emphasising these aspects of the Christian literature of the last third of the first century. Some questions however remain. Is the picture of

---

6 *The Unknown Paul*, 47.
7 See Romans 9-11; and in *Unknown Paul*, 41, 42.

Paul that has just been reviewed that which Jewish Christians wished to promote? It is not the picture with which they ultimately emerged from the dark period in which there is no evidence and only inferences are possible. A little later Paul will appear under the guise of Simon Magus, the origin of evil in the church. After the pairs, such as Cain and Abel, Esau and Jacob, have been listed the *Kerygmata of Peter* continues,

> He who follows this order can discern by whom Simon (= Paul), who as the first came before me to the Gentiles, was sent forth, and to whom I (= Peter) belong who appeared later than he did and came in upon him as light upon darkness, as knowledge upon ignorance, as healing upon sickness.[8]

This of course takes us beyond the period with which we are concerned. But we must ask whether Dr. Jervell's account of Matthew (for example) goes far enough.

Matthew's Jewish Christian attitude is painted in brighter colours in a recent book by M. D. Goulder,[9] a book to which I shall have occasion to return. Professor Goulder contrasts the attitude of Matthew, a "Petrine" gospel, with Mark, a "Pauline" gospel, with regard to the family of Jesus (pp. 8-15) and with regard to Peter himself (pp. 16-23). He contrasts the attitude to the Law of Matthew with that of Paul and Mark. "Disciples of Paul like Mark are a serious menace, suggesting that the food-laws have been abrogated, or the Fourth Commandment repealed. Nothing of the kind: the whole *Law and the Prophets* are valid, every *iota* ..., every crown on a letter, and they are valid *till heaven and earth pass away, till all is accomplished*. So teachers like Mark who go about *relaxing* even the least commandment (let alone the Ten Commandments!), and *teaching men so* in their Gospels, can hardly expect to go to heaven even; while people like Peter and James who have stood up for the validity of God's Law will be honoured there. The basis of religion is given by God in the first five books of the Bible, and of course this has to be kept" (p. 32). If Dr. Goulder is right, Matthew is much more aggressively anti-Pauline than Dr. Jervell allows. This tells us nothing about relative numbers; minorities are not infrequently aggressive. But Dr. Goulder's picture suggests a minority that is aware that it is losing, or is in danger of losing the battle, whereas Dr. Jervell suggests a minority that knows that it can and does exercise influence and is conscious of strength rather than weakness.

---

8   W. Schneemelcher, *New Testament Apocrypha*. Engl. ed. R. McL. Wilson, London 2nd. ed., 1991, Vol. 2 (Cambridge: James Clarke), 535 (= Clem. *Hom.* 2.17).
9   *A Tale of Two Missions* (London: SCM Press, 1994).

6   *Mighty Minorities*

If, when Matthew was written, there were those who defended the Law and believed that it was the business of Christians to observe it, there was a party which, without denying a kind of validity to the Law, opposed them, taking a view of the Law that superficially, but only superficially, resembled Paul's. The upholders of the Law are clearly in view in 1 Tim 1.7-10. They wish to be known as teachers of the Law (νομοδιδάσκαλοι), but they do not understand the Law or recognize that it is to be applied not to the virtuous but to those who need correction.[10] Legal controversies reappear in Tit 3.9, and in Tit 1.10 disorderly persons are found particularly among οἱ ἐκ τῆς περιτομῆς. These seem to be dissident members of the church and are therefore to be thought of as Jewish Christians. They are blamed (1.14) for giving heed to ἐντολαῖς ἀνθρώπων (cf. Mark 7.7).[11]

If we are to speak of majorities and minorities in the last decades of the first century we have a good deal of guessing to do, but there is no need to guess at the continuation of the controversies that marked Paul's career in the 40s and 50s,[12] though Acts itself suggests a context of consensus.[13] These observations are not contradictory; they are worth pursuing. Everyone knows that F. C. Baur based his understanding of early Christian history on the existence of controversy (if that is a strong enough word). Baur's account of the history has been widely abandoned; understandably, since Baur set it out in relation to the dates that he ascribed to New Testament documents. Since Baur's time many of these dates have been shown to be mistaken and with them Baur's whole view of New Testament history has been jettisoned—understandably, but in error. Baur was not the only scholar to observe the disputes that lie behind the New Testament; Lightfoot for example could see them too,[14] and Professor Goulder has now taken up the theme—exaggerating

---

10 If in v. 7 περὶ τίνων is taken as masculine rather than neuter there is an allusion to persons of whom the would-be νομοδιδάσκαλοι disapprove.
11 For ἐντολαί, F G have ἐντάλματα, possibly influenced by the Marcan passage.
12 See my "Pauline Controversies in the Post-Pauline Period", *NTS* 20 (1974), 229-45.
13 See my "Acts and Christian Consensus", *Context*. Festskrift til Peder Borgen (Trondheim: Tapir, 1988), 19-33.
14 See e.g. his *Galatians* (Grand Rapids, MI: Zondervan, 1957), 374; and cf. W. G. Kümmel, *Das Neue Testament im 20. Jahrhundert*. Stuttgarter Bibel-Studien 50 (Stuttgart: Katholisches Bibelwerk, 1970), 73: "... am Ende des 19. Jahrhunderts hatten sich diesem modifizierten Baurschen Geschichtsbild auch konservative Forscher wie ... J. B. Lightfoot angeschlossen."

it, I think, in places,[15] but demonstrating it convincingly. He recognizes Baur as a forerunner;[16] so also does Dr. Jervell,[17] though he makes the point that Baur's view of early Christian history is not that presented by Luke in Acts. Baur of course never claimed that it was.

I too believe that Baur was right in principle. The first age of Christianity was an age of conflict, and it is out of that conflict that the—more or less—settled church of the second century emerged. I am more than grateful for the version of Baur that Dr. Jervell and Dr. Goulder have given us. They are not, however, in full agreement with each other, and I am not in full agreement with either, indebted as I am to both. Dr. Jervell seems to me to have difficulty with Acts. Can Luke's evident enthusiasm for the Gentile mission be accounted for as bearing witness to the way in which the influential Jewish Christian minority found itself obliged to come to terms with the mission and at the same time impose its own conditions upon it? And was Luke subtle enough to invent a Pharisee Paul to gratify the Jewish Christians? or stupid enough not to see that they were foisting such a figure upon him? Acts is best explained as the honest but not always accurate product of an age of consensus,[18] written at a moment of peace when the old conflicts were no longer understood and new ones had not yet broken out. The point of principle over which I stumbled in Dr. Goulder's book is stated most plainly on pp. 8,9:

> The pillars had the authority of having been chosen by Jesus, and the authority of the Bible, which both sides agreed to be infallible; and in 48 they were running a scatter of churches with perhaps five thousand members, while Paul was pastor of a single church at Antioch with perhaps fifty. But Paul was better educated than they were, and he was a brilliant thinker; and he was possessed by an overmastering conviction that he was called by God. Convictions

---

15 For example, I do not think that Paul on his second mission "had to submit to the indignity of being supervised by a Jerusalem Christian, Silas" (p. 183). Is there any good reason for questioning the ἐπιλεξάμενος of Acts 15.40? Pages 70,71 are hardly strong enough. Or do we, with D, read ἐπιδεξάμενος?

16 "The theory I have proposed ... is not new in principle: it was in fact suggested in outline by Ferdinand Baur, Professor at Tübingen in Germany, in an article of 156 pages in 1831, and it was broadly accepted during most of the last century" (*A Tale*, 194). In this quotation the word *broadly* has to bear much weight; there was a good deal of opposition, especially perhaps in England, among those who had as well as those who had not read him.

17 "In spite of all criticism of Baur, especially with regard to Jewish Christianity after A.D. 70, his categories are still determinative—and rightly so" (*Unknown Paul*, 13).

18 See note 13.

8 *Mighty Minorities*

are always more powerful than institutions, and it was Paul who triumphed.[19]

Did Paul win? It is not only that institutions seem to have a good record against principles; we must not be misled by the number of Pauline epistles in the New Testament canon. Paul may have won in the long run (though that is questionable); in the short he did not.

The two main battles described within the New Testament itself are the affair at Antioch (Gal 2.11-18), of which Dr. Goulder (p. 3) says, "The Peter party, the *Petrines*, had won the round", and the council of Acts 15. Here (and this applies elsewhere also, where the story is not so clear) both Dr. Jervell and Dr. Goulder seem to have over-simplified the story— so too perhaps did Baur, whose long essay "Die Christuspartei in der korinthischen Gemeinde, der Gegensatz des petrinischen und paulini-schen Christenthums in der ältesten Kirche, der Apostel Paulus in Rom",[20] at least in its title omits one of the Corinthian parties. The earliest stages of conflict were fought out between not two but three groups. Of these, two groups, though they stood on opposite sides, both called themselves Hebrews (Ἑβραῖοι) and were radicals, though they stood at opposite ends of the spectrum. There was a Jerusalem group that used the title: they were Hebrews, Israelites, the seed of Abraham. They also spoke of themselves as servants of Christ (2 Cor 11.22,23); Paul denies them none of these titles, merely claiming that they applied to him also. He was more a servant of Christ than they, in that he had worked harder, suffered more. The irony with which Paul refers to them[21] identifies them with the similarly treated *pillars* of Galatians 2. But he too is a Hebrew; cf. also Phil 3.5.[22] By Ἑβραῖος Paul seems to mean one who is deeply concerned for the identity and destiny of his people, though it need not be said that he and James would understand the identity and destiny of the people of God in different ways. That they could understand and agree with each other, provided they went their separate ways, appears in Galatians 2, where Paul makes it clear that he will have no dealings with the false brothers whose aim was to bring his Gentiles Christians into slavery (Gal 2.4, ἵνα ἡμᾶς καταδουλώσουσιν) but was willing to accept the arrangement of two separate missions (2.7, 8). It was a

---

19 Cf. p. 3, "In the long run the Paulines won."
20 *Tübinger Zeitschrift für Theologie*, 1831, 61-206.
21 See my commentary on *The Second Epistle to the Corinthians* (London: Black, 1973), 278.
22 Cf. Rom. 11.1, where Paul does not use the word Hebrew; he is not dealing with opponents who used it.

superficially attractive arrangement, but it was bound to break down in a church with a mixed congregation, such as Antioch, and that it did break down is clear in Gal 2.11-14. It is also clear that there were Jewish Christians (false brothers, therefore claiming—though in Paul's opinion falsely—to be Christians) who insisted not only on food laws but on circumcision (2.3, 4). This insistence was to be found not only in Jerusalem but in Galatia also (6.12 et al.). There was, as Baur saw long ago,[23] no hope of full agreement between the radical left and the radical right. It may have been after the affair at Antioch that a centre party arose; according to Acts it had been in existence much earlier. At that earlier point (Acts 6.1) Luke calls them Hellenists, a word of no fixed meaning (cf. Acts 9.29; 11.20), and finds their founder in the martyred Stephen, a Jew of the Dispersion. There is no reason to doubt that this group existed; in some respects Jews of the Dispersion may have been easier to win for the new faith than Jews of Palestine. And the vacuum in the church called for filling. It was filled by Jews (and Gentiles, no doubt) who were prepared to compromise: No circumcision, but no offence at table to Jews who felt themselves obliged to observe the food laws; with complete repudiation of idolatry and loyalty to the one true Cod. This compromise, the "Apostolic Decree", is represented in Acts 15 as proposed by James, and not merely accepted but disseminated by Paul. It is certain not only that Paul in his extant correspondence does not mention the decree but that his teaching on food sacrificed to idols contradicts it. It is certain also that an influential party continued to assert the Law. As far as the New Testament goes it is unknown whether James accepted the Decree, but Hegesippus' account of his death represents him as venerated for his (Jewish) piety and righteousness (apud Eusebius, HE 2.23.4-18; cf. Josephus, Ant. 20.200f.

Paul did not win and James did not win. The centre party with their compromise Decree won. No doubt they began as a minority, but in the period A.D. 70-100 they were on the way to becoming a majority. It is their view of Paul that appears in Acts, where Paul is a kind of successor to the man whose death he approved (22.20); their Decree was recognized in the churches of Asia in which the Apocalypse circulated (Rev 2.14, 20) and became universal Christian practice.[24] In other respects too their understanding of Christian doctrine prevailed. It is hardly correct

---

23 James was prepared at most to tolerate Paul's mission to the Gentiles; he was not prepared to take part in it. See F. C. Baur, *Paulus* (Stuttgart, [1]1843, [2]1855), 125/142f.
24 See *Australian Biblical Review* 35 (1987), Special issue in Honour of Professor Eric Osborn, 54-59 (where there was space only for some of the evidence).

to call them (as Dr. Goulder does) "Petrines", for though they may have adopted Peter as a useful figure-head the man himself seems to have been too unstable and changeable to be a true leader; see Gal. 2.14 and other passages. This is a somewhat more complicated picture than the invaluable sketches drawn by Dr. Jervell and Dr. Goulder, but it seems to do more justice to the facts.[25]

---

25 Of these only a few have been mentioned here in what is no more than an attempt to enter into conversation with Professor Jervell. I hope to do more justice to the argument elsewhere.

Mysteries in the Gospel of Mark

Adela Yarbro Collins

Was the Gospel according to Mark written against a "mighty minority," Christian Jews who claimed the twelve as founders and Jerusalem as their center?[1] In this essay I would like to address this question by exploring the meaning of the "mystery of the kingdom of God," the identity of the mysterious young man who flees naked, and the reason why the Gospel ends the way it does. These topics may at first seem unrelated, but I will try to show that they each have profound significance for the meaning and purpose of the text as a whole.

In Mark 1:14-15, the teaching of Jesus is summarized as an announcement of the good news of God. This shorthand term is then explained as the proclamation that "the time is fulfilled and the kingdom of God has drawn near; repent and believe in the good news." The phrase "kingdom of God" appears again in the discussion of the purpose of the parables in 4:10 which reads, "When he was alone, those who were around him along with the twelve asked him about the parables." His answer is:

> *To you has been given the mystery (or secret) of the kingdom of God; but for those who are outside, everything comes in parables, in order that 'they may indeed look, but not see, and may indeed listen, but not understand; so that they may not turn again and be forgiven'* (4:11-12).

The tense of the verb "has been given" implies that the mystery of the kingdom of God was given to those "on the inside" at some time previously. The probable occasion is the telling of the parable of the sower. But even though the mystery has been *given*, it is clear that it has not yet been *comprehended* by the insiders, since they ask for an explanation of the parable.[2] But even when the parable is explained, the speech of Jesus

---

[1] I am happy to offer these reflections to Professor Jacob Jervell, who has taught us to think about early Christian history in new ways.

[2] Joel Marcus, *The Mystery of the Kingdom of God* (SBLDS 90; Atlanta, GA: Scholars Press, 1986), 70.

remains in large part figurative language. The fact that the explanation of the parable remains in large part behind an allegorical veil leads the audience to surmise that the mystery of the kingdom is explained more directly later in the Gospel.

Although the entire phrase "kingdom of God" does not appear between the summary of Jesus' message in chapter one and the discussion of the parables in chapter four, it seems to be significant that the notions of the kingdom, of Satan, and of speaking in parables all occur together, not only in the context of the parable of the sower in chapter four, but also in the Beelzebul controversy in chapter three. In chapter three, Jesus' rhetorical questions about Satan casting out Satan and a kingdom divided against itself are introduced with the words, "And he called them to him, and spoke to them in parables" (3:23). Thus the speech of Jesus about the kingdom in the first part of the Gospel is characterized as figurative speech, which conceals as much as it reveals.

Chapter four awakens the curiosity of the audience about the "mystery of the kingdom" which is obscurely hinted at in the discourse on parables. This curiosity leads to expectation for the revelation of the mystery. The clue as to where this occurs lies in the contrast between speech in parables and direct, plain speech. This contrast was well known in antiquity. Artemidorus, who wrote a work on the interpretation of dreams in the second century CE, stated that "The gods always speak the truth, but sometimes in simplicity (ἁπλῶς), sometimes in riddles (αἰνίσσονται)" (4.71).[3] An ancient reader familiar with this tradition may have perceived Jesus as a god walking the earth or as a prophet proclaiming and interpreting a message with a divine origin.

A contrast between figurative and simple or plain speech is made in chapter eight. After Peter's confession, Jesus began to teach them that the Son of Man must suffer, be killed, and rise from the dead (vs. 31). In the sentence immediately following, the narrator comments, "He said all this quite openly (παρρησίᾳ)." The use of this word, which is the opposite of "in parables" (ἐν παραβολαῖς), indicates that the necessity of the Messiah's suffering, death, and resurrection is the mystery of the kingdom of God.

The content or referent of the mystery of the kingdom of God is thus rather straightforward. Its reception, comprehension, and assimilation by human beings is another matter. According to chapter 4, those "outside" are given (only) speech in parables or riddles and are thus deliber-

---

3   See also John 16:25-29; *Epistle to Diognetus* 11:2.

ately prevented from receiving the mystery of the kingdom. This process occurs in accordance with the divine will, prophesied in Scripture and executed by Jesus.

What I would like to do now is clarify what Mark has to say about the human reception of this divine revelation by looking at some ideas and procedures that he has in common with the apostle Paul and by suggesting how Mark's use of older Scripture illuminates his own theological perspective.

In speaking about how the parables work for outsiders, Mark cites Isaiah 6:9-10, the words that Isaiah is supposed to say to the people of Judah. The context shows that the divine plan is to prevent repentance, because the Lord has determined to judge the people, "Until cities lie waste without inhabitant" (vs. 11). This passage was used by Paul to explain why the majority of the people of Israel did not accept Jesus as the Messiah (Rom 11:7-8). Mark uses the passage to characterize divine treatment of "those outside."

One of the mysteries of the Gospel of Mark itself, however, is that the qualities of figurative blindness and deafness attributed to the "outsiders" here are also attributed to "insiders" elsewhere in the Gospel. Mark does this by use of the motif of hardening, an image that Paul also used. As noted earlier, Paul cites the same passage from Isaiah that is cited in Mark 4. Paul prefaces the quotation with the remark, "Israel failed to obtain what it was seeking. The elect obtained it, but the rest were hardened" (Rom 11:7). The remark about hardening recalls an earlier passage in the letter, in which Paul states "For the scripture says to Pharaoh, 'I have raised you up for the very purpose of showing my power in you, so that my name may be proclaimed in all the earth.' So then he has mercy on whomever he wishes, and he hardens the heart of whomever he wishes" (Rom 9:17-18).

The first time that Mark uses the notion of hardening, he uses it in a similar way. In the story about the man with a withered hand in chapter three, Jesus is said to be both angry and grieved at the hardness of heart of those waiting to accuse him for healing on the sabbath. The anger and grief of Jesus may be understood either as directed against these opponents for their culpable decision to oppose him, or as an all too human, but temporary resistance to the will of God, analogous to the distress he will suffer in Gethsemane. This ambiguity is due to an analogous, traditional ambiguity in the notion of hardening, which goes back to the book of Exodus, which, as we have seen, Paul cites in Romans 9. In Exodus, God reveals to Moses, "I will harden his heart, so that he will not let the people go" (Exod 4:21). But the narrator nevertheless later says, "But when Pharaoh saw that the rain and the hail and the thunder had ceased, he sinned once more and hardened his heart, he and his officials. So the heart of Pharaoh was hardened, and he would not let the Israelites go, just as the Lord had spoken through Moses" (Exod 9:34-35). The hardening of Pharaoh's heart is both a divine act and a culpable decision made by Pharaoh himself.

Whereas the motif of hardening appears for the first time in Mark as a characteristic of the opponents of Jesus, the next time that the notion appears, it is associated with the disciples. This second occurrence is in the conclusion to the story in chapter six in which Jesus walks on the water and appears to the disciples as they struggle in a boat against the wind.[4] This story in Mark has important conceptual and verbal similarities with the ninth chapter of the book of Job, in which Job disputes the possibility of a theophany, that is, of the revelation of the divine nature or presence to humanity. Even if God passes by a human being, he or she could not perceive God's presence. Mark seems to be making an analogous point. His perspective is more evident in comparison with Matthew. Matthew ends his version of the story with the disciples' acclamation, "Truly you are the Son of God" (Matt 14:33). This is the typical, expected ending of a miracle story in general and of an epiphany in particular. Mark ends his story instead with the remark "And they were utterly astounded, for they did not understand about the loaves, but their hearts were hardened" (Mark 6:51-52). The parallel with Job suggests that we should not interpret the narrator's remark as a simple condemnation of the disciples for their obstinacy and sinful refusal to understand about the loaves, and, implicitly, about the walking on the water and the epiphany. They may be culpable, but there is a divine mystery at work as well. In light of the scriptural tradition in Exodus, which apparently was well known and frequently cited by early Christians, the reader should understand that it is God who has hardened the hearts of the disciples.

The motif of hardening appears again in the third boat scene, in which Jesus asks the disciples, "Why are you talking about having no bread? Do you not perceive or understand (συνίετε)?" (Mark 8:17). This

---

4 For a more detailed presentation of the argument summarized here, see Adela Yarbro Collins, "Rulers, Divine Men, and Walking on the Water (Mark 6:45-52)," in *Religious Propaganda and Missionary Competition in the New Testament World: Essays Honoring Dieter Georgi*, ed. L. Bormann, K. Del Tredici, and A. Standhartinger (NT.S 74; Leiden: Brill, 1994), 207-27.

question recalls the citation of Isaiah in 4:12, "in order that 'they may indeed look, but not see, and may indeed listen, but not understand (συνιῶσιν).'" Jesus asks a further question in the boat scene, "Are your hearts hardened?" (8:17). This question recalls the ending of the story in which Jesus walks on the water. The next question posed by Jesus is based on a passage in Jeremiah, but it is very similar in wording and perspective to the citation of Isaiah in chapter 4. It reads, "Do you have eyes and fail to see? Do you have ears and fail to hear?" (compare Jer 5:21). The context of the Jeremiah passage puts more responsibility on the people for their lack of understanding: they have a stubborn and rebellious heart. They are aware of God's power over (the) Sea, but this awareness does not lead to fear of the Lord (Jer 5:22-24). The responsibility need not be seen as simple or total, since, as Ezekiel and the author of 4 Ezra point out, God created humanity with a stony heart or an evil inclination.

The inability of the disciples to see the significance of Jesus' deeds is contrasted ironically with Jesus' ability to give sight to the blind man of Bethsaida, in the pericope that follows immediately. This miracle story introduces the middle section of Mark in which Jesus teaches the disciples repeatedly about his passion and about discipleship as sharing in it. This section ends with the healing of blind Bartimaeus, who again contrasts ironically with the disciples. Even while his physical eyes do not yet see, he "sees" that Jesus is the Son of David. That his understanding of Jesus' identity is not perfect becomes clear later in the narrative when Jesus disputes the idea that the Messiah is David's son. Nevertheless, he is able to follow Jesus "on the way." The narrator's comment, that he so follows Jesus, probably implies a deeper commitment than simply going along to see what will happen next.

Returning to the third boat scene in chapter 8, Jesus' question, "Do you have ears, and fail to hear?" recalls the healing of the deaf man in 7:31-37. The intertextual relationship with Jeremiah suggests that the mighty deeds of Jesus, healing deafness and blindness and multiplying the loaves, are analogous to God's victory over Sea. The response of the disciples is analogous to that of the people of Judah: the mighty deeds do not lead to the expected and proper response.[5]

Mark's use of the motifs of divine hardening and divine infliction of spiritual blindness and deafness implies that human nature is not capable of responding in the appropriate way to divine revelation. To a

---

5 Contrast the interpretation of Robert Tannehill, "The Disciples in Mark: The Function of a Narrative Role," *JR* 57 (1977), 400.

degree, the failure to respond is culpable. But, paradoxically, the human inability to respond is the result of divine activity. The only aspect of the Markan view of the interaction between the divine and the human that prevents despair is that the divine power continues to reach out and to engage the human world. I will return to this paradox when I try to explain why the Gospel ends the way it does.

But first I would like to turn to one of the most mysterious passages in Mark, mysterious in a different way. After Jesus was arrested, all of the disciples deserted him and fled. After making this remark, the narrator goes on, "And a certain young man was following him, wearing nothing but a linen cloth. They arrested him, but he left the linen cloth and fled naked" (14:51-52). The traditional interpretation is that this is the kind of detail that only an eye-witness could provide.[6] Some who hold this to be the testimony of an eye-witness also think that the young man was Mark himself, who inserted this cameo appearance as his signature, so to speak.[7] The main problem with this theory is that eye-witness testimony is usually introduced with some comment emphasizing its significance as such, for example, the remark about the one who saw the blood and water pour out of the side of Jesus in the crucifixion account in the Gospel of John (18:34-35). Thus the purpose of the evangelist in introducing the incident does not seem to be authorization of the text through the testimony of an eye-witness.

Further, the brief account is not well integrated into the narrative in a realistic manner. Why is he dressed in such a peculiar way, or rather nearly undressed? Why is he the only follower of Jesus who is seized by the arresting party? The text gives no clues about the answers to such questions.[8] This lack of historical verisimilitude has led to the conclusion that the young man is a fictional character, created to make a symbolic or metaphorical point.

For example, Frank Kermode, in his book *The Genesis of Secrecy*, argued that the young man's appearance represents the kind of random

---

6 For a list of commentators who hold that this passage reflects an actual incident, see Robin Scroggs and Kent I. Groff, "Baptism in Mark: Dying and Rising with Christ," *JBL* 92 (1973), 531, n. 1. See also the theories discussed by Albert Vanhoye, "La fuite du jeune homme nu (Mc 14,51-52)," *Bib* 52 (1971), 402.

7 For references, see Scroggs and Groff, "Baptism in Mark," 531, n. 2; Vanhoye, "La fuite du jeune homme," *Bib* 52 402, n. 1. Steven R. Johnson argues that the author has placed himself in the narrative as a young man who was a close follower of Jesus; the young man is both the paradigmatic disciple and the implied author; idem, "The Identity and Significance of the Neaniskos in Mark," *Forum* 8 (1992), 123-39.

event that characterizes ordinary experience and is analogous to the man in the macintosh in James Joyce's *Ulysses*, who just keeps popping up, although he has no significant narrative role.[9] This is an intriguing suggestion, but such a narrative device seems too modern and does not receive support from Mark's style elsewhere.

Nevertheless, the argument that the young man is a fictional, symbolic character is persuasive. One must ask, however, what the symbolic significance of the incident may have been in the original cultural context in which the Gospel was written. One possibility is that this short scene was introduced to depict the fulfillment of a prophecy recorded by Amos:

> *But you made the nazirites drink wine, and commanded the prophets, saying, "You shall not prophesy." So, I will press you down in your place, just as a cart presses down when it is full of sheaves. Flight shall perish from the swift, and the strong shall not retain their strength, nor shall the mighty save their lives; those who handle the bow shall not stand, and those who are swift of foot shall not save themselves, nor shall those who ride horses save their lives; and those who are stout of heart among the mighty shall flee away naked in that day, says the Lord.* (Amos 2:12-16)[10]

In favor of this interpretation is the fact that the passion narrative contains many allusions to Scripture with the implication that prophecy is being fulfilled in the events narrated. Against this solution, however, is

---

8 In 1958 at the Greek Orthodox monastery of Mar Saba, an eighteenth century copy of a fragment from a letter of Clement of Alexandria was discovered, which contains quotations from a work which Clement describes as a falsified version of a secret Gospel of Mark. This fragment, which was published in 1973, contains a passage which is said to have followed Mark 10:34 and which tells how Jesus raised a young man (νεανίσκος) from the dead and taught him the mystery of the kingdom of God. The question of the relation of this text to Mark 14:51-52 is unfortunately beyond the scope of this essay; see Hans-Martin Schenke, "The Mystery of the Gospel of Mark," *SecCen* 4 (1984), 65-82; Marvin W. Meyer, "The Youth in the Secret Gospel of Mark," *Semeia* 49 (1990), 129-53; idem, "The Youth in Secret Mark and the Beloved Disciple in John," *Gospel Origins and Christian Beginnings: In Honor of James M. Robinson* (ed. J. E. Goehring et al.; Sonoma, CA: Polebridge, 1990), 94-105.

9 Frank Kermode, *The Genesis of Secrecy: On the Interpretation of Narrative* (Cambridge, MA/London: Harvard University Press, 1979).

10 For discussions of this hypothesis, see Vanhoye, "La fuite du jeune homme," 403; John Knox, "A Note on Mark 14:51-52," in *The Joy of Study: Papers on New Testament and Related Subjects Presented to Honor Frederick Clifton Grant*, ed. S. E. Johnson (New York: Macmillan, 1951), 28; Herman Waetjen, "The Ending of Mark and the Gospel's Shift in Eschatology," *ASTI* 4 (1965), 117-18.

18   *Mighty Minorities*

the fact that there is no indication that the young man is particularly mighty or stout of heart.

A popular solution is the argument that the scene is added as a concrete illustration of the general flight of the disciples. The young man's nakedness emphasizes the shamefulness of his flight.[11] Support for this hypothesis may be found in the relationship between the warnings in chapter 13 and the failure of the disciples to heed them in the account of the passion. The warnings in Mark 13 consist of admonitions to keep awake and to watch. There is an interesting analogy in the book of Revelation:

> *See, I am coming like a thief! Blessed is the one who stays awake and is clothed, not going about naked and exposed to shame.* (Rev 16:15)

The author of Mark may have been familiar with such a saying and created the incident about the young man as a cautionary tale. But this interpretation does not take into account the way in which this short narrative foreshadows subsequent events in the Gospel. Furthermore, if it is recognized that public nakedness is indeed shameful in Hebrew and Jewish tradition, but not necessarily so in a wider Hellenistic context, interesting alternative interpretations become possible.[12]

The foreshadowing occurs through the use of the words "linen cloth" (σινδών) and "young man" (νεανίσκος). Each word occurs only in this passage and once more later in the passion narrative. The word "linen cloth" occurs in the story of Jesus' burial. Joseph of Arimathea wraps Jesus's body in a linen cloth before placing it in the tomb (15:46). It is a "young man" who announces the resurrection of Jesus to the women in the empty tomb (16:5).

Many scholars understand the young man in the tomb to be an angel. It is common, especially in Hebrew and Aramaic, but also in Jewish and Christian Greek texts, for an angel to be referred to as a "man" or a "young man."[13] Furthermore, he is said to be wearing a white robe, which belongs to the typical wardrobe of angels in contemporary texts.[14] But there is something very odd about the description of this young

---

11   Tannehill argues that the flight of the naked young man satirizes the pretensions of Christians who claim to be ready for martyrdom ("The Disciples in Mark," 403 and n. 38).
12   Vanhoye pointed out that, even in the Biblical tradition, the notions of flight and nakedness have positive aspects and uses ("La fuite du jeune homme," 405).
13   Dan 8:15-16; 9:21; 10:5; 2 Macc 3:26,33; Josephus *Ant.* 5.277.
14   Dan 7:9; 2 Macc 11:8-10; Acts 1:10.

man. He is said to be "sitting on the right side" (καθήμενον ἐν τοῖς δεξιοῖς). It is not stated on what he is sitting, to the right of whom or what he sits, or why he is on the right. The fact that there does not seem to be any reasonable literal meaning for this statement leads the reader to consider whether there may be a symbolic meaning.

The motif "sitting on the right" occurs earlier in the Gospel in Jesus' argument that the Messiah cannot be the son of David. In making his case, he cites the opening words of Psalm 110:

> *The Lord said to my Lord, "Sit at my right hand, until I put your enemies under your feet."* (Mark 12:36)

The reader should understand this to mean that Jesus, as the Messiah, will be enthroned at the right hand of God after his resurrection. This insight is reinforced by Jesus' answer to the high priest's question whether he is the Messiah, the son of the Blessed One:

> *Jesus said, "I am; and you will see the Son of Man seated at the right hand of the Power and coming with the clouds of heaven."* (14:62)

These passages suggest that the young man in the tomb symbolizes Jesus in his risen state. The white robe is worn both by angels and glorified human beings in contemporary texts. The seat on the right hand indicates that Jesus' words, as well as Psalm 110:1, have been fulfilled. As a character in the narrative, the young man may be understood as an angel. But the oddities in his presentation suggest that his role includes more than the simple announcement of the resurrection.

If the "young man" in the tomb symbolizes Jesus, perhaps the "young man" in Gethsemane does so as well. Here also two levels of meaning may be discerned. On the surface level of the narrative, the young man in Gethsemane is a disciple; "he was following Jesus" (συνηκολούθει αὐτῷ). But the brief scene in which he appears may also be understood as a symbolic anticipation of the resurrection of Jesus. This hypothesis is supported by the presence of another such symbolic anticipatory scene, namely, the transfiguration in chapter 9. It is further supported by the initial parallel between what happens to him and to Jesus: the servants of the high priest seize him, as they seized Jesus. No one else besides these two is seized.[15] The young man running away naked fore-

---

15 They seize Jesus: καὶ ἐκράτησαν αὐτόν (15:46); they seize the young man: καὶ κρατοῦσιν αὐτόν (15:51).

shadows Jesus' leaving the linen cloth behind and rising from the dead.[16]

If the young man symbolizes Jesus, why is he called "a *young* man"? It could be that Jesus was considered by the evangelist to have been a young man at the time of his arrest and death.[17] The two Greek words usually translated "young man," νεανίας and νεανίσκος, could signify a male person between the ages of 24 and 40. It is important to note, however, that both words also have the connotation of a subordinate person, even a servant. The ambiguity of the term makes possible a dual symbolic function: the young man, in both passages, can represent Jesus as the risen one and the follower who shares his fate.[18] From this point of view, neither the nakedness nor the flight is shameful. The risen one

---

16 In a footnote in an earlier book and then in a short essay, John Knox briefly suggested that the "whimsical story of the young man and the linen cloth" in 14:51-52 is a cryptic reference to the empty tomb; idem, *Christ the Lord* (Chicago, IL: Willett, Clark, 1945), 100; idem, "A Note on Mark 14:51-52," 28-29. Vanhoye, apparently independently of Knox, came to a similar conclusion ("La fuite du jeune homme," 405-6). Herman Waetjen also saw a relation between the young man of 14:51-52 and that of 16:5; he argued, however, that the former passage is a haggadah belonging to a genre of νεανίσκος stories and that it is the Joseph prototype (Gen 39:12; 41:40-43) which is the key to the significance of both youths and the cohesion which links them together as the same person ("The Ending of Mark," 117-20).

17 Scroggs and Groff observe, following E. Peterson, that the risen Jesus is often presented as a youth in the apocryphal acts literature ("Baptism in Mark," 535).

18 Scroggs and Groff argue that, "when seen against the backdrop of Christian baptismal practices, the appearance of the young man in both instances can best be explained as a symbolic pointer to the Christian initiate. The nakedness and flight in 14:51-52 symbolize dying with Christ; the reappearance of the young man in a new garment in 16:5 symbolizes rising with Christ" ("Baptism in Mark," 540). A problem with this interpretation, as the authors recognize, is that there is no early evidence for the practice of "the actual stripping off of the clothes of the candidate before immersion and the robing in a white garment after he had emerged from the water" (ibid., 537). The *Didache* says nothing about such a ritual act in its discussion of baptism (chapter 7) and the *Apostolic Tradition* attributed to Hippolytus states that the candidates shall take off their clothes before baptism, but put the same clothes on again afterward; see chapter 21 in the translation by Geoffrey J. Cuming, *Hippolytus: A Text for Students* (GLS 8; Bramcote Notts.: Grove Books, 1976), 18-20. John Dominic Crossan argued that "the *neaniskos*-messenger is not just the Christian initiate in general. It is the neophyte in the Mkan community and therefore it is that community itself, including Mk[;]" idem, "Empty Tomb and Absent Lord (Mark 16:1-8)," in *The Passion in Mark: Studies on Mark 14-16*, ed. Werner H. Kelber (Philadelphia, PA: Fortress, 1976), 148.

leaves behind the constraints of the earthly body and transcends the power of those who can seize and kill only the body.

The last mysterious aspect of the Gospel of Mark that I would like to discuss in this lecture is the ending. For the purposes of this discussion, I will assume that the Gospel originally ended with 16:8—"So they went out and fled from the tomb, for terror and amazement had seized them; and they said nothing to anyone, for they were afraid."

Those who conclude that this is the original ending of the Gospel have interpreted it in different ways. One possibility is to take it literally and historically and to conclude that the women never gave the message of the resurrection to the disciples.[19] According to this interpretation, the Gospel was written in large part to discredit the twelve, especially Peter, as leaders in the first century Christian Church.

Another approach is the argument that the evangelist used a literary device called the "suspended ending," a technique common in antiquity, whereby a particular work does not attempt to narrate the entire scope of a well known story.[20] The most famous example is the *Iliad*, which ends with the burial of Hector, and does not even narrate the outcome of the Trojan War. According to this interpretation, the fact that the evangelist did not narrate the appearance of the risen Jesus to the disciples in Galilee does not mean that he intended to deny that it occurred.

Most of those who take this literary approach assume that the women gave the message to the disciples eventually. But this construal of the ending makes it say the opposite of what it actually says, namely, that the women said nothing to anyone. They do this because they assume that, if the women did not give the message to the disciples, then the reunion in Galilee could not have occurred. If it did not, then Jesus' prediction that he would go before them to Galilee is falsified and he must be perceived as an unreliable character in the narrative.[21] These conclusions may be avoided by interpreting the ending in light of the theme of hardening which I discussed earlier in this lecture.

---

19 For example, Theodore J. Weeden, who argued that the women demonstrate a "negative, cowardly fear" and that this verse is part of Mark's "vendetta against the disciples" and the opponents that they represent; see idem, *Mark: Traditions in Conflict* (Philadelphia, PA: Fortress, 1971), 48.

20 J. Lee Magness, *Sense and Absence: Structure and Suspension in the Ending of Mark's Gospel* (SBL.SS; Atlanta, GA: Scholars Press, 1986).

21 Norman R. Petersen argued that, if 16:8 is taken literally, the readers must revise their understanding of Jesus as a reliable character in Mark's narrative; idem, "When is the End not the End? Literary Reflections on the Ending of Mark's Narrative," *Interpretation* 34 (1980), 151-66.

The connection may be found by beginning with the fear of the women mentioned in 16:8. This is a numinous fear, related to the pattern in the history of religions associated with epiphanies and theophanies.[22] Such fear is a typical feature of vision accounts, which often involve epiphanies of heavenly beings. In such accounts, however, the human visionaries are usually strengthened and encouraged by the beings who appear to them and enabled to listen to the message and follow the instructions of the revealer after the vision has ended.[23] In Mark 16:6, the angel does encourage the women not to be alarmed, but this admonition has no effect.

The interpretation of this passage, in which fear is evoked but no significant assistance is given in overcoming it, should occur in relation to expectations aroused by earlier parts of the narrative and its structural patterning.[24] The themes of hardening and spiritual blindness and deafness suggest that the Gospel of Mark is a series of secret manifestations of the divine presence at work in Jesus. No character other than Jesus is portrayed as able to understand these epiphanies in anything approaching a complete way and to respond appropriately. The fact that Jesus instructs Peter, James and John not to tell anyone about the transfiguration until after the resurrection does not necessarily mean that they will understand it fully when the resurrection has occurred. The reaction of the women in 16:8 is similar to the reaction of Peter to the transfiguration: "He did not know what to say, for they were terrified" (9:6).

Should we conclude then that Jesus is an unreliable character in Mark? I do not think so. The fact that the women do not communicate what the young man has said does not mean that the appearances in Galilee did not occur. It does mean that the initiative had to be taken once again by the divine side of the relationship. The disciples, being Galileans, would presumably have returned there after the Passover. The appearances would then have surprised them, in spite of Jesus' prediction, just as his arrest and death did. Mark assumes that some of the soil on which the seed falls will bear a hundredfold and some will bravely

---

22 See the discussion in Elizabeth Struthers Malbon, "Fallible Followers: Women and Men in the Gospel of Mark," *Semeia* 28 (1983), 29-48.

23 See, for example, Dan 8:18; 10:9-12; Rev 1:17-20; 4 Ezra 10:29-36.

24 Both Magness and Petersen argue that the ending of Mark should be interpreted in light of the structural patterning throughout the Gospel of Mark or in terms of the plotting of expectations and satisfactions; Magness, *Sense and Absence*, 100; Petersen, "Literary Reflections," 163. The conclusions of each of these scholars, however, differ from one another and from those drawn here.

proclaim the gospel, even when they are hauled before councils, governors, and kings. How will this be possible? Presumably by means of divine power. It is probably significant that the evangelist refers to those who continue to follow Jesus in the post-resurrection period as "the elect" (13:20,27). Those who follow are able to do so because they have been chosen.

The silence of the women is thus an intelligible response to the manifestation of divine power in the final scene of the Gospel, but it is not entirely appropriate and positive. If there is irony here, it lies in the contrast between the irrepressible speech of the healed leper and those who witness the healing of the deaf man in the face of commands to silence, on the one hand, and the stunned silence of the women in the face of a command to speak, on the other. The evangelist has not simply found an artful way to end the Gospel without rehearsing familiar facts. He has expressed something profound about the weakness and perversity of human nature in the encounter with the divine.

Returning to the question with which we began, we may ask how the characterization of the followers of Jesus relates to the context of the Gospel of Mark in the history of early Christianity. Johannes Schreiber and Joseph Tyson argued that the portrayal of the disciples in Mark must be seen as a literary device in the service of a polemic against a particular historical group in the Christian movement, namely, a conservative Jewish Christian community in Palestine which found no positive meaning in the death of Jesus, held to the long-established Jewish practices, and rejected the necessity of the Gentile mission.[25] This hypothesis finds some support in the recent analysis of the messianic secret in Mark by Heikki Räisänen.[26] It is an attractive theory, though difficult to prove. In any case, it is not incompatible with the theological interpretation offered above. Struggles for autonomy and power between majorities and minorities are never merely political. Such tension is usually connected also with fundamental differences of perspective on what it means to be human an how the human and the divine interact.

---

[25] Tyson argued that the leaders of this group were members of the family of Jesus ("The Blindness of the Disciples on Mark," *JBL* 80 [1961], 261-68); Schreiber, that they were Peter, James, and John ("Die Christologie des Markusevangeliums," *ZTK* 58 [1961], 175-83). Theodore J. Weeden agreed that the device served a polemical purpose, but defined that aim as an attack on a local Christological heresy (*Mark: Traditions in Conflict* [see above n. 19]).

[26] Heikki Räisänen, *The 'Messianic Secret' in Mark* (trans. Christopher Tuckett; Studies of the New Testament and Its World; Edinburgh: T. & T. Clark 1990).

Humble and Confident

On the So-Called Philosophers in Colossians

Lars Hartman

"May no one take you captive through his philosophy" (Col 2:8). The thinking and morality of this "philosophy", which is the main reason why the Letter to the Colossians was written,[1] are discussed in every commentary on the Epistle, in every text-book on New Testament Introduction, and, of course, in several other studies. But no agreement is in sight, nor does the present writer expect his treatment of the issue to have any such result. Nevertheless I shall propose a reconstruction of its ideology and relate it to the circumstance that the representatives of the "philosophy" evidently constitute a minority among the Christians in Colossae,[2] albeit a minority which seems to exert so great a pressure on the majority that it appears to be a "mighty minority".

These "philosophers"—which, for the sake of brevity, I shall call them in what follows—represent a minority; this may be inferred from a few details in Colossians. But apparently they do not form a minority in the usual sociological sense of the term; they certainly see themselves as a group, but do not lack power, are not regarded with contempt by the majority, and are not insulated or placed on a socially or culturally inferior level.[3]

I shall proceed as follows: firstly, I briefly collect those details in

---

1 I am of the opinion that the Colossians was written by a member of the Pauline school. I have argued this opinion in my commentary, *Kolosserbrevet* (Kommentar till Nya Testamentet 12, Uppsala: EFS-förlaget, 1986), 200-01. I agree with W. Schenk who maintains that the purpose of the Letter is more parenetic than is usually assumed; see W. Schenk, 'Der Kolosserbrief in der neueren Forschung (1945-1985)', *ANRW* II, 25:4 (Berlin, New York: de Gruyter, 1987), 3327-64, 3350.
2 When writing "Colossae", here and in the following, I am conscious of the fact that not only the author is a pseudo-Paul, but that it is also quite possible that Colossae is a pseudo-addressee. See, e.g., Schenk, op. cit., 3334-35.
3 See, e.g., A. M. Rose, 'Minorities', *International Encyclopedia of the Social Sciences* 9-10 (1968), 365-70.

Colossians which indicate the philosophers' minority status. Then I attempt to describe their ideology, and thirdly, consider how, according to the Letter, this "mighty minority" is related to the majority, in order, finally, to examine the other side of the relationship, viz. how the author depicts the attitudes of the majority to the minority, on the one hand considering their present attitude, which he thinks is unwarranted, and, on the other, the one he wants them to adopt.

1. The Representatives of the Philosophy as a Minority

The glimpses of the ideas of the philosophers indicate that they do not represent any of the contemporary thought systems, which we normally label philosophies, like Stoicism, Middle Platonism etc. On the contrary, they seem to exist on a local or possibly regional basis (cf. 4:15 and 2:1, on Laodicea).

The "somebody" of 2:8,16 and the "no one" of 2:4,18 suggest that the philosophers were not a large group, but actually a minority from a numerical point of view. They were, however, influential enough to worry the author and so numerous as to form a group which shared some cultic observances; whatever "festival, new moon, sabbaths" (2:16) denote, the enumeration implies something more than mere individual calculation. The same should hold true of the "service of the angels" (2:18), whatever this service may have meant. The rulings of 2:21, "do not handle, do not taste, do not touch" are characterized by the author as "rules and teachings of men", but can *per se* support the self-consciousness of the group.

2. The Philosophy.

Of course the author does not give us an objective, full and balanced picture of the phenomenon against which he warns his addressees. They knew what he had in mind, we do not. We can assume that he chose those features against which he wanted to direct his polemic, but we do not know how important they were to the representatives of the philosophy. Nor do we notice when he picks up slogans or turns of phrase typical for the group; the addressees would have heard the quotation marks and caught possible nuances of irony or parody—we do not.

My attempt to reconstruct the philosophy takes as its point of departure a couple of methodological considerations. I have divided the material in Colossians pertaining to the philosophy into three categories. In one I gather statements, items etc. which *certainly or almost certainly* tell us something about it. These are features which the author explicitly ascribes to it, and about which I assume that he is sure that the addressees cannot simply state that he lies or is wrong; if so, his argument would fail.

In a second group I bring together those features which *probably* refer to the philosophy. Thus, the writer's argument occasionally presupposes that the contents pertain to aspects of the philosophy. In other cases we can draw the conclusion *e silentio* that they should be taken into account. Thus, for example, if they had had a polytheistic faith, it is fair to assume that the author would have selected some weapons from the arsenal with which his tradition could provide him. Accordingly, I infer that the philosophers were monotheists in a sense of the word that the author could accept.

In a third group I gather those features which *possibly* characterize the philosophers. A glance at the commentaries on Colossians reveals a host of suggestions as to such features, often deduced from passages which are thought to allude to views held by the group.

In consequence of my manner of sifting the material on the philosophy I do not take into account the features of the third group until towards the end, in order then to see whether they naturally fit the pattern established on other, more reliable grounds.

Another presupposition of my discussion is that if we do not find a philosophy already known, in which the features of the philosophy can be discerned (and we do not), then, nevertheless, the reconstruction should be simple, combining features from as few other known philosophies as possible. This differentiates me from some colleagues, e.g. Martin Dibelius, according to whom the philosophy comprised elements from Iranian religion, Gnosticism, Judaism, astrology and, in addition, an otherwise unknown mystery cult.[4]

And now for my attempt to reconstruct the philosophy. First, then, features which *explicitly* apply to the philosophy: it represents some kind of wisdom (2:23), and its adherents apparently propagate their ideas with considerable energy and conviction; they are said to deceive with "persuasion through probabilities" (πιθανολογία, 2:4)[5] and to "take people captive" (2:8). They "condemn" and "disqualify" those who do not fol-

---

4   M. Dibelius, *An die Kolosser, Epheser, an Philemon* (HNT 12; Tübingen: Mohr [Siebeck], 3rd ed., rev. by H. Greeven, 1953). For an survey of the suggestions see F. F. Bruce, 'Colossian Problems, Part 3: The Colossian Heresy', *BS* 141 (1984), 195-208.
5   The noun has in itself no negative nuance of meaning, but denotes an argument based (only on) probabilities; thus Plato, *Theaet.* 162 E, opposes it to ἀπόδειξις.

low their rules for behavior (2:16,18). The nuances chosen by the writer indicate that they are very self-confident; he also accuses them of being "puffed up" (2:18).

Furthermore, the philosophy confronts people with regulations concerning what food and drink is allowed and what is not (2:16,21); it also requires observance of "festival, new moon and sabbaths" (2:16). Keeping their rules means "severe treatment of the body" (2:23) and "humility" (ταπεινοφροσύνη; 2:18,23). The word hardly has its ordinary Christian meaning (thus, though, in 3:12), nor the normal "secular" one, viz. "mean-spiritedness", etc. Rather it seems to stand for self-abasement or asceticism.[6] The author also mentions "worship of angels" (2:18) and "self-imposed piety" (ἐθελοθρησκία; 2:23), whatever these details mean.

Finally, the representative of the philosophy is said to "enter what he has seen" (2:18; ἃ ἑόρακεν ἐμβατεύων). The term is capable of several meanings and may refer to involvement in one's visions, to come into that which one has seen (as Joshua entered the promised land, Josh 19:49), or to "things one saw when entering", say, things shown to the initiate in a mystery cult; but in connection with a certain type of visions one also entered the divine Throne Hall with the heavenly court (cf., e.g., 2 Cor 12:2; Rev 4:1f.).

Certainly rules concerning food, calendar and sabbath were important to the Jews, but the author does not connect them with Judaism. If they were derived from any form of Judaism otherwise known to us, they would probably also have included the rule for which generations of Jews had been prepared to give their lives, viz. circumcision. In 2:11, 13, baptism is characterized as a spiritual circumcision, and sometimes this has been taken as a hint that the philosophy circumcised its members. But had the philosophy practised circumcision and required it of its adherents, then the author would most probably have polemicized against it. The rite was largely held to be repulsive and when the author's master, Paul, encountered Jewish demands that converted former Gentiles be circumcised, his polemics became almost choleric.[7]

---

6   E.g., E. Schweizer, *Der Brief an die Kolosser* (EKK; Zürich etc.: Benziger Verlag, Neukirchen-Vluyn: Neukirchener Verlag, 1976), 122.

7   The same position as that of the present writer is taken by P. T. O'Brien, *Colossians, Philemon* (WBC 44; Waco, TX: Word, 1982), 115. Others regard it as a possibility that the philosophy practised circumcision as a part of a mystery cult (not as a fulfillment of the Mosaic commandment); thus J. Gnilka, *Der Kolosserbrief* (HThK X:1; Freiburg etc.: Herder, 1980), 133, referring to Ewald, Lohse, Lohmeyer, Masson. Schenk, op. cit., 3350-53, argues that the philosophy was in fact a kind of Judaism.

Even if the people who maintained seemingly Jewish rules were not Jews, we need not go far to find another group who observed them. It was not sociologically delimited, but the behavioral pattern was with some variations well represented in the world of Early Christianity, viz., the so-called God-fearers, who, without becoming Jewish proselytes, adopted some features of Jewish practice and belief, such as monotheism, keeping the Sabbath and observing some of the food laws. But they were not circumcised and their social relationships with the Jews could be anything from close to fairly loose.[8]

It seems, however, that even if the said practice belonged to the God-fearers, it was not argued on purely Jewish grounds. Instead we can surmise other underlying reasons. These may also lie behind the other features mentioned, viz., the asceticism, the worship of angels, and the "seeing" of 2:18. Here we may as well add the details in Colossians which are *probably* pertinent to the philosophy. Thus, it claims to represent tradition (2:8). The writer argues that this tradition is (only) human (cf. 2:22); he may have spoken in contempt, but would presumably have expressed himself otherwise if the philosophy had meant that the traditions were of heavenly origin.

Furthermore, the rules are somehow connected with "the rulers and powers" (ἀρχαὶ καὶ ἐξουσίαι; 2:10,15), for when according to 2:14 the document containing the duties (the χειρόγραφον) was erased by being crucified, this meant a triumph over these "rulers and powers". This leads to the conclusion: "accordingly, nobody shall condemn you in matters of food and drink or concerning festival, new moon or sabbaths" (2:16). In 1:16 it is emphasized that the same rulers and powers are inferior to Christ, in that they owe their existence to him. The two nouns are often coupled (e.g., Luke 12:11; 20:20) and refer in, e.g., Eph 6:12 to cosmic, angelic powers (cf. 1 Cor 15:24).

Here, I suggest, we glimpse a second principal component in the philosophy, viz. an ideology which belongs to the so-called astral religion.[9] It is well known to scholars that in antiquity, e.g., the planets were held

---

8 For a balanced discussion of this problem, recently somewhat hotly debated, see S. J. D. Cohen, 'Crossing the Boundaries and Becoming a Jew,' *HThR* 82 (1989), 13-33.

9 See, *inter alia*, F. Cumont, 'Le mysticisme astral dans l'antiquité', *Académie Royale de Belgique: Bull. de la classe des lettres* 1909, 256-86; H. Greßmann, *Die hellenistische Gestirnreligion* (Beih. zur "Alten Orient" 1925:5; Leipzig: Hinrichs, 1925); A. J. Festugière, *La révélation d'Hermès Trismegiste I; L'astrologie et les sciences occultes* (Études bibliques; Paris: Lecoffre, 1944), 1-186; M. P. Nilsson, *Geschichte der griechischen Religion II* (HAW V.2.2; Munich: Beck'sche, 3rd edition 1974), 268-81, 598-601.

to be divine beings, that rainfalls, seasons etc. were thought to be governed by cosmic powers, and that, as the position of the sun affected the seasons, so human lives and destinies were influenced by stars and planets.

Jews and Christians were not alien to these views.[10] Thus, e.g., Philo meant that the universe was filled by God's different powers (δυνάμεις), e.g., the one through which everything came into being and was upheld, or the one through which he judged. Philo can also speak of spirits in the air who are "subordinate governors under the ruler of the All, so to speak the ears and eyes of the Great King which see and hear everything. Other philosophers call them spirits (δαίμονες), but the sacred word is wont to call them messengers (ἄγγελοι)" (*de somn.* 1:140-41). A fellow Jew, Paul, appears to have regarded things in a similar way. Thus, I find it permissible, slightly to paraphrase Rom 8:38f. as follows: "I am convinced that neither life nor death, neither angels (ἄγγελοι) nor rulers (ἀρχαί), neither anything present or coming, nor any powers (δυνάμεις), neither stars in their rising (ὕψωμα) nor such in decline (βάθος), indeed nothing created will be able to separate us from God's love in Christ Jesus our Lord."[11] One might even suppose that Paul's student who wrote Colossians had learnt from him of Christ's superiority to angels and powers and then adopted it in his own manner when polemicizing against the philosophy.

No doubt the rulers and powers to which Colossians refers belong to the cosmic potentates mentioned. But here is a crucial point: what is the connection between, on the one hand, such rulers and powers and, on the other, the rules advanced by the philosophy?

In the case of "festival, new moon and sabbaths" it is not too difficult to find a connection. The calendar was of course closely linked with that which was observed in the heaven. Although to a Jew the straightforward commandment was a sufficient argument for keeping the Sabbath and other festivals, he could also support his practice by referring to heavenly phenomena and to speculations on the number seven.[12]

Correct insight into calendar calculation and astronomy was a gift

---

10 See, e.g., J. H. Charlesworth, 'Jewish Interest in Astrology during the Hellenistic and Roman Period', *ANRW* II.20.2 (Berlin, New York: de Gruyter, 1987), 926-50.

11 See, e.g., H. Lietzmann, *An die Römer* (HNT 9; Tübingen: Mohr [Siebeck], 5th edition 1971), 88-89; H. Schlier, *Der Römerbrief* (HTK 6; Freiburg etc., 1977), 280-81. — A somewhat similar view is expressed in Plutarch, *de fato* 572 F-574 C (although the text is probably a pseudepigraph).

12 See Aristoboulos in Eus., *Praep. evang.* 13.12.13, and Philo, *de decal.* 158-61.

bestowed on particularly wise people. This is maintained by the author of *Astronomica* I.25-32:

> Deeper knowledge of heaven was first granted to earth by the gift of the gods. For who, if the gods wished to conceal it, would have guilefully stolen the secret of the skies, by which all things are ruled? (28) Who of but human understanding, would have essayed so great a task as to wish against heaven's wish to appear as god himself, (32) to reveal paths on high and paths beneath the bottom of the earth and stars obedient to appointed orbits through the void?[13]

The author of the Book of Wisdom is of a similar opinion, inasmuch as he maintains that the wisdom given from God also comprised knowledge of

> the construction of the world and of the effects of the elements, the beginning, the end and the midst of the times, the changes of the position of the sun ..., and the changes of the seasons, the course of the years and the positions of the stars. (Wis 7:17f.)

There are several testimonies among the ancient astrologers to the effect that in their view their study meant moving in the heavenly world, indeed, communing with divine beings. Thus, Seneca the older has this passage in his *Suasoriae*, referring to the views of the astrologers:

> the stars are available to us and we can mingle with the gods
> (*pateant nobis sidera et interesse numninibus liceat*; 4.1).

Ptolemy, the mathematician from the 2nd century CE, expressed himself in this manner:

> I know that I am mortal and born for a day, but when I follow the dense crowd of the stars in their orbits, my feet no longer touch the earth, but together with Zeus himself I satisfy myself with ambrosia, the godly food. (*Ant. Palatina* IX.577)

A context of this kind could be a suitable ideological framework when the author of Colossians states that the philosopher not only devotes himself to wisdom but also "enters upon that which he has seen" (2:18).

Such an attitude and such a "seeing" may be reflected in the following passage of the *Astronomica* II.115-23:

---

[13] Trans. G. R. Goold. Traditionally, the author is named Manilius, but the treatise is usually held to be pseudepigraphous.

> Who could know heaven save by heaven's gift and discover God save one who shares himself in the divine (*pars ipse deorum est*)? (117) Who could discern and compass in his narrow mind the vastness of this vaulted infinite, the dances of the stars, the blazing dome of heaven, and the planets' everlasting war against the signs ... (121) had not nature endowed our minds with divine vision (*ni sanctos animis oculos natura dedisset*), had turned to herself a kindred intelligence, and had prescribed so great a science (trans. G. P. Goold).

It is befitting one who would approach the dwellings of the gods to observe purity, and asceticism may serve this purpose. So thought also Vettius Valens, an astrologer from the 2nd century CE:

> when I arrived at the divine and awe-inspiring vision of the heavens I also wanted to cleanse my life from all evil and from every pollution and to take into consideration that my soul is immortal (τὴν ψυχὴν ἀθάνατον προλῆψαι [sic!]). Therefore also the divine seemed to commune (προσομιλεῖν) with me. (*Anthol.* VI.1.16)

Another example comes from Cleomedes, who attacked the way in which Epicuros dealt with astrology and burst out: Epicuros has been

> blinder than a mole, and no wonder, because, by Jove, it is not the affair of pleasure-loving people to find the true essence of things, but this should be done by those who have a virtuous character and put nothing before virtue and do not love "the healthy condition of the body".[14]

If the representatives of the philosophy heeded ideas like those mentioned in the preceding paragraph, the other rules they have defended also fit into the picture. These concerned not only pure and impure food but also some mortification and asceticism. They involved "severe treatment of the body" (ἀφειδία τοῦ σώματος) and ταπεινοφροσύνη (Col 2:18, 13). If we should hear a nuance of "humility" in the latter term, the writer may put it within invisible quotation-marks: "humility – indeed!".

The writer of Colossians does not think highly of this asceticism: he describes it as "without reason puffed up by a carnal mind" (2:18) and "a self-imposed piety" (ἐθελοθρησκία). When he characterizes it as a "worship of angels", this may be deprecatory (2:18), intimating that the rulers

---

14 Cleomedes, *de motu* II,1,86-87. It is difficult to date Cleomedes, but he is later than Poseidonios, to whom he often refers. The words within quotation-marks are from Epic. *fragm.* 668. —See further H. Strathmann, *Geschichte der frühchristlichen Askese I* (Leipzig: Deischertsche Verlagsbuchhandlung, 1914), 310-17.

and powers are degraded to messengers in a way reminiscent of Philo.

We saw that the philosophy has cited authorities to support its teachings. This is also a common feature among the representatives of astral religion, e.g. Vettius Valens (*Anthol.* VI.1.8f.) who speaks of "the old kings and rulers who cared for these things", quoting Nechepso, the more or less mythical Egyptian priest who, together with a certain Petosiris was also an authority on astrology. Actually, Vettius Valens' major work is largely made up of material from older authorities as befits its title, *Anthologiae*. The same holds true of the *Libri Matheseos* by Firmicus Maternus.

The conviction that one's ideology is of old and noble descent can inspire confidence; it can be further supported by the claim that one's belief and practice are closely related to the world of the divine. One lives in accordance with great cosmic patterns. In contrast the common simple people are regarded with contempt. This accounts for what we hear of the philosophy's judgment and dismissal of all others (2:16,18).

It remains to discuss material in Colossians which *possibly* represents the ideology of the philosophy. "Fullness"—"Pleroma" (πλήρωμα)—occurs twice in the Letter (1:19; 2:9), and was widely used by contemporary religious thinkers as a way of referring to the universal Deity. It appears in 2:9f. in a passage where the author maintains that by their union with Christ in baptism the addressees are united with the Pleroma. The passage *per se* is not a necessary link in the argument, but would function well in it, if the author indirectly said: you do not attain union with the Pleroma in the manner prescribed by the philosophy. In other words, the philosophy may well have claimed that it mediated a union with the divine All.[15]

In the passages quoted above as illustrations of the concepts of astral religion we also encountered turns of phrase which refer to the close communion between the divine and the astrologer. Here is a further example from *Astronomica*. The unknown author writes (IV.407):

---

15 In addition the writer claims (2:10): "in him (i.e., Christ)—and in no one else (σωματικῶς)—dwells the divine Pleroma, and you are filled in (or: through) him, the head of every ruler and power". —Sometimes the author's way of referring to a body of cosmic dimensions (1:18,24; 2:17,19) has been incorporated into the attempts to reconstruct the ideas of the philosophy. This assumes an underlying idea of the cosmos as being the body of the God of All. The idea might well be used for the author's cosmic Christology, but does not mean that the philosophy taught that, say, cosmos was the body of the Pleroma. Thus, I prefer not to take any of these features into consideration. See further E. Schweizer, σῶμα etc., *ThWNT* 7, 1024-91, 1035-36.

man must sacrifice himself in order that God be in him (*impendendus homo est, deus esse ut possit in ipso*).

Maybe the philosophers' wisdom also brought them into union with the Divine, when their life and speculations followed divine rules and complied with divine principles, and asceticism subdued the bad influence of the body.[16]

A couple of times we encounter the term "the elements of the world" (τὰ στοιχεῖα τοῦ κόσμου; 2:8,20), on which according to the writer the teachings of the philosophy depend (and not on Christ; 2:8). Almost all commentators regard this as tantamount to a technical term of the philosophy and try to find a reference for it in the culture and religion of the Roman Period.[17] Moreover it is inferred that these "elements of the world" and "the rulers and powers" are similar phenomena. Then, in 2:15 the author could as well have said that God disarmed and triumphed over the "elements" instead of, as now, over the "rulers and powers". This would be so, if either the elements are assumed to be the four (or five) elements, or stars, or cosmic powers which represent fundamental cosmic principles. It seems to me that the expression in 2:8 can as well be translated "according to cosmic fundamental principles". This takes into account both the context in Colossians and contemporary usage. If such a translation is accepted, there is still a relationship between "elements" and "rulers and powers", but the former do not belong to the same class of phenomena as the latter; instead rulers and powers are authoritative "according to cosmic fundamental principles" and for this very reason their rules should be upheld. In other words, either the elements are part of the doctrine of the philosophy or they are not, whatever is said about them at most complements what we already know, viz. that "rulers and powers" belong there.[18]

In fact, however, it seems to me that the writer has not picked up a

---

16 Another example is from Firmicus Maternus II.30,1: *oportet eum qui cotidie de diis vel cum diis loquitur, animum suum ita formare atque instruere, ut ad imitationem divinitatis semper accedat* ... (2) *Esto pudicus integer sobrius, parvo victu, parvis opibus contentus*.... Further material in Cumont, op. cit., 271-73.

17 See the survey in O'Brien, *Colossians*, 129-32.

18 In addition, there are good reasons to assume that the phrase actually has a vague reference. Only a few generations after Colossians, Clement of Alexandria understands it in two ways in his same book. Thus, in Strom. 1:11 he quotes Col 2:8 in support of a polemic against philosophers who think that the "elements" are gods, whereas in 6:8 he refers to the same passage to prove that a certain philosophy only devotes itself to "elementary" matters.

technical term from the philosophy, but has instead taken Paul to his help. Paul uses the term in Gal 4:3 (cf. Gal 4:9), a Letter which obviously also in other respects has provided the author with phrases and ideas, although he fills them with slightly different, or even quite different contents.[19] If this is so, the restriction I put forward in the preceding paragraph is even more justified.

A further detail which may shed light on the philosophy is the mention of a "circumcision not made by hands" (2:11), which stands for baptism and is contrasted to the pre-Christian life of the addressees when they "were dead because of the un-circumcision of (their) flesh" (2:13). It has been suggested that this implies that the philosophers practised circumcision, either because they were Jewish or for another reason. Above I have argued against such an assumption.[20]

I am even more doubtful concerning the suggestion that "do not touch" in 2:21 means sexual abstinence (cf. 1 Cor 7:1 and 1 Tim 4:3). The context does not favor such an understanding. For the following clause is best understood as referring to all the regulations of 2:21 ("do not handle, do not taste, do not touch"), characterizing them as concerned with objects that "perish with use"; this can hardly be maintained of women (as, e.g., of beans, which, e.g., the Neopythagoreans did not eat!).

Above, I quoted 2:18, "entering that which one has seen" and also briefly mentioned that it could refer to the initiate's entry into the shrine when he is shown pictures or symbols.[21] Was the philosophy involved in some sort of mystery cult, and is an affirmative answer supported by the use of μυστήριον in 1:26f. and 2:2? The suggestion was inspired by the History of Religion school's enthusiasm over the discovery of "influences" here and there and is nowadays rejected by the commentators.[22] The indications are vague and the obscure 2:18 might as well refer to phenomena seen in the context of astronomy and astrology without any linkage to a mystery cult.[23]

Thus, only one feature of my third group seems to fit smoothly into the picture composed of the details from the first two collections, viz., the mention of the Pleroma.

I shall now give a rough outline of the philosophy. I thereby also take into account that it almost certainly regarded its ideology as Christian, or

---

19 See E. P. Sanders, 'Literary Dependence in Colossians', *JBL* 85 (1966), 28–45.
20 See above and note 7.
21 See Dibelius, *Briefe*, 35.
22 E.g. Bornkamm, μυστήριον, *ThWNT* 4, 827-28; O'Brien, *Colossians*, 83-84.

to express myself more cautiously: their ideology was compatible with that held by people who regarded themselves as adherents to the religion which once was preached by Paul, but it should be refined and completed.

As a background we should recall various aspects of the cultural climate in the days of the Roman Empire, aspects which are more or less the same as those typical of the Hellenistic Age.

Official state religion and the *polis*-religion seem largely to have lost their ability to provide the citizens with the existential frames of reference which they desired. The syncretism which was a typical feature of the age meant a confusing ethnic and cultural pluralism in which many religions, philosophies and cults offered their solutions, also such as involved magic, mantics and astrology. Many individuals seem to have felt insecure and sought for meaning, structure, stability, perhaps for atonement with Tyche, or for support by powers stronger than destiny. Such support could be provided by joining this or that kind of association, by participating in higher wisdom, performing certain rites or following a particular way of life.

In such an environment Christianity spread, indeed at a remarkable speed, and its cultural climate determined the context of the Christian group which is called a philosophy in Colossians. In all probability, like so many Christians, they confessed Jesus as Lord, κύριος Ἰησοῦς. But in which sense? There were many κύριοι; already Paul could agree to that (1 Cor 8:5f.), and this group was obviously of another opinion than Paul, than his pupil Epaphras (presumably), and, of course, than the writer of Colossians, all of whom held that the κύριος position of Jesus was far superior to that of other κύριοι, cosmic rulers, stars, elementary powers. The philosophy may have conceded that Jesus Christ, as living in one

---

23 The vague phrase of 2:23, "in no honor" has been brought into the discussion of the philosophy. Here too those who think that it constituted something of a mystical association try to fit the expression into their suggested reconstruction; thus, they assume that the words echo a proclamation at the initiation to the effect that it was in honor of the initiand (e.g., E. Lohse, *Die Briefe an die Kolosser und an Philemon* (KEK IX/2; Göttingen: Vandenhoeck, 1968), 185f.; Gnilka, *Kolosserbrief*, 161). This is not impossible either, but the phrase is not *per se* a technical term at all. The main reason for assuming an external influence here is the rough construction of the sentence, which leads some interpreters to infer that the writer is using a series of technical terms of the philosophy, known by the addressees. This is, however, rather shaky ground for a reconstruction, and, in any case, the turn of phrase is so vague that it seems to me that attempts to find hidden allusions therein must remain pure conjecture.

way or another, was one of the κύριοι, but he was of less importance than certain others.

In order to be in harmony with the Pleroma, the Highest Being, who was in, over, under, behind and beyond everything, one must, according to the philosophy, ensure that one was reconciled (cf. 1:20,22) with the rulers and powers who reigned in the universe. The observance of certain calendar rules brought a certain contact with such lofty beings, already because rites of the new moon and living in a seven day cycle involved conformity to cosmic patterns, i.e. practices of so-called God-fearers, but they were adopted for non-Jewish or, rather, more-than-Jewish reasons.

It was, however, mandatory that people who wanted to live in harmony with the divine beings of the pure space did not pollute themselves—although we do not know what the philosophy regarded as polluting. But certainly the body was regarded with suspicion; it drew humans towards the earth and thus had to be subdued. Some forms of abstinence may have been the same as that of the God-fearers, and, as a matter of fact, here and there a Jew like Philo expresses himself in the same manner as his colleagues among, for example, the Stoics. Thus he can contrast hope (which causes the mind to depend on God) to desire, which causes the mind to "depend on the body, which nature created as a receptacle and a place of pleasures" (*de post.* 26). Indeed, he may maintain that the body is a polluted prison-house, from which man should try to escape, "its jailers being pleasures and lusts" (*migr.* 9).

In these matters the representatives of the philosophy apparently regarded Epaphras and his followers as unduly frivolous; they did not care about the calendar and they ate and drank and dealt with profane things and/or persons in such a way as to reject any possibility of reconciliation with the Fullness of the All. They themselves were freed to behold deep secrets and to be filled by heavenly light, whether their sessions dealt with horoscopes, astronomical observations and speculations or with other deep matters. In any case they were granted participation in extraordinary wisdom.

3. *The Philosophers' Attitude to the Majority.*

The conviction that one is infinitely more enlightened than the common people promotes either an attitude which involves a withdrawal into splendid isolation or of one of missionary zeal. Apparently the adherents of the philosophy took the second path. They devoted considerable energy to persuading others to join their group: they tried to "talk them over to them" (παραλογίζεσθαι; 2:4), indeed, spiritually to abduct them (συλαγωγεῖν; 2:8). In their propaganda they seem to combine practical issues and theoretical principles. Thus, they present the others with their rules—δόγματα; 2:14,20—and seem rigid in their assessment of those who do not follow them: they "judge" (κρίνειν; 2:16) and "disqualify" (παραβραβεύειν; 2:18) them. The practical rules were intimately connected with the ideology, an important topic of which seems to have been the insight into and good relationship with the Pleroma (cf. 1:19f.; 2:9). However, this knowledge of how to behave, and this contact with the Ultimate Fullness also seem to have resulted in arrogance (cf. 2:18, being puffed up).

In response to this attitude of the minority, the author, on the one hand, claims that Christ is superior to the authorities of the philosophy, they owe their existence to him (1:16), in him, personally, dwells the Pleroma (2:9), in his death and victorious resurrection the rulers and powers were put to shame and the rules which they authorized were nullified (2:14). Secondly, he denigrates the teachings and practices of the philosophy: the philosophers use πιθανολογία (2:4), i.e., unfair arguments to convince people,[24] their teaching consists only of shadows (2:17), "empty erring" (2:8), human and worldly inventions (2:8,23), it is not worthy of being called wisdom (2:23), and has no honor to it; instead of being an asceticism it rather indulges the flesh (2:23). In the Greek text the final phrase even sounds scornful with its alliterations and taking into account the itacism it goes in transcription: *ouk en timi tini pros plismonin tis sarkos*.[25]

4. The Majority as Confronted by the Minority

Apparently the majority has been impressed by the minority. They regarded them as a "mighty minority". Judging from how the writer urges them to behave, they felt uncertain: was that which they had learnt of Christian belief and life not accurate or sufficient? Was their hope for the future vain? Did they not "know" enough? Thus, the author exhorts and encourages them, sometimes through praising them for virtues in which he presumably fears they are lacking. So, I hear the impact of the minority's pressure on the majority in passages like the following: provided that they keep to the old Gospel (1:5,23) and do not surrender to

---

24 See above, note 5.
25 Cf. H. Lausberg, *Handbuch der literarischen Rhetorik* (Munich: Hueber, 1960), 661-71 (§434).

the philosophy, they have a firm hope of a heavenly heritage (1:5,12); thus, for a positive relationship to "heaven" they do not need the philosophy. If they faithfully hold on to what they have learnt from Epaphras concerning Christ, they have real and sufficient "knowledge" and understanding (1:6,9f.), indeed, of God's "mystery" (1:27; 2:2), i.e., the philosophy cannot offer anything better or more valid in these respects—on the contrary. This is so because they are baptized into the reign of the victor (1:13,16,20,22; 2:11-15), their Lord, Jesus Christ, and he is superior to the lords of the philosophers, viz. that which was held against the philosophy as I described it above, is also something that bolsters up the majority. In Christ they really meet the Pleroma (1:19; 2:9) and he, and no powers or potentates, is the Judge to whom they are responsible (1:22).

Rebuking the vociferous minority the writer also admonishes those among the majority who are tempted to align with the "wise", and maintains: already in this world you belong to a larger community, for the Gospel you have taken to yourselves prospers "in the whole world" (1:6), indeed, it is proclaimed "to every creature under heaven" (1:23). So the writer attempts to make the majority and the minority realize that, in a mundane perspective, the minority really is a minority, no matter how impressive it may sound.

Yet the small but apparently mighty minority in Colossae appears to have been convinced that it had found the Truth in a chaotic world, and that it belonged to a large, meaningful context in the contemporary world, in history, and, not least, in the heavenly realm. In what seems to have been a sturdy self-confidence, they obviously attempted to cozen the other Christians in Colossae and persuade them to realize the truth and so to leave their un-spiritual religion—so apparently the philosophers—in favor of the real thing. Of course they could not know that the future was not to belong to them but to the others, those more simple-minded Christians.

The Mighty Minority of Gnostic Christians

David Hellholm

In his provocative essay "The Mighty Minority" Professor Jacob Jervell developed Adolf Hilgenfeld's thesis that Jewish Christianity in the second part of the first century should be considered "a great power".[1] "Minority" Jervell understands clearly in numerical terms but "mighty" is as far as I can see nowhere distinctly defined as a theological, psychological, sociological or political entity. "The great power" is rather generally characterized as a phenomenon "determining the thinking, the theology, and the preaching of the Christian church."[2]

As far as I can see the terms "majority" and "minority" as characterizations of groups of Christians are not found in the New Testament writings, possibly with the exception of οἱ μικροί in Matthew, or these concepts are at the most extremely rare.[3]

1. "Minority" and "Majority" as Designations in Gnostic Writings

If the self-designation *"the little ones"* or *"the few"* in Jewish-Christian circles in the first century is scarce, it is all the more interesting to find this term as well as its contrast *"the many"* in Gnostic writings from the 2nd and 3rd century. There they are used precisely as self-designations of Gnostic Christians on the one hand and as their designation of antagonistic Christians on the other.

---

1 J. Jervell, "The Mighty Minority," in idem, *The Unknown Paul. Essays on Luke–Acts and Early Christian History*, Minneapolis, MN: Augsburg 1984, 26-51 (= *ST* 34 [1980], 13-38). A. Hilgenfeld, *Ketzergeschichte des Urchristentums*, Leipzig: Fues 1884 (repr. Hildesheim: Olms 1963), 445.
2 Jervell, "Mighty Minority," 26-27.
3 Cf. E. Schweizer, "Zur Struktur der hinter dem Matthäusevangelium stehende Gemeinde," in *ZNW* 65 (1974), 139.

Already in the *Gospel of Thomas* from Nag-Hammadi (NHC II.2. 32,10-51,28)[4] Jesus talks about *"the little ones"*; in log. 46 he says:[5]

> ... whichever one of you comes to be a *child* (ⲛ̄ⲕⲟⲩⲉⲓ) will be acquainted with the kingdom...

In its present context in the gnosticized form of Gos. Thom.[6] this term by all likelihood is a self-designation[7] in conformity with other designations such as

> the *solitary* (ⲙⲟⲛⲁⲭⲟⲥ) and *elect* (ⲉⲧⲥⲟⲧⲡ) (log. 49).[8]

This is confirmed by the subsequent logion in which Jesus tells his disciples to say to those who ask them if they are

> from the light, the place where the light came into being on its own accord ..., 'We are its *children* (ⲁⲛⲟⲛ ⲛⲉϥϣⲏⲣⲉ) and we are the *elect* (ⲁⲛⲟⲛ ⲛ̄ⲥⲱⲧⲡ) of the living Father' (log. 50).[9]

Not only the self-designation of the Gnostic Christians, however, are to be found in Gos. Thom. Also their designations of non-Gnostics is of interest, especially the usage of the term *"many"* (ϩⲁϩ).[10] In this connection log. 74 and 75 are instructive:

---

4 Text and transl.: B. Layton (text)/Th. O. Lambdin (transl.), "The Gospel of Thomas," in B. Layton (vol. ed.), *Nag Hammadi Codex II, 2-7* (NHS 20), Vol. 1, Leiden: Brill 1989, 52-93; M. Meyer, *The Gospel of Thomas. The Hidden Sayings of Jesus*, San Francisco, CA: Harper 1992. The translation by Lambdin has been used.
5 Cf. also Gos. Thom. log. 22.
6 E. Haenchen (*Die Botschaft des Thomas-Evangeliums*, Berlin: Töpelmann 1961) and many following him are convinced that Gos. Thom. is entirely Gnostic, while others like H. Koester, who interprets it as an early parallel to Q ("Introduction" to the edition by Layton/Lambdin, 38-49; "The Gospel of Thomas" in idem, *Ancient Christian Gospels. Their History and Development*, Philadelphia, PA: Trinity Press/London: SCM Press 1990, 75-128) and S. J. Patterson, who sees it in connection with an "Itinerant Radicalism" (*The Gospel of Thomas and Jesus*, Sonoma, CA: Polebridge Press 1993, 196-214) prefer to talk about its "Gnosticizing Interpretation" or "Esoteric Theology" (Koester, "Introduction," 44; idem, *Ancient Christian Gospels*, 124-28), or "Thomas' Gnosticizing Proclivity" (Patterson, ibid., 197-202).
7 See F. Siegert, "Selbstbezeichnungen der Gnostiker in den Nag-Hammadi-Texten," in *ZNW* 71 (1980), 129-32, here 131.
8 Cf. E. Haenchen, "Die Anthropologie des Thomas-Evangeliums," in H. D. Betz/L. Schottroff (eds.) *Neues Testament und christliche Existenz. FS Herbert Braun*, Tübingen: Mohr (Siebeck), 207-27, here 222.
9 Cf. Irenaeus, Adv. haer. 1.21.5; see M. Meyer, *The Gospel of Thomas*, 89. Further E. Haenchen, *Botschaft*, 39-41 and 44; S. J. Patterson, *Gospel of Thomas*, 200.
10 For further examples from Gnostic texts, see Siegert, "Selbstbezeichnungen," 132.

He said, 'O lord, there are *many* (ⲟⲩⲟⲛ) around the drinking trough, but there is nothing in the well' (log. 74).

Jesus said, '*Many* (ⲟⲩⲟⲛ) are standing at the door, but it is the *solitary* (ⲙ̄ⲙⲟⲛⲁⲭⲟⲥ) who will enter the bridal chamber' (log. 75).

Who exactly are meant shall be left open here, but that the *"many"* are others than Gnostic Christians and that they are seen as opponents to the Gnostics is beyond doubt. Stephen J. Patterson sets these Gnostic Christians in connection with the wandering radicals depicted in Didache 11-13, 2-3 John and James.[11] Since "the radicals' small voice against that of the majority of Christians would have offered little self-generating confidence (cf. Thom. 73)," only the "theological reflection within the framework of Gnosticism could result in a deeply felt conviction that the socially radical ethos one had chosen was not in vain".[12] They have become part of a larger cosmic scheme, after having been chosen by the Revealer. "It matters not what the majority believes (Thom. 74, 75) and that their own numbers dwindle. They are the *chosen few* (Thom. 23)."[13]

The terminological specifications given above return in a Gnostic Christian text from a somewhat later date, a text which is not a gospel as the Gos. Thom. but rather an apocalypse, viz. *The Apocalypse of Peter* from Nag-Hammadi (NHC VII.3. 70:13-84:14).[14]

The designation *"the little ones"* or *"the few"* (ⲛⲓⲕⲟⲩⲉⲓ) is found in 78:22, 79:19, and 80:11-(12). These passages are not by accident found in

---

11 Patterson, *Gospel of Thomas*, 200f., see also 133, 152f.
12 Patterson, ibid, 201.
13 Patterson ibid. (italics mine). A similar but somewhat different interpretation is found in Haenchen, "Anthropologie," 216: "Es scheinen *nicht viele* gewesen zu sein, welche diese von ThEv geforderte Isolierung aushielten und darin ihren Frieden fanden. Das beweisen die Sprüche 74 und 75" (italics mine).
14 Text and transl.: M. Krause/V. Girgis, "Die Petrusapokalypse," in F. Altheim/R. Stiehl (eds.), *Christentum am Roten Meer. Zweiter Band*, Berlin-New York: de Gruyter 1973, 152-79; J. Brashler, *The Coptic Apocalypse of Peter: A Genre Analysis and Interpretation*. PhD Diss. Claremont 1977. Transl.: Berliner Arbeitskreis für koptisch-gnostische Schriften (Federführend: A. Werner), "Die Apokalypse des Petrus. Die dritte Schrift aus Nag-Hammadi-Codex VII," in *TLZ* 99 (1974), 576-84; J. Brashler/A. Bullard, "Apocalypse of Peter," in J. M. Robinson et al. (eds.), *The Nag Hammadi Library in English*, Leiden: Brill/San Francisco: Harper 3rd. ed. 1988, 372-78; A. Werner, "The Coptic Gnostic Apocalypse of Peter," in W. Schneemelcher/R. McL. Wilson (eds.), *New Testament Apocrypha. Revised edition. Vol. 2*, Cambridge: Clarke/Louisville, KY: Westminster/John Knox Press 1992, 700-12. [German ed. Tübingen: Mohr (Siebeck) 1989, 633-43]. When not indicated otherwise the translation by Brashler/Bullard has been used.

the middle section of the Apoc. Pet. (73:14-80:23), which in the textanalysis presented below I have named "The revelation of the Savior about the heretical opposition". Who precisely these "little ones" are will have to be discussed in detail in the section below that deals with the ecclesiological understanding of the Gnostics behind the Apoc. Pet.

Also with regard to the designation of opponents in the Apoc. Pet. there are similarities with the Gos. Thom. Even though the specific term *"many"* (ⲟⲁϩ) is not to be found, they are nevertheless said to be "numerous" (ⲉⲛⲁϣⲱⲟⲩ [77:22]) or identified as *"multitude(s)"* (ⲟⲩⲙⲏⲏϣⲉ [73:23] or ϩⲉⲛⲙⲏⲏϣⲉ [80:3f.]). The summary of the revelation about the antagonistic opponents by Peter in the concluding dialogue with the Savior (79:32-80:22), after the Savior's revelation of the heresy has come to an end, is significant:

> ...there are *multitudes* that will mislead other *multitudes* of living ones... (80:3f.).

Here two "multitudes" are set up against each other: the "multitudes" representing a counterfeit will mislead the "multitudes of living ones". The question of who these numerous opponents are and how they relate to the "multitude of living ones", and if there is one unanimous opposition or several groups of opponents will have to be addressed below.

These characterizations of the opponents of the Gnostic Christians are—as was the case with the (self-)designations we saw earlier—found in the middle section of the Apoc. Pet. (73:14-80:23).

2. Structural Analysis of the Apocalypse of Peter

2.1. State of Scholarship

In present scholarship two interpretations of Apoc. Pet. that contradict each other have seen the light of day as far as the identification of the antignostic opponents to the Gnostic Christians is concerned.

Klaus Koschorke in his profound Heidelberg dissertation from 1976 advocated the view that there is *only one conflict* reflected in this document, namely the controversy between the Gnostic Christians and the so called Great (also labeled Catholic or Orthodox) Church, which constitutes the sole opposition as described in Apoc. Petr.[15]

---

15 K. Koschorke, *Die Polemik der Gnostiker gegen das kirchliche Christentum. Unter besonderer Berücksichtigung der Nag-Hammadi-Traktate "Apokalypse des Petrus" (NHC VII,3) und "Testimonium Veritatis" (NHC IX,3)* (NHS 12), Leiden: Brill 1978, passim, especially 14.

James Brashler and Andreas Werner on the other hand have argued primarily on the basis of the arrangement of the characterizations by means of "some ... others ... others ..." etc. that one should assume several points of conflict and thus several oppositional groups, orthodox as well as Gnostic.[16]

In order to be able to present further and hopefully more strict arguments in that discussion I shall provide a structural or, if preferable, compositional analysis of this apocalypse utilizing the text-linguistic method I have used elsewhere when analyzing other Jewish, Christian and Hellenistic texts of the same literary genre.[17]

2.2. Structural Textdelimitation

NOTATIONS FOR SYNTAGMATIC TEXTDELIMITATIONS[18]

^{1-n}ST	= subtexts of different grades
$^{1-n}ST^{1-n}$	= several subtexts of different grades
AA	= address appeal
DP	= dramatis personae
FM	= form media (e.g. narrative, discourse, monologue, dialogue etc.)
MS^{1-n}	= meta-communicative sentences of various intensional and extensional ranges
RM	= relational marker
SA^{1-n}	= substitutions on abstraction-level of different grades
SemM	= semantic marker
SM^{1-n}	= substitutions on meta-level
SMsurr	= substitutions on meta-level surrogate (verb instead of noun).

---

16 J. Brashler, *Apocalypse of Peter,* 222f.; idem, "Introduction to Apocalypse of Peter," in *The Nag Hammadi Library in English,* 372. A. Werner, "Apocalypse of Peter," 703; cf. also F. Wisse, "Peter, Apocalypse of," in *ABD,* Vol. 5, 269.

17 See D. Hellholm, *Das Visionenbuch des Hermas als Apocalypse. Formgeschichtliche und texttheoretische Studien zu einer literarischen Gattung* (ConBNT 13:1), Lund: Gleerup 1980; idem, "The Problem of Apocalyptic Genre and the Apocalypse of John," in A. Y. Collins (ed.), *Early Christian Apocalypticism: Genre and Social Setting* (= *Semeia* 36), Atlanta, GA: Scholars Press 1986, 13-64; idem, *Lucian's Icaromenippos. A Textlinguistic and Generic Investigation* (SO.S. XXVIII), Oslo – Copenhagen – Stockholm – Boston: Scandinavian University Press 1995 (forthcoming).

18 See my publications listed in n. 17, and in addition especially Hellholm, "Substitutionelle Gliederungsmerkmale und die Komposition des Matthäusevangeliums,", in T. Fornberg/D. Hellholm (eds.), *Texts and Contexts. Biblical Texts in Their Textual and Situational Contexts. FS Lars Hartman,* Oslo – Copenhagen – Stockholm – Boston: Scandinavian University Press 1995, 11-76, especially 22-33.

TEXTANALYSIS

⁰ST¹ Apocalypse of Peter (70:13) [SM¹: ΑΠΟΚΑΛΥΨΙΣ ΠΕΤΡΟΥ]

¹ST¹ INTRODUCTION TO VISIONS AND REVELATIONS (70:14-72:4)

²ST¹¹ Setting: Savior sitting in the temple instructing Peter (70:14-19)

²ST¹² Peter's narration of *monologue* by Savior as *angelus interpres* (70:20-72:4) [FM: monologue; DP: Savior → Peter; Address: Peter; MS: ⲡⲉⲭⲁϥ ⲛⲁⲓ̈ ⲭⲉ — *he said to me*]

³ST¹²¹ Introduction by means of a definition of the relationship between the Father as heavenly Originator, the Savior as Revealer, and the Gnostic Christians as Recipients of the revelation (70:20-71:15)

⁴ST¹²¹¹ Macarism of Gnostic Christians (70:20-32)

⁵ST¹²¹¹¹ The macarism of the elect (70:21f.)

⁵ST¹²¹¹² Identification of the Father as the *Originator* of revelation (70:23f.)

⁵ST¹²¹¹³ Self-identification of the Savior as *Revealer* of revelation and of his mission (70:25-32)

⁴ST¹²¹² Necessity of Revealer's appearance (70:32-71:9)

⁴ST¹²¹³ Epiphany of Revealer (71:9-15)

³ST¹²² Identification of Peter as *First Recipient* or *Transmitter* of revelation (71:15-72:4)

⁴ST¹²²¹ Paraenetic injunction to Peter (71:15-25)

⁴ST¹²²² Call to knowledge (71:25-72:4)

¹ST² TWO INTERCALATED REVELATIONS AND A CONCLUDING COMMISSION: (a) visions of Jesus' crucifixion (72:4-73:14 + 80:23-83:15), (b) revelation of the heresy of the opposition (73:14-80:22), and concluding commission (83:15-84:11) [SA¹: ⲛⲁⲓ̈ ⲇⲉ ⲉϥϫⲱ — *and as he was saying these things*; SM surr.: ⲁⲉⲓⲛⲁⲩ — *I saw* (= vision)]

²ST²¹ *First part of visions and interpretations of Jesus' crucifixion (72:5-73:14)*

³ST²¹¹ Vision of attack on Jesus and Peter by priests and people (72:5-9)

³ST²¹² Interpretation of vision by Savior in form of a dialogue with Peter (72:9-73:14) [FM: dialogue; DP: Savior/Peter; MS: ⲁⲭⲱ ⲡⲉⲭⲁϥ ⲛⲁⲓ̈ ⲭⲉ — *and he said to me*]

⁴ST²¹²¹ Savior's reference to former instructions about their blindness in form of scriptural allusion, and first instruction on technique for inducing visionary insight (72:9-17)

⁴ST²¹²² Peter's description of his failure to see (72:17-20)

⁴ST²¹²³ Savior's renewed instruction to Peter to make another attempt (72:20-21)

⁴ST²¹²⁴ Peter's second attempt and his successful vision of the descending

light upon the Savior (72:21-28) [SMsurr: ⲁⲉⲓⲛⲁⲩ — *I saw* (= vision); Conj.: γάρ — *for*]

⁴ST²¹²⁵ Savior's instruction to Peter to receive an interpreting audition (72:29-73:1)

⁴ST²¹²⁶ Peter's first and unsuccessful audition of the conversation between the priests and the scribes and his report thereof (73:1-5) [SMsurr: ⲁⲩⲱ ⲁⲉⲓⲥⲱⲧⲙ̄ — *and I listened*]

⁴ST²¹²⁷ Savior's renewed instruction to Peter to listen again (73:6-8)

⁴ST²¹²⁸ Peter's successful audition and report thereof (73:9-11) [SMsurr: ⲁⲩⲱ ⲁⲉⲓⲥⲱⲧⲙ̄ ⲟⲛ — *and I listened again*]

⁴ST²¹²⁹ Savior's reference to the attackers' blindness and deafness with recapitulation of initial scriptural allusion (73:11-14)

²ST²² *Revelation of the Savior about the heretical opposition and contrary anthropological principles as a demarcation line* (73:14-80:23) [AA: ⲥⲱⲧⲙ̄ —*listen*; Conj.: ⲇⲉ —*then*; SA²/SM: ϯⲛⲟⲩ ⲉⲛⲏ ⲉⲧⲟⲩⲱϣ ⲙⲙⲟⲟⲩ ⲛⲁⲕ ϩⲛ ⲟⲩⲙⲩⲥⲧⲏⲣⲓⲟⲛ—*to those things which will be told to you [= I tell you] in a mystery* (μυστήριον)]

³ST²²¹ Call to esoteric knowledge with motivation (73:14-23) [FM/DP: Peter addressed by Savior]

³ST²²² *First series* of prophecies of apostasy from Gnosis (73:23-75:7) [FM/DP: Savior informs Peter of the multitudes' action]

⁴ST²²²¹ Prediction of defection from Gnosis and persecution of Gnostic Christians (73:23-74:22)

⁵ST²²²¹¹ Description of defection of multitude (73:23-74:3)

⁵ST²²²¹² Resulting persecution of Gnostic Christians (74:4-12)

⁵ST²²²¹³ Content of false teaching (74:13-16)

⁵ST²²²¹⁴ Polemic against Paul as originator of false teaching (74:16-22)

⁴ST²²²² Description of multifarious appearances of orthodox heresy: first two characterizations (74:22-75:7)

⁵ST²²²²¹ *First* characterization: general defilement and internal contentions (74:22-27) [RM: ϩⲉⲛϩⲉⲓⲛⲉ ⲅⲁⲣ — *for some*]

⁵ST²²²²² *Second* characterization: heretics named after a man and a naked woman (74:27-75:7) [RM: ϩⲉⲛϩⲉⲓⲛⲉ ⲙⲉⲛ — *others*]

³ST²²³ *Digression*: contrary anthropologies and ecclesiological categorization— "dead" vs. "immortal souls" in two parallel sections (75:7-76:23)" [FM: simile; SemM: universally fundamental principles]

⁴ST²²³¹ *First section* dealing with the consequences of the principle: "like produces like" (75:7-76:4)

⁵ST²²³¹¹ Statement of principle: simile as scripture allusion (75:7-11)

5ST²²³¹² Description of mortal soul (75:12-26)

5ST²²³¹³ Description of immortal soul (75:26-76:4)

4ST²²³² *Second section* dealing with the consequences of the principle: "like produces like" (76:4-28)

5ST²²³²¹ Statement of principle: simile as scripture allusion (76:4-8)

5ST²²³²² Description of mortal soul (76:9-13)

5ST²²³²³ Description of immortal soul (76:14-17)

5ST²²³²⁴ Concluding negative statement of principle: "like returns to like", "for deaf and blind ones join with their own kind" (76:18-23)

3ST²²⁴ *Second series* of apostasies from Gnosis (76:24-79:31) [RM: resumption of series of characterizations; SemM: deceptive mysteries; Conj.: δέ]

4ST²²⁴¹ Prediction of defection from Gnosis (to deceptive mysteries) (76:24-26) [RM: ϩⲉⲛⲕⲟⲟⲩⲉ ⲇⲉ — *but others*]

5ST²²⁴¹¹ Description of defection (76:24)

5ST²²⁴¹² Content of false teaching (76:25-26)

4ST²²⁴² Description of multifarious appearances of heresy: last four characterizations (76:27-79:31)

5ST²²⁴²¹ *Third* characterization: claim of exclusive possession of truth (76:27-77:21) [RM: ϩⲉⲛϩⲟⲓⲛⲉ — *others*]

6ST²²⁴²¹¹ The claim to exclusiveness (76:27-77:3)

6ST²²⁴²¹² Justification for claim: the archontic powers (77:4-21)

5ST²²⁴²² *Fourth* characterization: the counterfeit of the true forgiveness (77:22-78:31) [RM: ϩⲉⲛⲕⲟⲟⲩⲉ ⲇⲉ ⲉⲛⲁϣⲱⲟⲩ — *and others who are numerous*]

6ST²²⁴²²¹ Messengers of error, who are numerous (77:22-33)

6ST²²⁴²²² Haimarmene exerted by the counterfeit (78:1-78:22)

6ST²²⁴²²³ Punishment of those who lead "the little ones astray" (78:23-31)

5ST²²⁴²³ *Fifth* characterization: *extra ecclesiam nulla salus* (78:31-79:21) [RM: ϩⲉⲛⲕⲟⲟⲩⲉ ⲇⲉ — *and others*]

6ST²²⁴²³¹ Description of "the true brotherhood" (78:31-79:7)

6ST²²⁴²³² Description of oppression of "the little ones" on the part of "the sisterhood" as a counterfeit (79:8-21)

5ST²²⁴²⁴ *Sixth* characterization: hierarchical structure of the heretic church: bishop and presbyters (79:22-31) [RM: ⲉⲩⲉϣⲱⲡⲉ ⲇⲉ ⲛ̄ϭⲓ ϩⲉⲛⲕⲟⲟⲩⲉ — *and there shall be others*]

3ST²²⁵ Concluding assurance of the final triumph of "the little ones" (*minority*) over "the multitude"(*majority*) in a *dialogue* between Peter and the Savior (79:32-80:23) [FM: dialogue; DP: Peter/Savior; MS: ⲁⲛⲟⲕ ⲇⲉ ⲡⲉⲭⲁⲓ — *and I said;* SA³: ϯⲣ̄ ϩⲟⲧⲉ ⲉⲧⲃⲉ ⲛⲏ ⲛ̄ⲧⲁⲕϫⲟⲟⲩ ⲛⲁⲓ̈ — *I am afraid because of what you have told me*]

⁴ST²²⁵¹ Peter's concern (79:32-80:7)

⁴ST²²⁵² Savior's assurance of victory (80:8-23) [MS: ⲡⲉϫⲉ ⲡⲥⲱⲧⲏⲣ ϫⲉ — *The Savior (σωτήρ) said*]

²ST²³ *Second part and completion of visions and interpretations of Jesus' crucifixion* (80:23-83:15) [AA: ⲁⲙⲟⲩ ⲟⲩⲛ — *Come therefore* (οὖν); SemM: *let us return to the completion of the will of the undefiled Father;* Modus: optative: ⲙⲁⲣⲟⲛ — *let us go!*]

³ST²³¹ *First* vision with interpretation (80:23-82:3)

⁴ST²³¹¹ Preparation for visionary experience (80:23-81:3)

⁵ST²³¹¹¹ Call to experiencing "the completion of the will of the undefiled Father" (80:23-26)

⁵ST²³¹¹² Description of approach of the priests and people (80:26-30)

⁵ST²³¹¹³ Appeal and assurance to Peter (80:31-81:3)

⁴ST²³¹² Vision report of the two figures on the cross and above it (81:4-14) [SA⁴: ⲛⲁⲓ̈ ⲛ̄ⲧⲁⲣⲉϥϫⲟⲟⲩ — *when he had said these things;* SMsurr: ⲁⲓ̈ⲛⲁⲩ — *I saw*]

⁴ST²³¹³ Interpretation in dialogue form (81:14-82:3) [FM: dialogue; MS: ⲡⲉϫⲁϥ ⲛⲁⲓ̈ ⲛ̄ϭⲓ ⲡⲥⲱⲧⲏⲣ ϫⲉ — *the Savior said to me*]

⁵ST²³¹³¹ Savior's interpretation of himself as the "living Jesus" and his "fleshly part" (σαρκικόν) (81:14-24)

⁵ST²³¹³² Peter's suggestion to escape (81:24-28)

⁵ST²³¹³³ Savior's rubuke of Peter and repeated declaration of the mistake by "the blind" (81:28-82:3)

³ST²³² *Second* vision with interpretation (82:4-83:15)

⁴ST²³²¹ Vision report of the Savior being filled with Pleroma (82:4-14) [SM: ⲁⲛⲟⲕ ⲇⲉ ⲁⲉⲓⲛⲁⲩ — *and* (δέ) *I saw*]

⁵ST²³²¹¹ Approach of the Pleroma [cf. 83:10-13] (82:4-6)

⁵ST²³²¹² Filling of the Soter with the pure spirit (82:7-9)

⁵ST²³²¹³ A great light surrounding the two figures of the Savior and the praising of the invisible angels (82:9-14)

⁴ST²³²² Peter's own testimonial assurance of his vision of the approach of figures representing different ranks of the Savior (82:15-16) [SemM: ⲁⲛⲟⲕ ⲇⲉ ⲉⲧⲁⲓ̈ⲛⲁⲩ — *and it is I who saw him* (or *and when I looked at him*)]

⁴ST²³²³ Savior's interpretation of vision and confirmation of Peter's vision (82:17-83:15)

^{5}ST^{23231} Savior's testimonial confirmation of the revelation of mysteries given to Peter (82:17-20)

^{5}ST^{23232} Interpretation of the σαρκικὸν σῶμα of the crucified as dinstinguished from the "living Soter", who is the νοερόν πνεῦμα, which "the blind ones", however, do not understand (82:21-83:15)

^{2}ST^{24} *Conclusion in form of a commission to transmit revelation to "the strangers (ἀλλογενής) who are not of this age (αἰών)"* (83:15-84:11) [SA^2: naï oyn etaknay; *these things that you saw*; DP: Peter → ἀλλογενής; Conj.: οὖν]

^{3}ST^{241} Commission itself (83:15-18)

^{3}ST^{242} Basis for commission in form of a substantiation partly by means of a self-quotation by Savior (= quotation from scripture) (83:19-84:6) [Conj.: γάρ]

^{4}ST^{2421} Reason for the commissioning Peter to transmit the revelations only to those of immortal essence (οὐσία) (83:19-26)

^{4}ST^{2422} Justification for commission by means of self-quotation by Savior (83:26-84:6) [Conj.: etbetai — *therefore*; Citation formula: aeixooc xe — *I have said*]

^{3}ST^{243} Exhortation and promise (84:7-11) [Conj.: οὖν]

^{4}ST^{2431} Exhortation to be strong (84:7-8)

^{4}ST^{2432} Reason in form of promise of Savior's presence (84:8-11) [Conj.: γάρ]

^{1}ST^3 CONCLUSION OF VISIONS AND REVELATIONS: Peter comes to his senses (84:12-13) [SA^1: naï ñtaqxooy — *when he had said these things*]

^{0}ST^2 Apocalypse of Peter (84:14) [SM^1: ΑΠΟΚΑΛΥΨΙΣ ΠΕΤΡΟΥ]

2.3. Comments on the Textanalysis

The textdelimitation provided above is in many ways indebted to the structural analysis of Apoc. Pet. given by James Brashler[19] and to relevant sections in the work by Klaus Koschorke,[20] who, however, does not bring a complete analysis of the entire text. By paying special attention to demarcation markers in the text, I have tried to arrive at a more precise delimitation than my precursors, especially of the macrostructure of the text. In what follows I shall comment in particular on the compositional macrostructure, which means that I shall limit myself to the delimitation of textsequences down to level two. The semantic and pragmatic-functional consequences of the textanalysis will be explicated in a subsequent paragraph dealing with the interpretation of this document.

---

19 Brashler, *Apocalypse of Peter*, 144-47.
20 Koschorke, *Polemik*, passim, especially 11-17.

DELIMITATION OF THE TEXT AS A WHOLE

In addition to the "superscript" at the beginning (70:13) and the "subscript" at the end (84:14) of the document, both formulated in Greek (ΑΠΟΚΑΛΥΨΙΣ ΠΕΤΡΟΥ), this text as a whole is clearly divided into three larger sections: (^{1}ST^1) "introduction to revelations" (70:14-72:4), (^{1}ST^2) "two intercalated revelations with a concluding commission" (72:4-84:11), and (^{1}ST^3) "conclusion of the revelations" (84:12-13). These three sections or textsequences are delimited by means of one and the same delimitation marker, the so called *substitution on abstraction level* (SA^1): "... and as he was saying *these things* (ⲛⲁⲓ)" (72:4); "... and when he had said *these things* (ⲛⲁⲓ)" (84:12). In addition the second section is set apart from the first by means of a *substitution on metalevel* (SM) or rather its surrogate (SMsurr): "I (sc. Peter) *saw*". And conversely the third section is set apart from the second by the opposite SMsurr: "he (sc. Peter) *came to his senses*".

DELIMITATION OF TEXTSEQUENCES ON LEVEL ONE

The first section on level one (^{1}ST^1), the "introduction" (70:14-72:4), is made up of two subsections: the first (^{2}ST^{11}) describing the Savior sitting in the temple instructing Peter (70:14-19); the second (^{2}ST^{12}) narrating Peter's report of the Savior's instruction about the Father as *Originator* of the revelation, himself as the *Revealer* and Peter as the *first Recipient* or rather the *Transmitter* (70:20-71:15). The Savior's monologue is clearly the dominating part in the introduction. The markers delimiting these two subsections are four: the change in *form media* (FM) from narrative to monological discourse; the change in the activity of *dramatis personae* (DP); the *address* by the Savior to Peter; finally the *meta-communicative sentence* (MS): "he (sc. Savior) *said* to me".

The second section on level one (^{1}ST^2), the "intercalated revelations with the concluding commission" (72:4-84:11), constitutes the main part of the document. It falls into four subsections: the first (^{2}ST^{21}) contains the "first part of visions and interpretations of Jesus' crucifixion" (72:5-73:14); the second (^{2}ST^{22}), sometimes called "middle section", encompasses the "revelation of the Savior about the heretical opponents" (73:14-80:23); the third (^{2}ST^{23}) is made up of the "second and completing part of visions and interpretations of Jesus' crucifixion" (80:23-83:15); the fourth and last subsection (^{2}ST^{24}) brings the "conclusion in form of a commission to transmit the revelation to the 'strangers who are not of this age'" (83:15-84:11). Noticeable here is the fact that the revelations regarding the heretical opposition in the "middle section" is enclosed by the two visionary sections about Jesus' crucifixion with concomitant interpretations. The importance of this structural intercalation will have to be addressed more closely below. The markers delimiting these subsections are of a somewhat diverse nature due to the construction of the text itself. The second subsection is set apart from the first by means of a *substitution on abstraction level* (SA^2) in combination with a *substitution on meta-level* (SM): "I (sc. Savior) *tell* you in a *mystery*"; an *address appeal* (AA) followed by the *conjunction* "then". The third subsection is set apart from the second by means of an *address appeal* (AA) followed by a change in *form media* (FM): "adhortatio" combined with a *semantic marker* (SemM) referring to a resumption and completion of the visions and interpretations of Jesus' crucifixion. The fourth subsection is set apart from the third by means of four markers: a *substitution on abstraction level* (SA^2) referring to the just completed visions with interpretations: *"these things* (ⲛⲁⲓ) that you saw" (83:15); a change in *form media* (FM): "commission"; a change in receptive *dramatis personae* (DP) (ἀλλογενής); a *conjunction*: οὖν.

The last section on level one (^{2}ST^3) is extremely short and consists merely of the remark that *"he* ([sic! *not I*; cf. 70:20] sc. Peter) came to his senses"(84:12-13).

Delimitation of Textsequences on Level Two

In order to save space I shall on this occasion limit my comments on level two to the second, and most important, subsections (^{2}ST^{21}, ^{2}ST^{22}, ^{2}ST^{23}, and ^{2}ST^{24}) on level one (^{1}ST^2).

The first subsection on level two (^{2}ST^{21}) within that section (^{1}ST^2), namely the "first part of visions and interpretations of Jesus' crucifixion" (72:5-73:14) is divided into two parts on level three: firstly (^{2}ST^{211}) the "vision of the attack on Jesus and Peter by the priests and the people" (72:5-9) and secondly (^{2}ST^{212}) the "interpretation of the vision by the Savior in form of a dialogue with Peter" (72:9-73:14). These two subtexts are divided by means of three markers in combination: a change in *form media* (FM): "dialogue"; a change in active and passive *dramatis personae* (DP): Savior/Peter; a *meta-communicative sentence* (MS): "and he said to me".

The second subsection on level two (^{2}ST^{22}) within the same section (^{1}ST^2), namely the "revelation of the Savior about the heretical opposition and the digression on anthropology and ecclesiology" ("the middle section" 73:14-80:23) is delimited into five further parts on level three:

the first (^{3}ST^{221}) contains "Peter's call to esoteric knowledge by the Savior" (73:14-23); the second part (^{3}ST^{222}) is made up of a "first series of two prophecies of apostasy from Gnosis" (73:23-75:7); the third part (^{3}ST^{223}) encompasses a "digression on contrary anthropological and ecclesiological convictions" (75:7-76:23); the fourth part (^{3}ST^{224}) contains a "second series of four prophecies of apostasies from Gnosis" (76:24-79:31), and the fifth part (^{3}ST^{225}) brings the "concluding assurance of the final triumph of the "minority" over the "majority" (79:32-80:23). These five subtexts are divided by way of a diversity of markers due to the nature of the text. The second subtext is set apart from the first through a change in *form media* (FM) in combination with a change in the status of the *dramatis personae* (DP): from Savior's direct address of Peter to Savior's information to Peter of the actions of the multitudes. The third subtext is set apart from the second through a change in *form media* (FM): simile and a *semantic marker* (SemM) emphasizing a universally valid and fundamental principle. The fourth subtext is set apart from the third by way of a change in *form media* (FM) in conjunction with a change in *dramatis personae* (DP): a resumption of characterizations; a *semantic marker* (SemM) introducing deceptive mysteries; *conjunction* δέ. The fifth subtext is marked off from the fourth by means of a change in *form media* (FM) from monologue to dialogue; a change in active and passive *dramatis personae* (DP); *a meta-communicative sentence* (MS): "and I *said*;" finally through a *substitution on abstraction level* of the third grade (SA^3): "... *what* you have told me".

The third subsection on level two (^{2}ST^{23}) within the same section (^{1}ST^2), namely the "second part and completion of visions and interpretations of Jesus crucifixion" (80:23-83:15) is delimited into two visions with concomitant interpretations by the Savior: the "vision of the two figures on and beside the cross with the Savior's interpretation" constitutes the first part (^{2}ST^{231}; 80:23-82:3) and the "vision of the Savior being filled with the Pleroma and its interpretation by the Savior" constitutes the second part (^{2}ST^{232}; 82:4-83:15). The markers setting these two Visions apart are a renewed surrogate of a *substitution on metalevel* (SMsurr): "and I *saw*" and the *conjunction* δέ.

The fourth subsection on level two (^{2}ST^{24}) within the same section (^{1}ST^2), namely the "conclusion in form of a commission" (83:15-84:4) is divided into three parts: firstly (^{3}ST^{241}) "the commission itself" (83:15-18); secondly (^{3}ST^{242}) the "basis for the commission" (83:19-84:6); finally (^{3}ST^{243}) the "exhortation and promise of Savior's presence" (84:7-11). The second subtext is set off from the first by means of a change in *form media* (FM) from commission to substantiation and the *conjunction* γάρ. The third subtext is separated from the second through the change in *form media* (FM) from substantiation to exhortation, and through the *conjunction* οὖν.

3. Interpretation of the Apocalypse of Peter

The question whether the Gnostic Christians behind the Apoc. Pet. are fighting one unanimous opposition in form of the Great Church or several oppositional groups from both the Orthodox Church and competing Gnostic circles should be answered on two levels: on the micro-structural level of exegesis of smaller units (due to lack of space here to a limited degree only, however) and on the macro-structural level of this document's composition and genre.[21]

If, as is often asserted, textsequences of different extent obtain their meaning and function only from a superior totality such as the macro-structure of the text as a whole or even the text-genre,[22] then we must address the question of composition and genre before we turn to the interpretation of individual passages.

3.1. Macro-Structural Composition

This document is divided—as we have seen—into three sections: the "conclusion" which is extremely short, and the "introduction" which in itself is a revelation; both will be dealt with in connection with the question of genre as will the superscript and the subscript.

The second section (^{1}ST^2) is as far as the macro-structural composition is concerned of great significance. In particular we should pay attention to the intercalation of "visions and interpretations of Jesus' crucifixion" with the surrounded "revelation of the oppositional heresy". On the literary level this very structure reveals that the author wants to intimate that there is a direct relationship between these three subsections, and that the surrounding parts concerning the crucifixion episode from the past is determinative for the "middle section" with regard to the present heresy. The surrounding "crucifixion sections" are

---

21 For these distinctions, see Hellholm, "Enthymemic Argumentation in Paul: The Case of Romans 6," in T. Engberg-Pedersen (ed.), *Paul in His Hellenistic Context*, Minneapolis, MN: Fortress/Edinburgh: T. & T. Clark 1995, 119-79, especially 122.

22 See Hellholm, "Amplificatio in the Macro-Structure of Romans," in S. E. Porter and Th. H. Olbricht (eds.), *Rhetoric and the New Testament. Essays from the 1992 Heidelberg Conference. FS Wilhelm Wuellner* (JSNTSup 90), Sheffield: JSOT Press 1993, 123-51, here 124f. with references.

given the form of visions and interpretations, since they are disclosed in retrospective, while the "heretical section" in the middle is given in form of direct revelations, since it is concerned with the present situation. Christology is in need of "flashback",[23] anthropology and soteriology not to the same extent! Therefore it seems adequate to begin by interpreting the surrounding crucifixion scenes and only thereafter turn to the revelation of the heretic opposition.

3.1.1. Visions and Interpretations of Jesus' Crucifixion

The first part of Peter's vision of the crucifixion scene reveals that the priests and the people attacking him and the Savior are without knowledge. Both at the beginning and at the end of the interpretation of the vision the Savior calls them "blind and deaf" (72:10-15 and 73:12-14). In addition to his "earthly" vision of the attackers Peter has another, "heavenly" vision of a "new light greater than the light of day", which "came down upon the Savior" (72:23-27). The development of these contrary visions takes place only in the second part of the visionary scene that follows upon the Savior's revelation about the opposition. In this introductory vision it was sufficient to point to the misunderstanding with regard to the priests, scribes and the people on the one hand, and the descending light upon the Savior on the other.

In the second part of Peter's revelation "the will of the undefiled Father" (80:25) is unfolded in two visions which then are interpreted by the Savior. In the first vision Peter sees two figures, one on the cross, the other above it. In the subsequent interpretation the Savior reveals the true nature of the two figures:

> He whom you saw on the tree, glad and laughing, this is the living Jesus. But this one into whose hands and feet they drive the nails is the fleshly (σαρκικόν) part which is the substitute (81:15-21).

The executioners of the crucifixion, who are Jews and not Romans,[24] are again characterized by the Savior as "blind ones" without knowledge (81:30-32).

Following immediately upon the first interpretation Peter had another vision (82:4-14) in which he saw someone about to approach him and the interpreting Savior. This figure was like the one who was laughing above the cross; he was <filled>[25] with the Holy Spirit and recog-

---

23 Brashler, *Apocalypse of Peter*, 129f., 132.
24 Cf. Koschorke, *Polemik*, 20: "Die Römer spielen überhaupt keine Rolle".

nized as the Savior. As in the first part of Peter's vision of the crucifixion scene (72:23-27) Peter also here sees a great indescribable light surrounding the two forms of the Savior.

Before the Savior communicates his interpretation of the vision, Peter gives his own testimony assuring that it is really he who experienced this vision of how the Savior was revealed (82:15-16).

The revelations given in these visions are characterized as "mysteries" (μυστήριον) by the Savior in his interpretation of the last vision. In greater detail than in the previous interpretations the *Christology* of these Gnostic Christians is revealed to Peter by the Savior functioning as *angelus interpres*.

Before the interpretation proper, however, the Savior confirms in a testimony of his own the truth and reliability of the revelations given to Peter (82:17-20).

As Klaus Koschorke convincingly has demonstrated, in the interpretation given by the Savior Peter learns first to distinguish between that part of the Savior, which is capable of suffering, his σαρκικὸν σῶμα and that part, which is not touched by suffering, his incorporeal body (ⲥⲱⲙⲁ ⲛⲁⲧⲥⲱⲙⲁ: 83:6-8).[26] Furthermore, Peter also learns about the complicated trichotomic nature (σῶμα/ψυχή/πνεῦμα) of the non-suffering part: (1) the non-corporeal σῶμα (83:6f.); (2) "the living Savior (σωτήρ), the primal part of him whom they seized" and who stood laughing at the executioners (82:28f.; cf. 81:18), since he knew "that they were born blind" (83:3); (3) the "I" of the Savior is his πνεῦμα νοερόν (83:8-10). These distinguishable forms of the Savior "entsprechen jeweils unterschiedliche Wesensformen des Erlösers".[27] What Peter in his vision saw coming toward the Savior was his νοερόν πλήρωμα, i.e. the Pleroma from the undefiled Father and it is this νοερόν πλήρωμα, "which unites the perfect (τέλειος) light with the pure Spirit" (83:13-15); Thus, Koschorke's conclusion is justified that "die Gestalt des 'Pleroma' den Soter in seiner Vollendung, in seiner eigentlichen Bestimmung (zeigt)".[28] This revelation about the *Savior's true nature* is the very conclusion of the revelation by the interpreting Savior of Peter's last vision in this document.

As we will see later the compositional structure of the crucifixion

---

25 Thus the emendation by Brashler, *Apocalypse of Peter*, 61; otherwise Werner, "Apocalypse of Peter," 709 with n. 35: "but it was <woven> in Holy Spirit", representing "the idea of the garment, such as is found in other Gnostic texts".

26 See Koschorke, *Polemik*, 24f.; Brashler, *Apocalypse of Peter*, 172f.

27 Koschorke, *Polemik*, 25; Brashler, ibid., 173.

28 Koschorke, ibid.

scenes is determinative for the semantic and pragmatic function of the Apoc. Pet. as a whole. Already now, however, we can begin to understand the importance of the arrangement of the crucifixion scenes around the "middle section" regarding the "heretical opposition". The three visions with their concomitant interpretations are arranged in such a way as to reach a climax at the very end of the third vision. The first is of an introductory art, the second deals with the corporeal vs. the incorporeal nature of the Savior, while the third is concerned with the trichotomic nature of the non-suffering part and the Savior's relation to the Pleroma.

Even if the central theme in these visions clearly is *Christology*, there are indications that also in these parts of the Apoc. Pet. the teaching of the opposition is on the agenda. In all three visionary accounts we encounter the characterization of the priests, the scribes, the people, and the executioners as being "blind and deaf", they are even called "born blind" in the last interpretation (83:3). Of course, here the opponents of the Savior are mentioned; the oppositional heretics are not directly mentioned but they are certainly intended as can be seen from the use of these characterizations also at the very end of the "digression" in the "middle section" (76:21-23).

3.1.2. Savior's Revelation to Peter Regarding the Heretical Opposition

Contrary to the "crucifixion sections" the "middle section" does not consist of visions and subsequent interpretations but is altogether made up of the Savior's revelation to Peter about the heretical opposition. However, it is equally well organized as the surrounding crucifixion sections. Also within this "middle section" (73:14-80:23) we find another intercalation between the two surrounding series of characterizations of apostasy from Gnosis (73:14-75:5 and 76:24-80:23) and the "digression"[29] (75:5-76:23) programmatically addressing the *anthropological* concepts that lead to *ecclesiological* positioning. In two parallel sections dealing with the universally fundamental principle of "like produces like" the contrast between mortal and immortal souls is addressed, this time though not on the Christological but on the anthropological level. Each section begins with a general simile in form of a reminding scriptural reference

---

29 Cf. Koschorke, *Polemik*, 50; Brashler, *Apocalypse of Peter*, 222f.; Werner, "Apocalypse of Peter," 702. With digression I here mean: "eine selbständige Texteinheit, deren Thema komplementär ... zum Hauptthema (ist)" (H. Plett, *Einführung in die rhetorische Textanalyse*, 3rd ed., Hamburg: Buske 1975, 54).

(75:7-11; cf. Matt 7:18 par.; 12:35; Jas 3:11-12, and 76:4-8; cf. Matt 7:16-18 par.). Each simile is followed by an explication of the principle in regard to the souls, the mortal and the immortal: the mortal souls "love the creatures of the matter (ὕλη) which came forth with them" (75:24-26); the immortal souls remain "in the Eternal One, the One of life and immortality of the life which they resemble" (76:15-17).

The preceding and succeeding sub-sections are structured in such a way that *before* the "digression" we encounter a call by the Savior to esoteric knowledge (73:14-23), which is followed by a first series of prophecies of apostasy from Gnosis (73:23-75:5). After a prediction of defection from Gnosis and persecution of Gnostic Christians the *first two* characterizations of the opponents are given. *After* the "digression" the series of characterizations is resumed (76:24-79:31), and after a new prediction of defection has been given *another four* characterizations of the opponents are launched. In conclusion an assurance of the final triumph of the Gnostic Christians is conveyed to Peter by the Savior (79:32-80:23). This is the compositional organization of the Savior's revelation about the heretical opposition to Peter.

3.1.3. Result of the Compositional Structure of the Apocalypse of Peter

What does this analysis of the composition of our text mean in regard to our initial question concerning the identification of the heretical opponents in this document? If our attempt has any validity it ought to be obvious that this text—in the words of Klaus Koschorke—"in seinem Grundgerüst von prägnanter Klarheit und darüber hinaus ... von hoher Aussagekraft (ist)".[30] If this is true, then we should also expect the problem of identity of the opposition to be solved on the basis firstly of the *Christological* concepts developed in the surrounding "visions of the Savior's crucifixion" and secondly on the basis of *anthropological* concepts revealed in the "digression" placed in the center of the "revelation of the heresy". In order to gain a net-result from my structural analysis and thus to arrive at a proper understanding of this text I shall now within limits address the semantics of content and the pragmatics of function.

3.2. Elements of Theology under Dispute and Their Distribution in the Apocalypse of Peter

When turning to the theological perspectives two aspects will be considered: (1) The most important elements of the theology under dispute

---

30 Koschorke, *Polemik*, 14.

between the adversaries; (2) The location of these various elements in the compositional structure of the document as presented above. The most essential theological element deliberated upon in the Apocalypse of Peter are: Christology, Anthropology, Soteriology and Ecclesiology.[31]

3.2.1. The Concept of Christology

The concept of Christology requires a twofold treatment: Firstly with regard to the Savior's relation to the undefiled Father and secondly with regard to the true nature of the Savior himself.

The concept of a dualistic cosmology, which plays such an important role in Gnostic systems, is nowhere really developed in this text but rather presupposed or only indirectly attested. In fact it serves merely as the background for the Christological and anthropological dualism. The superior deity is named the "Eternal One" (76:14-17) or the "Invisible One" (81:2), the "Undefiled Father" (80:25), or the "Father who is above the heavens" (70:22). His counterpart is the "Father of their (sc. the multitude's [sic!]) error (πλάνη)" (73:27) with his archons (77:4-8).

The inner relation between the Father, the Savior, and the elect, i.e. the true Christians, is disclosed programmatically and unmistakably in Gnostic categories in the introductory macarism of the elect presented to Peter by the Savior in his role as *angelus interpres*:

> Blessed are those who belong to the Father, <who> is above the heavens, he who has revealed life through me to those who come from life, since I have reminded (them of it) (70: 21-25).[32]

From this text it is obvious that there exists a unity of substance between the Father, the Savior, and the Gnostics, even though the latter are in need of being reminded of their eternal origin. The Savior's role is that of the Revealer of the "will of the undefiled Father" (80:25f.). The Revealer is identified with the "heavenly Son of Man",[33] and he and the receiving Gnostics are consubstantial (71:9-15).[34]

---

31 In "The Mighty Minority" Jervell has payed special attention to the theological elements: "Christology," "Salvation," "Ecclesiology," and "Paul" (*Unknow Paul*, 40f.).
32 Transl. Werner, "Apocalypse of Peter," in loc. with n. 17.
33 See Brashler, *Apocalypse of Peter*, 163f.
34 Cf. Birger A. Pearson, "The Apocalypse of Peter and Canonical 2 Peter,' in J. E. Goehring Ch. W. Hedrick, J. T. Sanders, H. D. Betz (eds.), *Gnosticism & the Early Christian World. FS James M. Robinson*, Sonoma, CA 1990, 67-74, here 72: "For the author of the Apocalypse of Peter—this is typical of Gnosticism in general—the elect, i.e., those who have received *gnosis*, share the divine nature of the Savior, being 'consubstantial' (ⲛ̄ϣⲃⲏⲣ ⲛ̄ⲟⲩⲥⲓⲁ = ὁμοούσιος, 71:14-15) with him".

Regarding the true nature of the Savior himself I shall be brief here, since this topic was dealt with already in § 3.1.1. As we saw earlier the most elaborate interpretation of the crucifixion scenes is found in the Savior's interpretation of Peter's last vision (82:21-83:15). It is only the fleshly part of the Savior that is capable of suffering.[35] The suffering Jesus is called the "firstborn" and thus unequivocally said to be a part of the demiurgical creation; he is further named the "House of demons (δαίμων) and the stony vessel in which they dwell",[36] which by all likelihood refers to the fleshly body as the territory occupied by the demons. Also such designations as "<the man> of Elohim" (cf. Mark 15:34 parr.) and "<the man> of the cross (σταυρός)"[37] (cf. 1 Cor 1:23; 2:2; Gal 3:1) indicate the fleshly character of the suffering Jesus: "Sie weis[en] den Gekreuzigten als Geschöpf jener demiurgischen Macht aus, die dieses ihr eignes Gebilde am 'Holz' vernichtet hat...".[38] In their "blindness" they have destroyed their own creation, "for the son of their own glory instead of my servant they have put to shame", confirms the interpreting Savior. In contrast to the σαρκικὸν σῶμα which is put to death, the "living Jesus" cannot be touched by the archons and executioners, since his body is incorporeal. This is the essential distinction to be made concerning the Christological predications in the Apocalypse of Peter.

The distribution of the Christological delineation is almost exclusively concentrated to the crucifixion sections with their visions and interpretations (^{2}ST^{21}; 72:5-73:14 and ^{2}ST^{23}; 80:23-83:15) that surround the heresy section. This confirms my assumption from the macro-structural delimitation that the surrounding crucifixion sections are determinative for understanding the "middle section" also from the point of view of their semantic content.

3.2.2. The Concept of Anthropology

The fundamental principle governing all anthropological statements in Apoc. Pet. is the hellenistic principle developed in Gnosticism: τὸ γὰρ ὅμοιον τῷ ὁμοίῳ νοητόν — *For like is known by like* (Corp. Herm. XI.20).[39]

This principle is depicted in two parallel sections (75:7-76:4 and 76:4-23). The structural composition with two similes followed by explica-

---

35 For the following, see Koschorke, *Polemik*, 21.
36 Cf. Werner, ibid., 712 n. 37: "Here evidently use is made of the legend according to which Solomon imprisoned demons in pitchers. Cf. Testim. Truth (NHC IX 3, p. 70.10-14) and on this B. A. Pearson, NHS XV, 193 and note".
37 Transl. Werner, ibid.; see below p. 64 n. 49.
38 Koschorke, *Polemik*, 21.

tions is demonstrated above pp. 47f. and 57f. The explications bring the correlation of the pictures with the issue itself without, however, carrying out an explicit *tertium comparationis* interpretation.[40]

The principle "like is known by like" is *per definitionem* a relational principle and is described as such in both similes in positive as well as in negative terms by means of the verbs "produce" and "gather from" respectively. This is further developed in the explications. There are two kinds of souls:[41] (a) The souls of "these ages" (75:16; 83:18), which love matter (ὕλη) and which will encounter eternal destruction and death (75:19-26,31; 76:13). Like ὕλη they have their *origin* in what is not good (75:11-12) and since they are from "this place" (83:30f.) they have nothing to remember, they are "mortal souls" (75:31f.). (b) The souls who are not from this world, where they are "strangers (ἀλλογενής)" (83:17), are "from life" (70:24) and are "immortal" (75:14,26f.), of "immortal essence (οὐσία) (83:23). There *origin* is "from the truth" (75:13) and they "remain in the Eternal One, the One of life and immortality" (76:15f.). They are capable of remembering their origin, if through a Revealer they are reminded thereof (70:23-25).

The distribution of anthropological statements in our text is not as concentrated to one section as are the the Christological predications. However, they are most developed in the "digression" ($^3ST^{223}$; 75:7-76:23) of the "middle section" ($^2ST^{22}$). In addition anthropological statements are found in particular in the "introductory macarism" ($^4ST^{1211}$; 70:20-32) and in the "concluding commission" ($^2ST^{24}$; 83:15-84:11).

3.2.3. The Concept of Soteriology

As in practically all Early Christian Writings also in Apoc. Pet. Christology and soteriology are closely interconnected. When dealing with the notion of soteriology three questions will have to be discussed: How is

---

39 Text: A. D. Nock/A.-J. Festugière, *Corpus hermeticum. Tome 1*, Paris: Les belles lettres, 1972. For further examples and literature, see J. Jervell, *Imago Dei. Gen 1,26f. im Spätjudentum, in der Gnosis und in den paulinischen Briefen* (FRLANT 76), Göttingen: Vandenhoeck & Ruprecht, 1960, 130; H. Conzelmann, *Der erste Brief an die Korinther* (KEK 5), 2nd ed., Göttingen: Vandenhoeck & Ruprecht, 1981, 91.

40 In the correlation of the second simile A. Werner, "Apocalypse of Peter," in loc. and in n. 26 restores the text so that the *tertium* actually is given: "But that (other soul) comes from the eternal (tree), the (tree) of life and immortality". This is unlikely. Brashler, *Apocalypse of Peter*, in loc. and Brashler/Bullard, "Apocalypse of Peter," in loc. in my opinion translate correctly: "...the Eternal One, the One of life..."; so also Koschorke, *Polemik*, 73.

41 Cf. Koschorke, ibid., 72-74.

salvation brought?, What is salvation?, and Who will receive salvation?

How is salvation brought?

The most succinct text in Apoc. Pet. as far as the question of "how" is concerned is the Savior's macarism (70:21-25) in the introductory monologue, already quoted and discussed above in connection with the treatment of Christology. Here it is stated that the heavenly, undefiled Father has revealed life through the Savior. Thus, the Father is the *Originator* and the Savior the *Revealer* of the message of redemption.

What is salvation?

The mission of the Revealer is to "illuminate" (71:4) the consubstantial souls, to call them to "knowledge" (71:21), and to "remind" them of their heavenly origin and reveal life to them (70:23-25), i.e. to free them from "matter (ὕλη)" (cf. 75:24). This is the μυστήριον which has been revealed to the elect and of which they are reminded again in this text. Thus, also in this apocalypse salvation is accomplished through γνῶσις, i.e. through knowledge of

> Who we were, What we have become, Where we were, Whither we have been cast, Whither we hasten, From what we have been set free.[42]

From the structure of Apoc. Pet., however, we can easily discern that the revelation given here is more specific than the general Gnostic awakening call, the reminder of the heavenly origin and promise of redemption from this world. The major purpose of the revelation given in Apoc. Pet. is directly stated in 71:25-27, where the interpreting Savior says, "He (sc. the Savior) called you so that you would know him in the proper way."[43] This programmatic statement is found at the end of the introductory monologue and is fully developed in the visions and interpretations of the crucifixion. What is at stake here is evidently the question of a true Christology, i.e. a correct understanding of the nature of the Savior.

Who will receive salvation?

The answer to this question is grounded in the principle of "likeness" (ⲉⲓⲛⲉ) discussed above.[44] Only those who have their origin in the Eternal

---

42 Clem. Alex., *Excerpta ex Theodoto*, 78.
43 Transl. Brashler, *Apocalypse of Peter*, in loc.
44 See n. 34 and § 3.2.2.

One and resemble him (76:15-17), who are "consubstantial" with the "heavenly Son of Man" (71:14f.) can be reminded of their "immortal essence" (83:23). They are also the only ones, who are able to recognize the true nature of the Savior, the "living Jesus", who cannot suffer death on the tree.

The "mortal souls", who have their origin in this world and are consubstantial with ὕλη, have nothing to remember and falsely believe that the sarkic figure on the tree, who is the creation of the archons (75:25), is the real Savior. Therefore they are incapable of accepting the "Erlösungslehre" of the Gnostic Christians; on the contrary they are in fact combatting it. "So haben die Gnostiker und ihre orthodoxen Opponenten nichts miteinander gemein,"[45] for "deaf and blind ones join with their own kind" (76:21-23).

Is this a doctrine of ontological–deterministic predestination as Brashler insists,[46] or are there passages that soften a strict determinism as Koschorke maintains?[47] The answer is particularly important in view of our attempt to identify the "multitude" (majority) and the "little ones" (minority), and can only be answered in connection with the detailed interpretation of passages entailing this terminology. In order to avoid duplication and to save space these passages will be dealt with in the following paragraph on ecclesiology.

3.2.4. The Concept of Ecclesiology

The passages dealing with ecclesiology are for the most part localized in the "middle" or "heresy section" ($^2ST^{22}$; 73:14-80:23). The general and most essential critique of the heretical opponents is that they "hold fast to the name of a dead man" (74:13f.).[48] This is evident from the structure of this section, since it makes up the "content of the false teaching" as described in the "predictions of defection from Gnosis" ($^4ST^{2221}$). Only in subsequent sections are the "multifarious appearances of the heresy" reported. The worship of a "dead man" in fact unveils the opposition to be the Great Church, which is called heretic (–αἵρεσις; 74:22). The "dead man" (74:13f.; 78:17) in the "revelation about the present heresy" is, of course, identical with that form of the Savior, who is capable of suffering in the "retrospective crucifixion scenes" and a result of the *Pauline* influ-

---

45 Koschorke, *Polemik*, 73.
46 Brashler, *Apocalypse of Peter*, 203 et passim.
47 Koschorke, ibid., 74.
48 Koschorke, ibid., 42.

ence, especially the designation of the Savior as "<the man> of the Cross" (cf. 74:16-22; 82:21-26).[49] Consequently, there is a direct connection between the Christology in the surrounding sections and that in the middle one.

According to one important passage at the beginning of the "heresy section" (73:23-28) the Gnostic Christians were once of a significant number,[50] since at first a "multitude" accepted the Gnostic teaching, but later turned away "according to the will of the Father of their error". Thus, this defection is described as a defection from the "will of the undefiled Father", i.e. from Gnostic Christianity. Also after the specified characterizations, in the "concluding assurance" of the Savior in his dialogue with Peter ($^3ST^{225}$), Peter—in a *summary* of the foregoing visions and interpretations—repeats and specifies what was said in 73:23-28:

> Indeed (μέν) there are *multitudes* that will mislead other *multitudes* of living ones (80:2-4).

In spite of the similarities between these two passages, which secures the identity of the "gnostic multitude(s)", there are two divergences that are noticeable: (a) the existence of *two multitudes*, and (b) the multitude of living ones are *actively* being misled by the multitude of orthodox Christians. This reflects a different situation than the one in the beginning. Now those "who oppose the truth" are "numerous".[51]

The designation "little ones" is more difficult to unravel as the opposite interpretations indicate. Koschorke asserts that they are the ordinary churchmembers, who are being deceived by their leaders.[52] Brashler and Werner on the other hand maintain that the Gnostics called themselves the "little ones", and thus constitutes a self-designation.[53] Both interpretations are problematic, since the purpose of this Apocalypse seems to have a double function: (1) to strengthen the elect, especially emphasized in the paraenetic sections and (2) to bring hope to the deceived ones. Koschorke must work with two different groups of "multitudes" in the Great Church: the "apostates" (73:23f.) and the "ordinary churchmembers" (80:4), and also explain how the "leaders of the Church" (79:21-31), who "will rule over the little ones" can be called a "multitude" (80:3).

---

49 See especially Koschorke, ibid., 21f., 40-46; Werner, "Apocalypse of Peter," 703 and n. 38. See further above p. 60 ad n. 37.
50 See Brashler, ibid., 137.
51 Cf. Brashler, ibid., 217.
52 Koschorke, ibid., 81 and especially 84.
53 Brashler, ibid., 154; Werner, "Apocalypse of Peter," 704.

Furthermore, it is hard to believe that the "little ones"—if they were ordinary churchmembers—can be said to have been taken prisoners (79:21) or that these "little ones" alone will be victorious (80:15f.). Brashler's and Werner's solution is equally problematic, since if the "little ones" were Gnostics, why do they have to be "released" (78:31) and how can they "be ruled over" (80:31)? In spite of Koschorke's objection[54] the best solution seems to be that the "little ones" designates two types of "immortal souls": (1) deceived "immortal souls", who were reminded but have *forgotten* who they really are (77:10; 76:27-77:22) and thus in need of being *reminded again*, and (2) Gnostic Christians who *have been reminded* of their origin but encounter the danger of being deceived by the majority in the Great Church and thus are in need of being *strengthened* in particular in their belief in the Gnostic Christology and anthropology. "Therefore," the Savior commands Peter to present "these things that you saw to the strangers (ἀλλογενής), who are not of this age", those who "were chosen by virtue of their immortal essence (οὐσία)" (83:15-22), i.e. "the little ones", whether deceived or not.

The Gnostic Christians, once a majority, have been severely decimated, since a "multitude of living ones" have been lead astray and gone over to the Great Church (79:32-80:7). They are evidently an outnumbered minority,[55] but sure of their *superior* knowledge of who they are and hoping for their *mighty* victory at the end of this age promised them by the Savior through Peter's revelation:

> For a time determined for them [the misleading multitude –DH] in proportion to their error they will rule over the little ones. And after the completion of the error, the never-aging one of the immortal understanding shall become young, and they (the little ones) shall rule over those who are their rulers. (80:9-17)

These are the signs of the "'Mighty' Minority of Gnostic Christians" as portrayed in the Coptic Gnostic Apocalypse of Peter.

3.3. *The Apocalypse of Peter and Its Genre*

Martin Krause is with some hesitation prepared to accept this document as an apocalypse.[56] Koschorke almost completely overlooks the rele-

---

54 Koschorke, ibid., 82-85.
55 Cf. Brashler, *Apocalypse of Peter*, 225.
56 M. Krause, "Die literarischen Gattungen der Apokalypsen von Nag Hammadi", in D. Hellholm (ed.), *Apocalypticism in the Mediterranean World and the Near East*, Tübingen: Mohr (Siebeck), 2nd ed., 1989, 621-37, here 627f.

vance of this question, while Brashler and Werner emphasize the significance of the generic form for the function of the text.[57] In this regard two questions become pertinent: Why an apocalypse? and Why to Peter? These questions deserve a more adequate treatment than can be given here, where I can only hint at a few answers.

Besides the visions, the *angelus interpres*, the pseudonymity and the title, the most striking feature of an apocalypse is found in the introduction, where the hierarchical revelation embedment with God as the *Originator*, the Savior as the *Revealer* and Peter as the *Transmitter* shows great similarities with other apocalypses.[58] The reason for choosing this form is evident: the Gnostic Community is in a deep crisis, threatened as it is by the Great Church. Their members need to be strengthened and comforted in order to prevent further defection. But also the "misled little ones", who are now under the dominion of the leaders of the Great Church, are in need of being reminded anew of their true origin and essence in order to be saved. For this the authority of an apocalypse revealed by the Savior himself as *angelus interpres* is necessitated.

As Peter is claimed by the Great Church as its leader, the Gnostic Community now claims him as its founder and leader, "to whom these mysteries have been given so that you (sc. Peter) could know *through revelation*" the true and saving nature of the Savior (82:19-20).[59]

Three of the apocalypses from Nag Hammadi—The Apocalypse of Peter, The Acts of Peter and the Twelve, and The First Apocryphon of James—recount, how Peter receives special revelation through visions, and as Elaine H. Pagels has shown, "they share three premises: *first*, that the apostles lack understanding and power, and therefore need further revelation to remedy their deficiencies; *second*, that such direct access to Christ is available through visions long after the resurrection; and *third*, that such revelations are granted only to certain persons and not to others".[60]

---

57 Brashler, *Apocalypse of Peter*, 121-57; Werner, "Apocalypse of Peter," 703.
58 Cf. Hellholm, The Visions He Saw or: To Encounter the Future in Writing. An Analysis of the Prologue of John's Apocalyptic Letter", in T. Jennings (ed.), *Text and Logos. The Humanistic Interpretation of the New Testament. FS H. Boers* (Scholars Press Homage Series), Atlanta, GA: Scholars Press 1990, 109-46.
59 Cf. Koschorke, *Polemik*, 32-35; Brashler, *Apocalypse of Peter*, 206-16.
60 Elaine H. Pagels, "Visions Appearances, and Apostolic Authority: Gnostic and Orthodox Traditions," in B. Aland (ed.), *Gnosis. FS Hans Jonas*, Göttingen: Vandenhoeck & Ruprecht 1978, 415-30, here 424.

The Markan Community and the "Mighty Minority"

Donald Juel

Exegetical revolutions occur infrequently. When they do, they are often forced by historical events. The Holocaust is a watershed for Bible readers as much as for students of history and politics. The New Testament will never look the same since Christian involvement in the tragedy has been seared into our collective memories. Revolutions may also come about because of new discoveries. The Qumran Scrolls and the works unearthed at Nag Hammadi have required a new narrative of the first century within which to locate the New Testament. Revolutions will not occur, however, until an interpreter asks a new question. For many in my generation, Jacob Jervell has served as a catalyst for a remarkable shift in New Testament studies by posing those new questions. My seminar with Prof. Jervell on the Acts of the Apostles at Yale University in 1970 was the beginning of an exegetical revolution for me. What set it in motion was a series of questions about the implied audience of Acts, the reconstruction of which is nicely captured in the phrase "mighty minority." It is with gratitude for those new questions that I undertake a brief study of the audience in the Gospel of Mark.

The Implied Audience

For whom was the book we know as the "Gospel according to Mark" written? We do not know. That must first be said. There is no explicit identification of an audience, just as there is no explicit mention of an author. The host of conjectures by commentators are just that: conjectures. Some guesses are more educated than others; some are more interesting than others. Any guesses will finally have to rely on clues in the narrative. In recent parlance, hazarding an educated guess about the Markan audience is known as reconstructing an "implied audience"— taking as evidence what the author expects readers to know, what they are interested in.[1] While the distance between an implied audience and an actual, flesh and blood group in the past may be impossible to bridge, some impression of an audience can be formed.

Such reconstruction is not a frivolous exercise. For some, who believe literature is only meaningful in its "original" setting, such work is crucial. According to this view, a biblical work "means" what it "meant" to an ancient group for whom it was written. Even those of a more literary bent, however, who are convinced that the Bible's meaning to contemporary audiences is not confined to what a work meant to other readers, will find that the exercise of attending to an implied audience can discipline and shape present readings. We may discover there are things we are expected to know. Study of that implied knowledge may deepen our appreciation of the work. Sometimes knowledge can make sense of something previously unintelligible. Awareness of the ethos of scriptural argument in the ancient world, for example, illumines some of the obscure arguments in Paul's letters and the Gospels—obscure because we have not been trained to make or appreciate such arguments.

I will argue that such reconstruction of an implied audience is not only useful to contemporary interpreters but that it is theologically necessary.

Identity and Labels

The most obvious feature of Mark's implied audience is that they speak and read Greek. There was a time when that was enough to convince scholars that the work was written for Gentiles. The last decades have witnessed a flurry of scholarship on Greek-speaking Judaism, however, and the assumption that Greek works could not be written to Jewish groups can no longer be made. Hellenized Judaism was not only the fertile ground from which early Christianity sprang; as Jervell has argued, Greek-speaking Jews were also among the intended audience of some of the Gospels.

Who were these Greek-speaking and Greek-reading people for whom Mark wrote? Not surprisingly, opinions vary among commentators. The tradition that Mark was written in Rome probably goes back as far as Papias, who believed the author of the Gospel, "Mark" was Peter's

---

[1] Two standard discussions of "audience" are Seymour Chatman's *Story and Discourse: Narrative Structure in Fiction and Film* (Ithica: Cornell University Press, 1978), and Wayne Booth's *The Rhetoric of Fiction* (Chicago: University of Chicago Press, 1983). For a brief discussion of the categories in regard to Mark's Gospel see D. Juel, *A Master of Surprise: Mark Interpreted* (Minneapolis: Fortress, 1994), 128-31.

"interpreter."[2] The notion still has modern advocates. Vincent Taylor still speaks for many: "The Gospel was probably written for the use of the Church in Rome."[3] Not surprisingly, other proposals have been made. Larry Hurtado, for example, will speak only of a location "outside Palestine."[4] Howard Kee locates the composition in southern Syria.[5]

While opinions may vary on the location of the Gospel's composition, commentators are remarkably consistent on certain matters. Virtually everyone employs the term "Christian" to describe the movement out of which Mark comes and to which readers are invited.[6] Yet if there is anything about which we may be certain, it is that Mark's audience did not know they were "Christians." The label does not appear in the Gospel, and its use in virtually all scholarly literature is a misleading anachro-

---

2   For an assessment of Papias' testimony, see my "From Papias to Perrin," *Master of Surprise*, 11-30.
3   *The Gospel according to St. Mark* (London: Macmillan, 1963), 32. So also Robert Gundry, *Mark* (Grand Rapids: Eerdmans, 1993), 1045.
4   *Mark* (San Francisco: Harper and Row, 1983), xix: "The only positive conclusion to draw is that Mark wrote for Gentile Christians located somewhere outside Palestine." William Lane (Mark [Grand Rapids: Eerdmans, 1974], 25), believes it "apparent, moreover, that Mark prepared his Gospel for Gentile Christians who were familiar with the OT in the Greek version, and who needed an explanation of Palestinian customs and practices." Mary Ann Tolbert (*Sowing the Gospel* [Minneapolis: Fortress, 1989], 304, believes Mark was not written to a community but to individuals. The "individuals," however, are still identified as "individual Christians experiencing persecution because of their faith." Robert Gundry (*Mark*, 1045) cites Clement's *Adumbrationes* as suggesting Mark wrote for Caesar's knights:

> Especially in Rome, the center of power and culture, and more especially among these knights, representing Roman power and culture, death by crucifixion would be repugnant and an apology for the cross, such as Mark's, would be called for.

More cautious is Williamson (*Mark* [Atlanta: John Knox, 1983], 25), who prefers to make no judgment about the particularities of the community within which and for whom the Gospel was written. He does so in the interest of focusing on present engagement with the Gospel. One must ask, however, if such focus on the present is not purchased at the expense of any particularity. The process of translation alone presumes a sense of the world out of which the Gospel came. And without some awareness of the Gospel's particularity, it is not clear how readers can adequately defend against the tyranny of individual experience and cultural bias.
5   Howard Kee, *Community of the New Age* (Philadelphia: Westminster, 1977), 176-77.
6   This is the case even with someone like Joel Marcus, whose *The Way of the Lord: Christological Exegesis of the Old Testament in the Gospel of Mark* (Louisville: Westminster/John Knox, 1992), emphasizes the great similarity between Mark's and other Jewish forms of scriptural interpretation.

nism, obscuring significant questions that arise as soon as the absence of "Christian" is taken seriously. In its modern setting, "Christian" stands over against "Muslim" and "Jew" as a coherent religious alternative. The absence of such a label in "Christian" literature prior to the last decades of the second century should raise questions about the identity of those who confessed Jesus as "Christ" and "Son of God."

How would believers in Jesus among Mark's implied audience identify themselves? We can hazard guesses about the social circumstances of the implied audience, but by what name would they have recognized themselves? By what name would they have been identified by others? Over against what and whom did they define themselves? To be specific, given the location of the story, the cast of characters, the concerns about sabbath and purity, and the presence of scriptural language and titles, did these believers in Jesus understand themselves as something other than "Jews"? That might well seem to be the case in the Fourth Gospel, where "the Jews" appears as a designation for those on the outside. The absence of a corresponding label for Jesus' followers, however, and the positive use of "Israelite" in 1:47, do not give evidence even in the Fourth Gospel of a religious identity distinct from those available in Jewish tradition. What is the case in Mark's Gospel?

Traditional labels are remarkably absent in Mark. Where they do occur, the usage suggests familiarity with Israel's tradition. The term λαός occurs only twice (and as a variant in 11:32). The second occurrence (14:2: the chief priests and scribes fear "a riot among the people"), may or may not reflect knowledge of traditional usage. The first, however, is in a citation of Isaiah ("This people honors me with their lips, but their hearts are far from me" [Mark 7:6—a passage that merits further attention]). "The people" is tied here to Israel, the people of God.

The term "Israel" occurs only twice. The first is in Jesus' citation of the *Shema* in 12:29 ("Hear, O Israel... .") in response to a lawyer's question about the greatest commandment. The second is in the passion narrative, in the mockery of the chief priests and scribes ("Let the Christ, the King of Israel, come down now from the cross"). "Israel" is thus employed only by Jews among Jews.

Only slightly more common is the term Ἰουδαῖος. Of the six occurrences in Mark, five appear in the passion narrative in the expression "the King of the Jews." The term is employed only by Gentiles. The single exception—and the only occurrence outside the passion narrative—is in chapter 7, where the narrator adds an explanation about practices among "all the Jews."

The term ἔθνη, while not common, appears in significant places. In Jesus' final prediction of his passion and resurrection, he speaks of being condemned to death by the "scribes, chief priests, and elders," who will "deliver him over to the Gentiles" (10:33). Romans are identified by a category that distinguishes them from Jews—though significantly, it is not "the Jews" of whom Jesus speaks but the "scribes, chief priests, and elders."

A few verses later, Jesus employs "Gentile" in a way one would expect from a Jew. "You know that among the Gentiles those whom they recognize as their rulers lord it over them, and their great ones are tyrants over them. But it is not so among you" (10:42). The disciples are to view Gentile ways as a foil. There is little suggestion that Mark's implied audience is to hear the verses in any other way. For Gentile leaders, the words might be experienced as judgment—but there would have to be convincing evidence elsewhere that the "implied audience" included Gentile rulers. An appreciation of the contrast between "Gentile ways" and how it will be among the faithful can be presumed.

The next two occurrences, in 11:17 and 13:10, speak of the inclusion of Gentiles in God's mission. After driving money changers and merchants out of the temple courts, Jesus cites a passage from Isaiah as justification for his actions: "My house shall be called a house of prayer for all the Gentiles" (Mark 11:17, citing Isa 56:7). A bit later, speaking to his inner circle of disciples, Jesus promises that "first the gospel must be preached to all the Gentiles." The NRSV translates the term in both cases as "nations." In view of earlier usage, there is little justification for translating "nations." "Nations" are to be distinguished from Israel. Jesus' indictment of the temple has something to do with a failure to make a place for Gentiles; Jesus' forecast of what is to come promises a future not bounded by the confines of Israel. In both cases, however, precedent is established from within Israel's tradition. The first is warranted by a quotation from Isaiah; Jesus' promise "to all the Gentiles" is little more than a restatement of God's promises to Abraham in Genesis about his seed serving as a blessing "for all the Gentiles." The perspective from which the inclusion of Gentiles is promised is thoroughly Jewish.

Closely related to ἔθνος is the term "Greek" in 7:26. The woman with whom Jesus has an exchange is identified as a "Greek, a Syrophoenician by birth." The NRSV translates, "Now the woman was a Gentile, of Syrophoenician origin." Justification for such translation can be found in the regular juxtaposition of "Jew" and "Greek" in Paul's letters and in Acts.

Remarkable is the inference Vincent Taylor draws from the terminology:

> Mark describes the woman as 'a Greek' ... and since he further characterizes her as a [Syrophoenician by birth], it is probable that he means 'a pagan' or 'Gentile,' a sign that he has Gentile readers in mind. (Taylor, 349)

The terminology suggests nothing of the sort about Mark's implied audience. The identification of the woman as a "Greek" would be of no more or less interest to a Gentile than to a Jewish audience. As the story continues, it would in fact appear that Jesus reflects Jewish prejudice and is concerned about protecting Jewish sensibilities. Gentile readers may of course appreciate the story, but only with a sense that their place is not at the table with "the children" but on the floor with the dogs.

What do we learn from observing the various labels Mark employs? They are not particularly common in the Gospel, and we are given no explicit sense of what labels would be appropriate to insiders. How would the disciples have understood themselves? Some are introduced by their profession: Simon and Andrew, James and John are fishermen; Levi is a tax collector. Like the common people, they are not Pharisees or Sadducees—though Pharisees apparently expect Jesus' disciples to be more careful about sabbath observance (2:23-28), and some are surprised the disciples do not observe fasts (2:18-22). Jesus' followers do not qualify as lawyers, scribes, elders, or chief priests. Yet they are surely not "Gentiles" or "Greeks," since exceptional characters, like the Syrophoenician woman, are clearly marked.

"Jews" is probably the most apt label available, if only because the disciples are included in the group Pilate describes collectively in identifying Jesus as "King of the Jews." Yet it is not clear the disciples would have used the label "Jew" to describe themselves. In Mark, there is a clear difference in the way "Jews" and Gentiles speak. "Jew" is never employed as a self-reference. And when the chief priests and scribes mock the crucified Jesus, they do not speak of him as "the King of the Jews" but as "the Christ the King of Israel." They would presumably prefer the designation "children of Israel" or "Israelites," consonant with the scriptural, "Hear, O Israel" cited earlier in the narrative.

The narrator is consistent in this regard. Gentiles refer to Jews as "Jews;" Jews do not. What, then, of Mark's implied readers? Ought readers to regard them as "Jews" or "children of Israel"? Does the reader, in other words, assume the perspective of a Jew or a Gentile in hearing the story?

One piece of evidence might be the sole passage in which "Jew" is used outside the passion narrative. It is employed by the narrator in an explanatory note. In the context of Jesus' debate with the Pharisees and scribes about washing, the narrator explains:

> For the Pharisees, and all the Jews, do not eat unless they thoroughly wash their hands, thus observing the tradition of the elders; and they do not eat anything from the market unless they wash it; and there are also many other traditions that they observe, the washing of cups, pots, and bronze kettles. (Mark 7:3-4)

Such a comment is intended for readers unfamiliar with the intricacies of Pharisaic practice. A reasonable assumption is that Mark's "Gentile" audience needed information about practices among "Jews." There are problems with such an interpretation, however. The narrator has offered no explanations earlier in the narrative about purity laws, dietary practices, sabbath regulations, and scriptural citations, implying that readers would be familiar with such matters. It is not clear, furthermore, what is meant by "all the Jews". The narrative has already featured a class of people identified as "sinners and tax collectors" with whom Jesus associates and eats. These people are not Greeks—not Gentiles. Yet they do not observe the proper dietary rules. Nor, we learn, do some of Jesus' disciples. Does that mean they are not "Jews"? Given what we have learned already in the narrative, the comment cannot be taken as evidence that the narrator is ignorant of divisions among Jews. Of all the Gospel writers, Mark is the most careful to differentiate among Pharisees, Sadducees, Herodians, scribes, chief priests, and elders.

Perhaps we need a category like "non-observant" Jews to do justice to the narrative. We know of such categories from Jewish literature. The label *"am haaretz"* could be applied to people who belonged to Israel but were not "proper." Mark's sketch is not so different. It is in fact more complex. "Jews" occupy a whole spectrum with respect to observance of the law. At the one end are Pharisees, clearly observant. But we learn of at least one other group that is curious about matters of piety. We are not told they are observant, but these people know that the religious fast, and they wonder why Jesus' followers do not: "Why do John's disciples and the disciples of the Pharisees fast, but your disciples do not fast?" (2:18) The questioners are not identified as disciples of either John or the Pharisees. We are to presume they are neither. They serve as common people with some respect for marks of traditional piety. Other members of Abraham's family are even less respectable. They make up the "crowds" who come to Jesus. Lowest of all are the "sinners and tax collectors," people with whom Jesus eats, thus scandalizing the pious.

The narrator thus depicts a community that ranges from pious Pharisees to impious sinners and tax collectors, with several distinctions in between. And from the perspective of the narrator, all these groups would be included by Pilate and the Romans within the category of "Jews."

So who are "all the Jews" who observe such careful ritual practice according to the "tradition of the elders"? Appealing to compositional reconstruction to solve the problem ("unthinking redaction") is tempting but probably unconvincing. More plausible would be to view "all the Jews" in 7:3 from the Pharisaic perspective. The Pharisees—and all observant Jews—are careful about washing. Such behavior is hardly typical of all those whom Romans would have regarded as "Jews," however. Even if the explanatory comment about washing is intended for non-Jews among the readership who are unfamiliar with Pharisaic practices, the question still remains whether the reader shares the perspective of one inside the Jewish community or that of the Romans.

Jewish Concerns

Here, I must be brief. I have argued elsewhere that the "Markan Community" implied by the narrative is expected to know a great deal about Jewish matters and to share Jewish concerns. Readers are expected to know the scriptures. "As it is written" appears at the beginning of the Gospel; allusions to and echoes of Israel's scriptures appear throughout and are essential to an appreciation of the story.[7] Readers are not only expected to know the scriptures, but are to understand the intricacies of learned scriptural argument (esp. 12:24-27 and 35-37).

The controversy stories in the opening chapters and the more extended controversies in chapter 12 suggest a readership invested in matters relating to observance of the law. Jesus deals explicitly with dietary laws, sabbath regulations, matters of purity, payment of taxes to Romans, belief in the resurrection, and the relationship of temple sacrifices to keeping the commandments. And while Jesus consistently transgresses sacred boundaries and issues rulings that place him far outside the "hedge" the later Rabbis would place around the torah, departures

---

7 Juel, *Master of Surprise*, 133-39; Marcus, *The Way of the Lord*.

from traditional practices are marked, addressed, and justified, often by appeal to the scriptures.

Finally, language used to speak about Jesus belongs within the scriptural heritage of Israel. Terms like "prophet," "Christ," "Son of God" and "Son of David" had enjoyed currency within Greek-speaking Jewish communities long before Mark wrote. While influence of hellenism on the use of such biblical conceptions had been great, the context within which they belong is nevertheless Jewish.

The Mighty Minority

In view of all this data, I find highly questionable the traditional identification of Mark's implied audience as "Gentile Christian." The label "Christian" does not appear, and one might well ask how anyone could imagine that Mark was written for a "Gentile" audience. The christological (and theological) conceptions are thoroughly Jewish. The conflict that drives the story has to do with Jesus and the Law. Jesus' death is interpreted in conjunction with the end of the temple.[8] Characterization of Mark's readership as Gentile owes more to a model of first-century "Christian" history than to any data in the Gospel—and it is precisely that model Jervell has so thoroughly reconstructed.

The "mighty minority" is as significant a feature in Mark's Gospel as in Luke-Acts. That Mark was written to believers in Jesus seems clear. That those believers understood themselves to be "Christians" is simply untrue. That the implied audience included Gentiles is highly likely, as Jesus' promise in 13:10 anticipates. Inclusion of Gentiles in no way implies the demise of Israel, however, as the citation of Isaiah 56:7 in 11:17 shows. Such "replacement" theology, common throughout the history of the church, can find no justification in Mark. Jesus' polemic against the temple and its leaders is specific: it is the "scribes, chief priests, and elders" whose future is tied to the temple. They—not all Israel—are the wicked tenants who will be punished.[9]

How other Jewish communities would have read Mark's Gospel is an interesting question. The lack of explicit polemics in Mark of the sort found in Matthew, Luke, and John perhaps suggests that tensions within the Jewish community had not yet reached the point where boundaries

---

8 Juel, *Messiah and Temple* (Missoula, Mont: Scholars Press, 1977).
9 Care is not always exercised by commentators at this point. It is common to see in these verses "the rejection of Israel." Even the destruction of the temple is read in overly broad terms. Howard Kee (*Community*, 150) speaks of the "cursing of Israel as the planting of God."

had to be drawn and some family members excluded. If pressed, however, I expect the community implied by the Markan narrative would lay claim to all the traditional categories, from "Jews" to "children of Israel" to "the people of God." And I want to be as clear as Jervell was in his essays on Luke-Acts: the "Israel" here is not a new Israel, but the one Israel of God with whom Gentiles may eat but whose status as the elect of God is not called into question.

A Matter of Theological Consequence

A question begs for consideration: What difference does the reconstruction of an "implied" audience make for contemporary reading of the New Testament? The result of the renewed appreciation of the "mighty minority" in the New Testament will be, in part, the discovery of a new strangeness. While it may be significant that our ancestors in the faith spoke languages other than ours, more striking is the discovery that a significant majority of them were children of Abraham according to the flesh; that they regarded the Law as God-given and the election of Israel by God as "irrevocable" (to use the language of Paul). Many Christians will experience this discovery as a radical decentering, much like a Copernican revolution. And such decentering may prove as fruitful for Christian theology as the Copernican revolution was for science.

What if Jesus was uninterested in Gentiles? What if the Gospel writers were most concerned with "Jewish" issues, even if among their audience were a significant number of Gentiles? The difference between actual readers and an implied readership may function theologically as the law, as Paul understood it:

> Now we know that whatever the law says, it speaks to those who are under the law, so that every mouth may be silenced, and the whole world may be held accountable to God. For "no human being will be justified in his sight," by deeds prescribed by the law, for through the law comes the knowledge of sin. (Romans 3:19)

The "sin" which such reconstruction of an implied audience may address is the pretense of Gentile Christians who claim the promises of the New Testament—and the Old—as if by natural right. The experience of the distance between the implied and the actual readership may identify the roots of anti-semitism. Nowhere does Mark's Gospel speak of a "new Israel" built on the ruins of the old. Nor does the Gospel speak of an abrogation of the law with the same rigor and consistency as Paul. A careful reader might well ask on what basis Gentiles, who are to be satisfied with the children's crumbs, are actually invited to sit at the table with the heirs of Abraham and Sarah. Such an invitation would belong in the category of God's election of Israel.

Such a revolution might create new interest in Paul's reflection about such matters in Romans 9-11, and it might even make it easier for contemporary Christians to experience the grace of God as something utterly unmerited—and to understand what "justification of the ungodly" really means.

There should be no mistake. Christian readers are not Jews. We live on the other side of a watershed. To deny the difference is disrespectful to Jews as well as to the Christian tradition. The discovery of a "mighty minority" in the early church and at the center of the Gospels' implied audiences will place the Jewish/Christian issue in a rather different light. If the New Testament provides no "replacement theology" (which Prof. Jervell has so eloquently and convincingly argued); if each of the Gospels in its own way presumes an observant Jewish community of believers in Jesus as its theological center, what can it mean to be "the church" without that mighty minority—and what is the status of contemporary Jews who do not believe Jesus to be Israel's Messiah and God's Son? Jervell's work does not provide an answer but opens a whole new agenda for Christian reflection.

An Early Christian Inscription in the Musei Capitolini

Peter Lampe

At Rome's Via Latina a marble inscription was found. Its fragments are preserved at the Musei Capitolini in Rome.

)τρα δ' ἐμοὶ παστῶν δᾳδουχοῦσιν συ(

)ᾳπίνας πεινοῦσιν ἐν ἡμετέρο(

)γοῦντες γενέτην καὶ υἱέα δοξάζον(

)γῆς ἔνθα μόνης καὶ ἀληθείης ῥύ(.[1]

After C. Scholten[2] rekindled the debate about the Valentinian character of this epigraph, a fresh look is needed. I will try to fill in the blanks and to translate:

---

1 Cf. L. Moretti, "Iscrizioni greche inedite di Roma": BCACR 75 (1953-55), 83-86; M. Raoss, "Iscrizione cristiana-greca di Roma anteriore al terzo secolo?": *Aevum* 37 (1963), 11-30; A. Coppo, "Contributo all'interpretazione di un'epigrafe greca cristiana dei Musei Capitolini": *RivAC* 46 (1970), 97- 138; M. Guarducci, "Valentiniani a Roma": *MDAI.R* 80 (1973), 169-89; Guarducci, "Ancora sui Valentiniani a Roma": *MDAI.R* 81 (1974), 341-43; Guarducci, "Iscrizione cristiana del II secolo nei Musei Capitolini": *BCACR* 79 (1963-64), 117-34; P. Lampe, *Die stadtrömischen Christen in den ersten beiden Jahrhunderten* (Tübingen: Mohr, 2nd ed. 1989), 257-61. Manlio Simonetti (orally) was the first to suspect a Valentinian origin of the inscription, followed by M. Guarducci.

2 "Gibt es Quellen zur Sozialgeschichte der Valentinianer Roms?": *ZNW* 79 (1988), 244-61.

Co(brothers; συνάδελφοι) of the bridal chambers celebrate

with torches the (ba)ths (λουτρά) for me;[3]

They hunger for (ban)quets (εἰλαπίνας) in ou(r rooms;

ἡμετέροισι δόμοισι),[4]

(La)uding the Father[5] and praisin(g; δοξάζοντες)

the Son;

O, may there be flow(ing; ῥύσις εἴη) of the only (sp)ring (πηγῆς)[6]

and of the truth in that very place (or: then).

The length of the completions at the left and right margins fits well, as I cross-checked by means of a computer-assisted photo montage, using letters from within the inscription itself to fill in the blanks (see plate II at the end of the article).[7]

---

3 In connection with an accusative, δαδουχέω ("to carry a torch, to illuminate") means "to celebrate" (e.g. "to celebrate mysteries" Them. *Or.* 5.71a). —Instead of συνάδελφοι an analogous term could be read too, e.g., σύντεκνοι "co-children," "foster-siblings" (*Corpus fabularum Aesopicarum*, ed. A. Hausrath – H. Hunger, 147.2.9; *Ancient Greek Inscriptions in the British Museum* 1010). Metrically this reading would create a spondaic hexameter.

4 This is the epic meaning of δόμος. Cf., e.g., H. G. Liddell – R. Scott, *A Greek-English Lexicon* (Oxford: Clarendon Press, 9th edition 1982), s.v. The meter requires a plural form. Another possibility would be "in our dining rooms" (ἡμετέροις ἀναγαίοις), cf. Mark 14:15. ἡμετέροισι δόμοισι, however, fits better in its length, having one letter less.

5 Possible parallel terms to δοξάζον- are ὑμνοῦντες, αἰνοῦντες, or σεμνοῦντες.

6 Other possibilities would be: "of the only light" (αὐγῆς), or even the Valentinian technical term σιγῆς ("of the only silence"). —Moretti ("Iscrizioni," 83) proposed στοργῆς. But a) if we filled in four missing letters at the beginning of the line, this line would be too long, starting further to the left than the previous lines. b) Moretti's translation of υἱέα δοξάζοντες στοργῆς as "compiacendosi col figlio per l'amore" hardly is convincing. c) "Spring" better matches the metaphor of "flowing." —Moretti (ibid., 83) also pondered μονῆς ("abiding") instead of μόνης. But how does line 4 make sense this way? By translating μονῆς … ῥῦ[σίς μοι] (sic) as "è per me la difesa della tranquillità" Moretti only provokes questions. If there is the pos- sibility for another, smoother reading, we definitely should choose it. —ἔνθα denotes either place or time (Liddell – Scott, s.v.).

7 Photos, however, *cannot* help to decide about the reading of individual letters, as Scholten assumes ("Quellen," 246 and 249 n. 21). For the deficiencies of this method, see, e.g., E. Meyer, *Einführung in die lateinische Epigraphik*, (Darmstadt: Wissenschaftliche Buchgesellschaft, 1983), 103.

Also metrically the completions fit well. The four epigraphic lines represent hexameters:

λουτρὰ δ' ἐ ǀ μοὶ πασ ǀ τῶν δᾳ ǀ δουχοῦ ǀ σιν συνά ǀ δελφοι

εἰλαπίν ǀ ας πει ǀ νοῦσιν ἐν ǀ ἡμετέ ǀ ροισι δό ǀ μοισι

ὑμνοῦν ǀ τες γενέ ǀ την καὶ ǀ υἱέα ǀ δοξά ǀ ζοντες

πηγῆς ǀ ἔνθα μό ǀ νης καὶ ἀλ ǀ ηθεί ǀ ης ῥύσις ǀ εἴη.[8]

‒ ◡ ◡ ǀ ‒ ‒ ǀ ‒ ‒ ǀ ‒ ‒ ǀ ‒ ◡ ◡ ǀ ‒ ‒

‒ ◡ ◡ ǀ ‒ ‒ ǀ ‒ ◡ ◡ ǀ ‒ ◡ ◡ ǀ ‒ ◡ ◡ ǀ ‒ ◡

‒ ‒ ǀ ‒ ◡ ◡ ǀ ‒ ‒ ǀ ‒ ◡ ◡ ǀ ‒ ‒ ǀ ‒ ◡

‒ ‒ ǀ ‒ ◡ ◡ ǀ ‒ ◡ ◡ ǀ ‒ ‒ ǀ ‒ ◡ ◡ ǀ ‒ ‒

Paleographically the inscription most likely dates into the 2nd century at the time of the Antonines, as M. Guarducci has shown comparing several hundred texts.[9] If the inscription is Christian, it represents one of the earliest epigraphic Christian documents. A detailed discussion of the epigraph therefore is justified.

I.

C. Scholten has questioned the Valentinian interpretation proposed by M. Simonetti, M. Guarducci and myself (notes 1 and 2). Scholten denies a Christian (M. Raoss) or religious reading. Instead the epigraph is supposed to represent a pagan wedding inscription, as one learns from scattered hints in his article (pp. 253, 250, 247). Scholten does not inform us which secular wedding inscriptions could be seen in parallel to our epi-

---

8 For καί as short sound, cf., e.g., Homer *Il.* 5.300. Guarducci ("Valentiniani," 170), following Coppo, "Contributo" completes with ῥύσις ἐστίν at the end. ἐστίν, however, would make line 4 too long in comparison with the other lines.

9 M. Guarducci ("Valentiniani," 169-70, and "Iscrizione," 127-32) outdates older attempts to date: 1st-2nd cent. C.E. (Moretti, "Iscrizioni, 83); 3rd cent. C.E. or later (J. and L. Robert, reviewing Moretti in *REG* 71 [1958], 359-60; Raoss, "Iscrizione," 30).

82   *Mighty Minorities*

graph. He does not try to show how the praising of father and son (line 3) and the flowing of truth (line 4) could be interpreted in the framework of a secular nuptial inscription. In fact, Scholten does not even make an effort to fill in the missing letters in order to obtain a text that makes sense. His alternative is no real alternative, as long as he does not take the trouble to spell out a complete reading and translation on his own and to find parallels that could make his version plausible. Any attempt to disprove other readings runs aground as long as no solid alternative is offered.

As Scholten did not do it himself, we must test a pagan secular reading on our own.

(a) In the first line one clearly can read "of the bridal chambers" and "they celebrate with torches for me." How do both fit into a sentence that makes sense?

At a pagan wedding the bride's way from her parental house to the groom's house—i.e., to the nuptial chamber—was indeed illuminated with torches at nightfall; torch-bearers led the procession.[10] In Plautus *Cas.* 1.1.30 this custom is called *lucere novae nuptae facem*. In a pagan interpretation thus the "for me" in our inscription would have to be spoken by a bride.[11] At the beginning of the line we would have to read λέκ)τρα,[12] if the line were to make sense: They "carry torches to the beds of the bridal chambers for me." δε in this case would be the enclitic particle -δε, which is added to an accusative in order to denote motion towards something (e.g., Homer *Od.* 8.292 λέκτρονδε = "to bed").

Very quickly, however, difficulties arise for a pagan reading of this line.

• The plurals in "beds" and "bridal chambers" would be awkward, since only one bride ("for me") is guided to her nuptial bed.

• Wedding songs used to be sung by friends and not by the bride herself.[13]

---

10 Cf., e.g., the materials in J. Marquardt, *Das Privatleben der Römer*, I (1886; Darmstadt: Wissenschaftliche Buchgesellschaft, reprint of the 2nd ed. 1975), 53-56.

11 Not by the groom, as Moretti ("Iscrizioni," 84) assumed. If the groom were referred to in our epigraph, this would be in line 3 in the third person—if at all.

12 Or φίλ)τρα ("love")? Moretti's ("Iscrizioni," 83) reading στοιβάδ᾽ ἐμοὶ (στοιβάς "bed") is impossible. Moretti falsely reads an Iota, where there clearly was a Γ, Τ, Ε or Σ.

13 Cf., e.g., Catull *Carm.* 62; 61.36-40; Marquardt, *Privatleben*, 54. Already Moretti ("Iscrizioni," 84-85) admitted that our poem does not match well with the Greco-Roman wedding customs.

- In the pagan nuptial procession young boys carried the torches for the bride,[14] not any "*co-*(...)." In which way could the torch-bearers be labelled "co-" in relation to the bride in a pagan nuptial setting?
- In a pagan setting the festive banquet used to take place *before* the procession with torches, not after, as our epigraphical lines 1 and 2 would suggest.[15]

On the whole a pagan reading of line 1 does not seem plausible. Our Christian reading "baths" at the beginning of the line, on the other hand, does not create problems. βάπτισμα and λουτρόν are interchangeable, in both Valentinian and other Christian texts (cf., e.g., Justin *Apol*. I 61.3; Clem. Alex. *Exc. ex Theod*. 4.78). According to Justin (*Apol*. I 65), Christian baptism used to take place *before* the congregation celebrated the eucharist, which matches the sequence of baptisms (line 1) and "banquets" (line 2) in our inscription.

After a Christian provenience of line 1 has been conceded, the question of the particularly Valentinian character has to be raised. With παστοί ("bridal chambers"), a Valentinian keynote is hit. Not only is the nuptial theme a predominant subject in Valentinianism, the Valentinian motif of the "bridal chamber" stands for the eschatological union of the pneumatics (the "images") with their angels in the *pleroma*. In this world this union is anticipated in the sacramental rituals.[16]

The expression "co-brothers / co-children of the bridal chambers"

---

14 *tollite, o pueri, faces:* Catull *Carm*. 61.114. See the materials in Marquardt, *Privatleben*, 55-56.

15 See, e.g., Catull *Carm*. 62.3 and Marquardt, *Privatleben*, 52-53. —The next meal for the guests was not served before the following day at the after-celebration called *repotia* (cf. Marquardt, ibid., 57). But line 2 cannot refer to the *repotia*, since both lines 1 and 3 focus on the wedding day itself (procession, wedding songs). —Moretti ("Iscrizioni," 85) quoted texts which talk about a dinner given by the groom (Cic. *ad Quint. fr*. II 3.7; Juv. 6.202). Marquardt (ibid., 53 n. 1), however, put these texts in the right light. According to the usual custom, first the banquet in the bride's paternal house took place and afterwards the bride's procession from there to the groom's house.

16 E.g. Iren. 1.21.3-4; 1.13.3,6; 1.7.1,5; Clem. *Exc. ex Theod*. 63.2; 64; 65.1; 36.2; Heracleon in Orig. *CommJohn* 13.11; 10.19; *Gos. Phil*. from Nag Hammadi (NHC II 3) logia 68; 76; 87; 102; 122; 124; 126-127; 60-61; 66-67; 73; 79; 80; 82; 95; cf. also *Tri. Trac*. NHC I 5 (122. 12ss); Clem. *Strom*. 3.1.1; Tert. *adv. Val*. 30-32. J.-M. Sevrin ("Les noces spirituelles dans l'évangile selon Philippe": *Muséon* 87 [1974], 143-93) correctly observed that the sacramental anticipation of the eschatological "bridal chamber" probably did not take place in a separate "bridal chamber" sacrament, as many scholars have thought (this possibility, however, is not totally ruled out by Sevrin 192), but rather in the rituals of anointing, baptizing, eucharist and liturgical kiss.

(see n. 3) corresponds well to the Valentinian self-description as "children of the bridal chamber" in *Gos. Phil.* logia 87; 102; 127.

If probability points in the Christian-Valentinian direction, we have to cross check whether the rest of the line can be understood in a Valentinian light. δᾳδουχῶ ("to illuminate with torches," "to celebrate with torches") denotes the celebration of the Eleusinian mysteries in Clemens Alex. *Protrep.* 2.12; Themistius *Or.* 5.71a and other texts. And Tertullian, indeed, reproaches the Valentinians for Eleusinian influence (*adv. Val.* 1).

Baptisms (λουτρά, "baths") are celebrated by the Valentinians[17] as one form of anticipation of the eschatological "bridal chamber."[18] The torches fit this well. They are not only a traditional Roman nuptial symbol: for the Valentinians the "bridal chamber" is also particularly characterized by light and the receiving of light,[19] so that the torches could have a double symbolic value.

The plural in "bridal chambers" is a problem for *any* reading of the inscription, but in the Valentinian frame of reference it seems to create the *smallest* problem: In the *pleroma* the pneumatics unite themselves with their angels (plurals), which might have inspired the unprecedented plural in our epigraph.

(b) Line 2 by itself is neutral when it comes to deciding between a Christian and pagan reading. Festive dinners were of course celebrated both in pagan and Christian contexts. In a Christian framework εἰλαπίνη might allude to the eucharistic meal, as it parallels λουτρόν/baptism in line 1. Christian εἰλαπίναι are mentioned in Justin *Dial.* 10.1: Justin quotes the pagan defamation that "after the banquet" (μετὰ τὴν εἰλαπίνην) the Christians extinguish the lights and practice improper sex. True, the epic-poetic εἰλαπίνη would be only a periphrastic term for the eucharist; there is no certain evidence for a technical eucharistic usage of εἰλαπίνη before the 7th century C.E.[20] But this does not rule out a possible eucharistic reading of our line. In a poetic text like ours, nobody with

---

17 Cf., e.g., *Gos. Phil.* logia 68; 76; Iren. 1.21.3; Clemens Alex. *Exc. ex Theod.* 78.2.
18 See Sevrin, "Les noces," in n. 16.
19 *Gos. Phil.* logia 127; 122; for further references see Sevrin, "Les noces," 169-71. For the torch as Roman nuptial symbol, see Marquardt, *Privatleben*, 55. For those who want to maintain the hypothesis of a separate Valentinian "bridal chamber" sacrament, it also would be possible to read λέκτρα ("couches," "bridal beds") in line 1 as a direct reference to this sacrament.
20 See Raoss, "Iscrizione," 28 n. 53.

some sense for the genre would require a technical term for the eucharist.

In itself line 2 is open for both pagan and Christian interpretations. Because of line 1, however, we have to cross check whether line 2 can be understood in a Valentinian light. This creates no problem. Eucharistic celebrations by the Valentinians are evidenced in, e.g., Iren. 1.13.2; *Gos. Phil.* logion 68; Clemens Alex. *Exc. ex Theod.* 82.1. Like the baptism, the eucharist anticipates the eschatological "bridal chamber" for the Valentinians.[21]

(c) The praising of Father and Son in line 3 is easily understood in a Christian frame of reference. Scholten (246-47) claims that γενέτης does not denote God in Christian texts before Gregory of Nazianz. This is not true. Jews in Egypt and Christians sang of God as γενέτης much earlier. In Egypt in the 2nd cent. B.C.E.,[22] the Jewish Sibyl (III 604; cf. also III 550) called God the γενέτης of all human beings. Between 80 and 130 C.E. in Egypt,[23] the Jewish Sibyl prayed to God as "begetter of all" (παγγενέτωρ; V 328). The hymn to Christ in Sibyll. VI starts out: "I speak from my heart of the great famous son (υἱόν) of the Immortal, to whom the Most High, his begetter (γενέτης), gave a throne to possess:"

Ἀθανάτου μέγαν υἱὸν ἀοίδιμον ἐκ φρενὸς αὐδῶ,
ᾧ θρόνον ὕψιστος γενέτης παρέδωκε λαβέσθαι.

These are hexameters as in our inscription. The hymn sings about Christ's life, his baptism in the Jordan River, and his cross. Lactantius (*Div. Inst.* 4.15.3,25; 4.13.21; 4.18.20) quotes this song; it therefore was composed some time *before* ca. 300 C.E. As the metric quality is better than in most texts of the 3rd century, we might want to date it into the 2nd century C.E., without certainty however. The geographical provenance is unknown.

As Scholten did not even try to spell out a pagan reading of line 3, we have to test this alternative on our own. Anyone would have a hard time finding pagan nuptial inscriptions in which the bride's father-in-law was praised[24] or in which the groom was revered as "son." I see, however,

---

21 See n. 16.
22 For place and date, see J. J. Collins, "Sibylline Oracles": *OTP* 1 (1983), 354-55.
23 For place and date, see Collins, ibid., 390-91.
24 If at all, the bride's father could be honored (Claudianus *Fescennina* 13). The bride's father, however, is not mentioned by our inscription: Line 3 talks about a son and not about a daughter.

the possibility of interpreting "son" as Hymen(aeus), the god of marriage, who could be sung of at weddings (e.g. Catull *Carm.* 61-62) and who was called son of the Muses (Schol. Pindar *Pythia* 4.313) or "Urania's offspring" ("*Uraniae genus*," Catull *Carm.* 61.2). The γενέτης would be Hymen's father (Apollo or Dionysus). However, even this reading has serious problems. Why is there only mention of the father and not of the mother? Even stranger would be for Hymen to be referred to only by his sonship, and not by his name or any other title. Metrically it would have been possible to say Ὑμένα (accusative of Ὑμήν) instead of υἱέα. As Hymen's name was a frequent refrain in wedding songs (e.g. Catull. *Carm.* 61-62), it would have been unusual to paraphrase this god's identity without mention of his name. Not even the father's name is given. The absolute "Father" and "Son" are much more easily understood in a Christian reading of line 3 than in a pagan one.

The last step will be again to cross check whether the line remains plausible in a Valentinian framework. The combination Father – Son – Bridal Chamber, indeed, occurs again in, e.g., *Gos. Phil.* logion 82. And in Clemens' *Excerpta ex Theodoto* (1.6-7) the Valentinians refer to the son (υἱός) as Μονογενής of the father (πατήρ), which comes at least close to the terminology of our epigraphical line. "Father," "Son" and "Monogenes" are also dealt with in the *Valentinian Exposition* Nag Hamm. XI 2.22-25,28,36-37. Moreover, in the liturgical fragments of a Valentinian celebration of baptism and the eucharist (Nag Hamm. XI 2.40,43) glory is sung "to thee, the Father in the Son." "Jesus Christ" is referred to as "the Monogenes," and the Valentinian celebrants of the eucharist sing "O Father ... [Glory] be to thee through thy Son [and] thy offspring (MICE, γεννητός) Jesus Christ." True, the specific term γενέτης itself does not occur in the few *Greek* Valentinian texts that we have. In Valentinus' Egyptian homeland, however, the Jews had been calling God γενέτης for a long time, and Christian hymnic hexameters picked up this term, as we saw above.

(d) In line 4 the pendulum swings again into the Christian direction. So far we have no single pagan wedding text in which the "flowing of truth" plays a role. A Christian reading of line 4 on the other hand runs smoothly. The "flowing of the only spring" is a common Christian motif derived from Judaism. The Septuagint calls God πηγὴν ὕδατος ζωῆς (Jer 2:13; cf. also, e.g., *Barn.* 11.2; Ezek 47; Isa 55:1). Justin quotes Jer 2:13 and interprets Christ as πηγὴν ζῶσαν (*Dial.* 19.2).[25] According to 1 Cor 10:4, Israel "drank from" Christ. But we do not even have to interpret the spring narrowly as Christ. John 4:14 leaves the identity of "spring" and Christ unsettled. According to Rev 21:6 (cf. 7:17), "he who sat upon the throne ... will give from the fountain (πηγή) of the water of life." This spring is the site of abundance from which the life prepared by Christ flows. μόνης is easily understood in this light. And μόνη πηγή is paralleled by several Christian and Jewish texts, even in connection with ἀλήθεια ("truth") as in our epigraphical line.[26]

We have to ask our Valentinian cross-check question again. Like line 3, line 4 represents common Christian motifs and therefore is possible also as a Valentinian verse if line 1 suggests a Valentinian reading of the whole poem. It was characteristic of the Valentinians to use common Christian language ("*similia enim loquentes fidelibus*" Iren. 3.17.4; "*communem fidem adfirmant*" Tert. adv. Val. 1).

Again, the poetic, metric form fits well with Valentinus' style. Even Ionic dialect (ἀληθείη) is echoed,[27] just as in Valentinus' only preserved poetic fragment (Hipp. *ref.* 6.37.6-8) where an ionic form (αἴθρης) can be found.

For the Valentinians, ἀλήθεια "existed since the beginning" (*Gos. Phil.* logion 16). It is nutrition for eternal life given by Jesus (93). It can be interpreted christologically (47), and the "bridal chamber" is for those who have the ἀλήθεια (110 + 73; 127; 123-125). More than six motifs of our poem, ἀλήθεια, "co(children) of the bridal chambers," water ("baths," "spring," "flowing"), fire and light ("to illuminate with torches"), "Father," and "Son," are found again in logia 66-67 ("It is from water and fire and light that the child of the bridal chamber [came into being] ...Truth did not come into the world naked ... The bridal chamber and the image must enter through the image into the truth: this is the restoration. Not only must those who produce the name of the Father and the Son and the Holy Spirit do so ...").

To sum up the Christian reading of the marble epigraph: In the first person a host (line 1), opening his or her rooms (line 2) for Christian ritu-

---

25 In Justin's version of the OT text God talks about the "living spring" in the third person; αὐτόν, therefore, only can denote Christ. —In the previous sentence Justin talks about τὸ βάπτισμα τὸ τῆς ζωῆς (19.2), which is also called λουτρόν in 13.1; 14.1. Justin's combination of βάπτισμα/λουτρόν and Christ-πηγή parallels our inscription.

26 Epiphanius *Haer.* GCS 25, 157.22-23: ἥτις μόνη ἐστὶ πηγή σωτηρίας καὶ πίστις ἀληθείας. Athanasius *Epist. ad Afros episcopos* PG 26.1033.12-13: καταλείψαντες τὴν μόνην πηγήν τοῦ ζῶντος ὕδατος. Cf. also Philo *vit. Mos.* 1.48.8 (ed. Cohn): λόγον, ὃς μόνος ἐστὶν ἀρετῶν ἀρχή τε καὶ πηγή; Athanasius *Contra Sabellianos* PG 28.97.30ss; PsOrigenes *Fragmenta in Psalmos* 58.17,18 (ed. Pitra).

27 Cf. Guarducci ("Valentiniani"), 181; ἀληθείη as in Homer.

als, speaks.[28] At the host's residence, the congregation regularly celebrates baptisms (line 1) and looks forward to the eucharistic meals afterwards (line 2), singing praise to the Father and the Son (line 3). When and where the rituals are celebrated, there is "flowing of the only spring and of the truth" (line 4), the speaker hopes. The image of flowing at the end fits well with the baptismal baths at the beginning of the poem.

The most logical conclusion is that the epigraph was displayed in the room where the baptisms took place. The eucharists were celebrated in this room and/or in adjacent accommodations of the same house, with line 2 b using the plural. The inscription fits Justin's description (*Apol.* I 61; 65), according to which Christian eucharists were celebrated *after* the baptismal rituals and often in *different* accommodations, since the baptisms required a locality with a water supply.

The Valentinian character is suggested by verse 1, and the following lines can be easily understood in a Valentinian frame of reference. Valentinians celebrated the sacraments as anticipations of the eschatological unions ("bridal chamber") of the pneumatics with their angels.

II.

The δέ in line 1 does not suggest that the four verses once were part of a larger poem. The letter δ was inserted for poetic reasons to avoid an hiatus between the two vowels α and ε. Also epigrams by Pittacus and Timon, e.g., start out with an unexpected δέ, without reference to a previous context (Μεγαρεῖς δὲ φεῦγε πάντας· εἰσὶ γὰρ πικροί: *Anthologia Graeca*, ed. H. Beckby, 11.440; 11.296). Likewise in Homer *Od.* 4.400, a story is begun with δέ.

On our marble slab clearly neither a previous nor a subsequent text was inscribed. Except for occasional abrasions, the slab's upper edge runs parallel to the first row of letters. More importantly, the free space between the upper edge and this first row equals the height of two epi-

---

28 The dative ἐμοί in line 1 can be interpreted as "for me," "in my interest," "to my delight" (*dativus commodi*) or as *dativus ethicus*. The latter denotes that a speaker is mentally and emotionally involved in the action, i.e. the baptisms, that he or she talks about. Cf., e.g., R. Kühner – B. Gerth, *Ausführliche Grammatik der griechischen Sprache: Satzlehre, I* (Hannover: Hahnsche Buchhandlung, 4th ed. 1955), 423 with numerous examples where μοι is used in this way. —ἐμοί hardly indicates that the speaker talks about his or her own baptism. The end of line 2 strongly advocates that a host is speaking. —ἡμέτερος can stand for ἐμός from Homer's time to the third century C.E. (Liddell - Scott, *s.v.*).

graphical lines, i.e. the height of two rows of letters plus the free space between these two rows. We thus observe the result of a stone-mason's calculations, and the preserved upper edge of the slab is more or less identical with the upper edge that the stone-mason had in his hands. No previous text has broken off.

The same is true about the end of the epigraph. The margin below the last row of letters is more than 25 percent higher than the said upper margin. This layout makes it highly improbable that our four verses were followed by more text. Taking the extant epigraphical evidence into account, usually big spaces were not left in between paragraphs. Space was expensive, especially on marble slabs which had to be imported to Rome. In Rome therefore marble was used much less often for inscriptions than at other places such as Greece.[29]

Scholten's speculations after all are unfounded. He objected (253 n. 43) that our epigraph could be "the rest of a bigger inscription" and that this larger text could have been not only a pagan nuptial, but alternatively also a funereal epigraph (without specifying the details of this other reading either). No, our inscription represents a rounded-off unit, without conventional grave inscription formulas, without names.

In spite of the handicap that no internal clue hints at a funereal interpretation, let us hypothesize for a moment that external evidence pointed into this direction. Let us hypothesize that the epigraph was attached to a mausoleum and not to a suburban house at the Via Latina, as we concluded above. How could the epigraph be understood on the basis of this assumption? The implied author of the inscription would be a deceased person speaking about his or her own funeral: "Co(brothers) carry torches to beds of bridal chambers for me." True, torches are not only a symbol of the wedding, but of the funeral as well.[30] But an explicit nuptial motif (here παστῶν) usually is absent in burial contexts. Only in one text (Herodas 4.56) is there a *question* whether or not the term παστός could mean "shrine." In which 2nd century frame of reference would it be possible to state that death gave access to "beds of bridal chambers?" On the basis of a funereal hypothesis, again the Valentinian perspective would give possible meaning to this line—if at all.

What would ἔνθα mean in line 4? Where and when is there "flowing of the only spring and of the truth" in a funereal context? ἔνθα could

---

29 Cf., e.g., Meyer, *Epigraphik*, 17, 84. Already Moretti ("Iscrizioni," 83) observed correctly that parts of the slab's original *lower* edge are also preserved.
30 Cf., e.g., Marquardt, *Privatleben*, 55, 343-45.

refer back to the "beds of bridal chambers" in line 1, and then again only a Valentinian reading of verse 4 would be plausible to some extent, with a specific funereal aspect, however, missing in this line.

The "banquets" in line 2 could be interpreted as the funeral repast and the annual meals at the grave. The tomb would be referred to as "our rooms."[31] But why would anybody *"hunger"* for these repasts, as line 2 states? A hunger for non-funereal, eucharistic meals in a suburban house ("in our rooms") makes much more sense.

At the pagan funeral the *deceased* was praised,[32] not the "Father" and the "Son." Whoever wants to maintain a funereal hypothesis, probably has to admit that a Christian reading of line 3 remains the most probable one, and that a specific funeral aspect is absent in this verse.

In conclusion, the epigraph was a Valentinian inscription at the Via Latina. Rather than at a burial site, it was displayed in a suburban house where Valentinians celebrated sacramental rituals. Only this latter interpretation allows a coherent understanding of all lines, running into the least number of difficulties compared to the other alternatives.

III.

The Valentinian congregation at the suburban section of the Via Latina adds to the number of known second-century Valentinian groups in Rome—if it was not identical with one of them. These Roman Valentinian groups gathered around teachers such as Valentinus, Heracleon, Ptolemaios and Florinus.[33]

Our epigraph exemplifies what has been shown from other sources: Early Christianity in Rome consisted of "minorities," i.e. of various house churches with different theological orientations. Second-century Rome saw: Christian groups following Valentinian, Marcionite, Carpocratian, Theodotian, Modalistic, Montanist, or Quartodecimanian teachings; Cerdo-followers; house churches of (what was only later called) "orthodox" faith; a Jewish Christian circle which still observed the Torah; groups with a logos-theology that was too complicated for less educated Christians; circles which believed in the millennium and others which did not.[34]

---

31 Cf., e.g., Marquardt, *Privatleben*, 378-85, 369. For the tomb as "domus" cf., e.g., CIL III 2165; 3171; V 2255; VIII 7541; 8751; 9949.
32 Cf., e.g., Marquardt, *Privatleben*, 352, 357-60.
33 See Lampe, *Die stadtrömischen Christen*, 251-68.
34 For this multicolored spectrum, see Lampe, ibid., 316-18, 321-24, 455.

All these groups met in private homes.[35] There was no local center for Roman Christianity. The individual house churches, scattered over the city, were loosely connected.[36] Some sent portions of their eucharists to other Christian islands in town to express church unity with them. Also letters were sent between the Christian groups in the city.[37] Communication with persons or congregations *outside* of Rome often was coordinated among the groups. As a result, outsiders could perceive the various Roman house churches as "the Roman church."[38] A monarchical bishop, however, who oversaw at least the "orthodox" house churches in the city, did not come into existence before the second half of the second century. Earlier, the various house churches were led solely by their own presbyters,[39] who met only occasionally at conventions on a level above the local house church.[40]

On the whole, the various Christian groups in town tolerated each other. With few exceptions,[41] no Christian group in town labelled another as heretical before the last decade of the second century. It was not until bishop Victor (ca. 189 – 199 C.E.) that house churches, which thought of themselves as orthodox, started to excommunicate other groups on a larger scale. Victor cut the ties to the Quartodecimanians, Montanists, Theodotians—and to the Valentinians.[42]

The Valentinians themselves always emphasized their feeling of unity with the other "psychic" Christians. For "pneumatic" Valentinians, the "psychic" understanding of the Christian faith was not wrong, it

---

35 See ibid., 306-20.
36 See ibid., 317.
37 See ibid., 324-35, 339.
38 See ibid., 335-36.
39 See ibid., 334-45.
40 See the material in Lampe, ibid., 338-39.
41 See Lampe, ibid., 330-32, 456. Marcion and his adherents were excluded from church community with the other Christian groups in town in the 140s C.E. Cerdo was not excommunicated but withdrew *himself* from this community in the 130s. The circle of Torah-observing Jewish Christians isolated itself in order to maintain its purity. For the relationship between Justin's group and the Valentinians, see n. 42.
42 See Lampe, ibid., 324-34. For the Valentinians, see ibid., 327-29. Irenaeus had called Victor's attention to the danger of Florinus' convictions. The advocates of the logos-theology (Justin, Irenaeus) were the first to fight the Valentinians. Justin attacked the Valentinians not in his *Apology* but in his later *Dialogue* (35.5-6), assuring that his own house church had no sense of community with Valentinians. However, Justin's critical attitude does not seem to have infected other house churches in Rome. Even Victor still expressed church unity with Florinus in his first years of office, until Irenaeus alerted him of the Valentinian "heresy."

only was deepened in the esoteric Valentinian gatherings.[43] Valentinians were eager to stress the continuity between the normal Christians' faith and their own. The Valentinian Roman teacher Ptolemaios used common Christian language in his letter to the lady Flora.[44] Our Valentinian inscription in lines 3 and 4 picks up common Christian motifs. The Valentinian "minorities" hated the label "Valentinian," which was attached to them by outsiders.[45] They did not want to be anything other than Christians.

Plate I

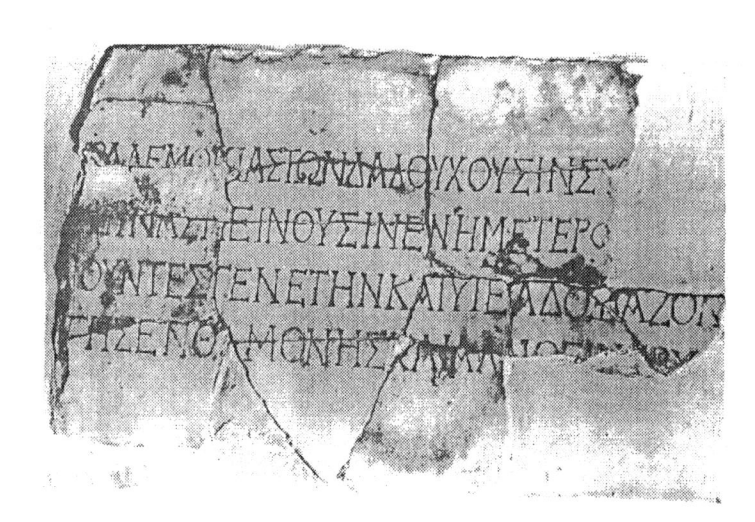

Plate II

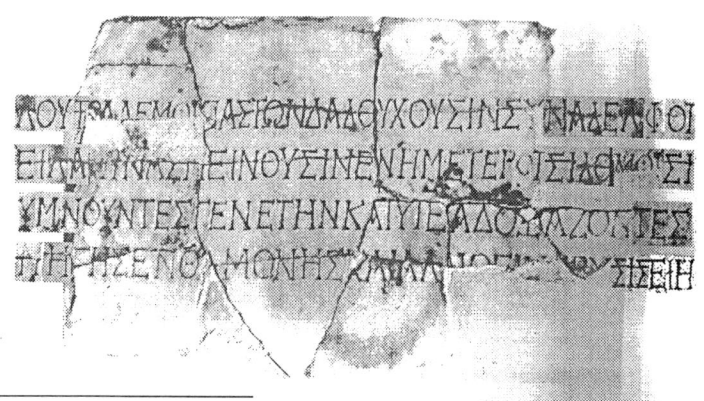

---

43 See Lampe, ibid., 325-29, 255-56.
44 See ibid., 256.
45 See ibid., 326, n. 76.

How Mighty was the Mighty Minority?

Edvin Larsson

Jacob Jervell has made many contributions in the course of his scholarly career to the study of the history of early Christianity, especially as this is recorded in Acts: here, his numerous investigations have often proved to be challenges to dominant views within contemporary scholarship. Although he accepts redaction-criticism, he has questioned many of its basic assumptions, as we see for example in his 1962 article on the problem of traditions in Acts.[1] Against the dominant opinion, he maintained that the early church offered conditions for the formation of traditions about the apostles and their activity. His most challenging view, however, is his understanding of the role of Jews and Jewish Christians in the early church, especially in his interpretation of Luke-Acts. He maintains that there is no anti-Jewish tendency in the Lucan writings;[2] on the contrary, Luke does not presuppose that the Jewish people as a whole have rejected the Christian kerygma. However, the message of Jesus Christ has divided the Jewish people into believers and unbelievers.[3] In Luke's view, the believing Jews are Israel, the people of God, purged of unbelievers. Faith in Christ has given the Gentiles the possibility of incorporation into this people of God. According to Jervell, the Gentile mission started at the very beginning; it was not simply a consequence of the Jewish rejection of the gospel. In Luke's view, this mission was the fulfilment of the scriptures. This is the theoretical basis of Jervell's exposition.

How about the historical development? According to the consensus-

---

1 J. Jervell, "The Problem of Traditions in Acts", in: *ST* 16 (1962), 25-41 also in idem, *Luke and the people of God* (Minneapolis: Augsburg, 1972), 19-39.
2 Cf. J. B. Tyson, "Jews and Judaism in Luke-Acts. Reading as a God-fearer" (Seminar paper delivered at the SNTS-conference in Madrid 1992). A position opposite that of Jervell and Tyson is represented by J. T. Sanders, *The Jews in Luke-Acts* (Philadelphia: Fortress Press, 1987).
3 Jervell, "The Divided People of God. The Restoration of Israel and Salvation for the Gentiles", in: *ST* 19 (1965), 68-96; also in *Luke*, 41-74.

interpretation, Jewish Christianity ceased to exist after the fall of Jerusalem in AD 70, apart from small sects which survived for a few centuries. In Jervell's view, Jewish Christianity survived the fall of Jerusalem and established itself like other Jewish groups such as Pharisaic Judaism. The increasing number of Gentiles who joined the church posed problems, however: for how could Israel, the people of God, have room for a majority of Gentiles? The tensions and conflicts became apparent at the apostolic council. The apostolic decree is to be regarded as a sign of a new restrictive attitude towards the Gentile Christians, who now threaten to become the dominating majority.

In the period from 70 to 100, Gentile Christians doubtless formed a majority in the church. In spite of its numerical inferiority, Jewish Christianity was able to dominate the life and the thinking in most of the churches. This leads Jervell to label Jewish Christianity "the mighty minority".[4] In an attempt to define this manifold phenomenon, Jervell states: "Jewish Christians refuse to separate Christianity from the religious, political, and cultural fate of Israel—and there is but one Israel."[5] This rise of a self-conscious Jewish Christianity with its own profile inevitably led to a revival of Jewish elements in the church as a whole. Jervell sees the important role of the mighty minority in the anti-Pauline attitude and propaganda which are discernible in Gal 2:11ff., Rom 15:30ff., and Acts 21:20ff. Paul's Jewish Christian opponents are themselves recognisable at, e.g., 2 Cor 11:22ff., Phil 3:2ff., and Gal *passim*. According to Jervell, the influence of the mighty minority even affected Paul himself: he contrasts the apostle's attitude towards the Jews in 1 Thess 2:14-16 with his exposition of the fate of Israel in Rom 9-11. The Lucan picture of Paul as a Law-abiding Christian Pharisee is also born of the necessity to take account of the mighty minority.

There is no doubt that Jervell's thesis about the mighty minority has called attention to a neglected factor in the development of early Christianity. In what follows, I shall discuss his approach, especially his thesis about the role of Jewish Christianity; but let me state at the outset that I am in agreement with him about many of his basic assumptions: Luke-Acts are not products of Gentile Christianity; Jewish Christianity did not vanish at the fall of Jerusalem; Acts has an apologetic character, defending the (Pauline) Gentile mission; Jewish Christianity functions as a

---

4 Jervell, "The Mighty Minority", in: *ST* 34 (1980), 13-38. Also in idem, *The Unknown Paul. Essays on Luke-Acts and Early Christian History* (Minneapolis: Augsburg, 1984), 26-51.
5 *The Unknown Paul*, 33.

mighty minority. But it is precisely this last topic that I wish to discuss. I suspect that the influence of the mighty minority was not so overwhelming as Jervell assumes. There are other ways of explaining the legalistic, "Judaising" tendencies in the second and third post-apostolic generations. Judaising traits within the church are not necessarily due to inspiration from Jewish Christianity. One could ask, for instance, about the role of radical Judaism in the period from 60 to 70. What about pressure from the Zealot movement, always prepared to detect and persecute "unJewish" groups and individuals?[6] It is by no means improbable that political tensions in these years forced the Church to make an accommodation to Judaism which in other circumstances might have taken a more modest form. Such a development could, of course, be in accordance with the intentions of Jewish Christianity, but if that is the case, its influence in the church is due to external factors, and not only to its own spiritual strength.

Leaving this somewhat hypothetical discussion, I should like to recall another Scandinavian scholar, Johannes Munck, who likewise made a very interesting contribution to the Jewish-Christian problem.[7] His approach differs strongly from Jervell's. In Munck's view, Christianity was never a movement within Judaism, but was a new religion from the start. Jewish Christianity was destroyed at the fall of Jerusalem. Later groups labelled as Jewish Christians do not have their origin in this primitive movement, but are derived from Gentile Christianity. The Jewish-Christian apostles had set a Jewish-Christian stamp on this Gentile-Christian church, which also accepted the LXX as their scriptural text. The ecclesiastical tradition they inherited contained Jewish elements. Out of all this, a new Jewish Christianity emerged which had nothing to do with the original Jewish Christian community in Jerusalem. Its members were Judaisers in the sense that they observed the Law—but not in a Pharisaic fashion (circumcision was not required). In Munck's opinion, this Judaising tendency was due to their use of the LXX with its stress on the Law.[8]

According to Jervell, Jewish Christianity formed the very centre of

---

[6] Especially the *sicarii* were feared because of their terror-activity. See Josephus, *Bell.*, 2:254-56.

[7] J. Munck, "Jewish Christianity in post-Apostolic times", in *NTS* 6 (1959-60), 103-16. Cf. idem, *Paulus und die Heilsgeschichte* ([Acta Jutlandica. Aarskrift for Aarhus Universitet 26:1. Teologisk serie 6], Aarhus: Universitetsforlaget/København: Munksgaard, 1954).

[8] Munck, art. cit., 110.

the early Church. It functioned as a mighty minority. In Munck's view, primitive Jewish Christianity vanished at the fall of Jerusalem. Postapostolic Jewish Christianity was a product of the Gentile Christian church.

Munck was probably wrong in his general view of Jewish Christianity and its development, but I suspect that he was correct to maintain that many Jewish traits and Judaising tendencies were caused by other factors, and like Munck I assume that the use of the LXX among Gentile Christians was decisively important in the re-Judaising process in the early church. The development proposed here is in fact likely, if one takes into consideration the situation of Gentile Christianity. The Gentiles, who previously had been living "far off", had now been "brought near" through the message of Christ and his work (Eph 2:13). From a psychological point of view, it is by no means surprising that they should have become (with converts' customary zeal) more Judaising than their Jewish Christian missionaries (cf. the Galatians and Paul). In this connection, it was naturally of great importance that their scripture offered rules for religious belief and praxis.[9] This is how I take the process to have proceeded in the apostolic and post-apostolic church. I intend to substantiate this understanding of the development by analysing relevant themes in the Epistle to the Hebrews. I have dealt in previous articles with the supposed "Jewishness" of this letter.[10] My intention here is to extend the discussion to include the question of the mighty minority.

At first sight, the letter to the Hebrews gives the impression of being a genuine Jewish-Christian writing. This seems in fact to be the oldest opinion, reflected already in the (secondary) title Πρὸς Ἑβραίους.[11] This title seems to indicate that the author (whose identity is less important than that of the addressees)[12] has a Jewish Christian community in mind. Such an interpretation is in itself quite natural. The author's whole argumentation takes its orientation from the Old Testament. His typological use of scripture seems to fit well into a Christian milieu with a Jewish background. Only in such a context does it seem appropriate to

---

9 Munck, ibid.
10 E. Larsson, "Om Hebreerbrevets syfte", in SEÅ 37-38 (1972-73), 296-309. Also in: Människan inför bibeln (Arlöv: Skeab/Verbum 1982), 197-210. Idem, "Sonen och änglarna i Hebreerbrevet 1-2", in Asheim et al. (eds.), Israel – Kristus – Kirken. FS Sverre Aalen (Oslo-Bergen-Tromsø: Universitetsforlaget, 1979), 91-108.
11 Jervell, The unknown Paul, 48ff. thinks of Jewish Christians. For the recent discussion, see H. Fr. Weiß, Der Brief an die Hebräer. KEK XIII – 15. Aufl. (Göttingen: Vandenhoeck & Ruprecht, 1991), 67ff.
12 The suggestions regarding the identity of the author are numerous: Paul, Apollos, Barnabas, Luke, Priscilla (according to Harnack). See Weiß, Hebräer, 61ff.

make a detailed presentation of how the Jewish temple cult has been replaced once and for all by Christ's sacrifice. Advocates of this understanding often assume that the author intends to lead his Jewish Christian readers deeper into the mysteries of faith in Christ, or alternatively that he is compelled to combat Judaising tendencies among them. The latter point of view often includes the assumption that he wants to prevent their relapse into Judaism.[13] Nevertheless, this idea presents problems.

As is well known, a critical point is found at 6:1f., where the author speaks of the basic catechetical instruction the readers once received. The elements enumerated here do not fit, if the author is addressing exclusively Christians of Jewish descent, for these would hardly need catechetical instruction about faith in God, the resurrection of the dead and eternal judgment. These *topoi* would on the other hand seem to be very fitting, if the readers are Gentile Christians. People with a pagan past are likely to need exactly such an instruction. One can also add, in favour of this view, the warnings against apostasy from the living God (3:12; cf. 11:6).

There are, however, strong arguments against the idea of the addressees being Gentile Christians. There are no clear references in the exhortations to vices and weaknesses which could be attributed with certainty to the readers' pagan background. One would also need to explain why the author—if he is addressing Gentile Christians—chooses to deal with such specific Old Testament *topoi* as the tabernacle, the sacrificial cult, the priesthood etc. This choice does not appear self-evident, even if one takes into consideration the readers' assumed acquaintance with the Old Testament (LXX).

The attempts mentioned so far at a solution of the identity of the addressees are hardly convincing.[14] One negative conclusion seems, however, to be possible: solutions based on firm convictions regarding

---

13 So Jervell, *Unknown Paul*, 48ff. Cf. the grand article of E. Gräßer, "Der Hebräerbrief 1938-1963", in: *ThR* 30 (1964), 138-236, here 147.

14 H. Hegermann, *Der Brief an die Hebräer*, ThHK XVI (Berlin: Evangelische Verlagsanstalt, 1988), 10, suggests that the addressees are Gentile Christians. So also H. Braun, *An die Hebräer*. HNT 14 (Tübingen: Mohr [Siebeck] 1984), 2. E. Gräßer, *An die Hebräer*. EKK XVII/1 (Zürich: Benziger/Neukirchen: Neukirchener 1990), 24f. maintains that the letter is addressed to the church as a whole. The number of attempts at a solution is increased by assumptions that the letter is directed to a particular group—Jewish Christian or Gentile Christians—within a congregation. These hypotheses do not, however, provide any certain solution regarding the identity of the addressees.

the Jewish or Gentile origin of the addressees do not lead to any unequivocal conclusions. The question concerning the origin does not, in fact, play any demonstrable role in Hebrews. Nor does the relationship between Jewish Christians and Gentile Christians within the community appear as a problem in this epistle. When such a problem is suggested, it is most likely read into Hebrews on the analogy of problems one encounters in the Pauline letters. The question of the origin may therefore be left unanswered without any loss, at least at the outset. The author's lack of interest in the origin of his readers is an indication that we are at a rather late stage in the development of early Christianity. This probably means that the author simply regards his addressees as Christians. Most of them may belong to the second and third Christian generations. The question of origin has lost its importance, although one may assume that there would also be new converts among the addressees. At the same time, the founding period of the community does not seem to lie very far back: it still makes sense to speak about it. Presumably there are still members alive who experienced the founding period. The congregation has a glorious past, of which the present generation ought to be aware, and to which the author appeals (10:32ff.).

I have affirmed up to now that the addressees of Hebrews are to be labelled simply as Christians, with no special relationship to Judaism or to pagan religion. The question now arises what the purpose of the author might be, and what problem he is tackling. Even a superficial reading of the letter clearly shows that Old Testament and Jewish issues are at stake. This fact seems to undermine my previous statement that the question of Jewish or Gentile origin is of no significance to the readers. Nevertheless, I wish to maintain that the *origin* of the addressees is of no consequence in this connection. The readers are "Judaising" simply as Christians. This is the problem for the author. In order to substantiate this suggestion, it is necessary to discuss further the purpose of the letter. This includes considering what the author reveals about the readers and their situation.

The author makes positive as well as negative statements about his addressees. They themselves did not hear the preaching of Jesus, but they have his word as a reliable tradition (2:14).[15] They have demonstrated in a laudable way their Christian life by serving "the saints" in

---

15 Weiß, *Hebräer*, 78 emphasizes the author's consciousness of his dependency on the early Christian tradition and adds: "Auch wenn er bei der Aneignung und Auslegung dieser Tradition durchaus seine eigenen Wege gegangen ist, versteht er sich selbst ganz in der Kontinuität dieser Tradition".

the love of God (6:10). The most positive statements are found in 10:32ff., where the author reminds the readers of the time when they "were enlightened". They were then exposed to sufferings, abuse, affliction, public dishonour. They were imprisoned, their property was plundered. They endured all this joyfully and showed sincere solidarity with those who shared the same sufferings, for they knew that something more valuable than any earthly reward awaited them.

The author also makes negative statements. The addressees have become dull of hearing, so that it is difficult to teach them (5:11), although by now they ought to have been able to teach others. Instead, they need elementary instruction (5:12). This makes the situation extremely serious. The author urgently warns his readers against the risk of apostasy (6:2ff.; 8:4-8; 10:26-31; 12:15-17). It is an ominous sign that some of them have begun neglecting the assemblies of the community (10:25). The addressees are in danger of losing their confidence (10:35). They run the risk of growing weary and faint-hearted. They fear sufferings and try to avoid them (12:1-11).

This is some of the direct information about the addressees of Hebrews. One may also draw some conclusions indirectly. The author seems to presuppose a certain degree of education on the part of his readers—in spite of his severe criticism of their lack of insight into the fundamentals of the Christian faith. His estimate of their intellectual ability can be discerned from his academic language and his sophisticated argumentation. Lastly, and most importantly, he presupposes that they possess a considerable knowledge of the Old Testament.

What then is the real problem of Hebrews? I have already suggested that the author seems to be confronted by a Christian community (group) which for some reason is "Judaising". It appears that his attitude on the part of the readers cannot be derived from their Jewish origin, nor is it due to influence from Jewish propaganda. There is no demonstrable anti-Jewish polemic in Hebrews. In spite of this, Old Testament and Jewish issues are dealt with by the author in a way which indicates that they were of great importance to his addressees.

Many scholars, realizing the untenability of the traditional idea of Hebrews as a rebuttal of Judaism or of Judaising tendencies among Jewish-born Christian readers, try to explain the situation in another way. They rightly concentrate on the author's exhortations. There seem to be possibilities of recovering, at least to some extent, the situation of the addressees from this paraenetic material. The central role of the paraenesis in the total conception of Hebrews has become increasingly clear to

New Testament scholarship during the last decades. This is due mainly to the studies of O. Michel. For excellent reasons, he maintains that the paraenesis are the author's real concern.[16] The extensive theoretical expositions function as basis and illustrations of the exhortations. The "dogmatic" parts thus serve the paraenetic intention. Michel has gradually found strong support from other interpreters, although one can discern a certain reluctance in the most recent commentator of Hebrews.[17] But even in recent interpretation, the role of paraenesis is emphasized. These observations about the exhortatory material are important for the classification of Hebrews' literary type: it may be designated a sermon. In German scholarship it has been labelled "eine zugesandte Predigt", i.e., a sermon that it sent to a congregation to be read aloud.[18] Since it is sent by the author to readers known to himself, but living in another place, it is easy to understand how the sermon has taken on some epistolary traits.

Having accepted Hebrews as some kind of sermon, and realizing the role of the paraenesis, scholars try to explain the situation of the addressees and the purpose of the author. Attempts at a solution differ widely. According to some, the delay of the *parousia* is the decisive factor.[19] This has created laxity and bewilderment among the addressees, and the author has to deal with this situation. E. Käsemann understood the motif

---

16 O. Michel, *Der Brief an die Hebräer*. KEK XIII – 14. Aufl.; 8. Aufl. dieser Auslegung (Göttingen: Vandenhoeck & Ruprecht 1984). This emphasizing of the role of the paraenesis dominates the interpretation of Michel. The high evaluation of the paraenetic material is not entirely new, but no scholar had previously made use of this idea to the same extent as Michel.

17 Weiß, *Hebräer*, 45, remarks that although the Christological and Soteriological expositions are issuing in paraenesis, this does not mean, that these "doctrinal" passages "lediglich eine 'Funktion der Paränese' darstellen". In spite of this reservation Weiß stresses the importance of the paraenetic material. Among other recent interpreters one finds a similar evaluation, see e.g. Hegermann, *Hebräer*, 4ff., Braun, *Hebräer*, 1f.

18 This understanding of the literary type of Hebrews was initiated already by J. Berger, "Der Brief an die Hebräer, eine Homilie", in *Götting. Theol. Bibl.* III 3 (1797), 449-59. Berger's view of the writing is to a considerable extent accepted by modern scholarship. A certain reluctance is discernible by Gräßer, *Hebräer*, 15 when he says: "Die Kennzeichnung als 'zugesandte Predigt' kann den Befund zur Not erklären". See the excellent overview by W. Übelacker, *Der Hebräerbrief als Appell. I. Untersuchungen zu exordium, narratio und postscriptum (Hebr 1-2 und 13,22-25)*. CB.NT 21 (Stockholm: Almqvist & Wiksell International, 1989), 17-26.

19 So E. Gräßer already in his study *Der Glaube im Hebräerbrief*. MThSt 2 (Marburg: Elwert 1965).

of *wandering* as the central idea of Hebrews. By emphasising this motif, the author is trying to convince his readers that they must surmount their weariness and break the ties that bind the church to the world.[20] O. Michel and C. Spicq think of defective knowledge on the part of the addressees.[21] According to G. Theißen, the weakness of the readers is a sacramentalism without ethical sincerity. The author wants to snatch them out of their sacramental security by arousing their fear of the God who is a "consuming fire" (12:29).[22] Überlacker speaks of the addressees' want of faith in the grace of God and their scepticism regarding the consequences of the sacrifice of Christ.[23]

I do not intend to discuss these attempts at a solution. For my part, it is enough to point to one difficulty which all interpretations have in common: they are not able to give a reasonable explanation of Hebrews' Old Testament and Jewish orientation. Why does the author bring into play this magnificent Old Testament theology? Why does he use such peculiar themes as the tabernacle, the sacrificial institution, the priesthood, the role of Melchizedek and his relation to Christ? Why all this, if the intention is simply to undergird general Christian exhortations?

Faced with this difficulty, one could conclude that we had better return to the traditional notion. In my view, this is neither necessary nor advisable. The arguments against this solution retain their weight. Instead, I shall attempt to present an explanation which does justice to Hebrews' Old Testament-Jewish orientation without exposing itself to the criticism which is often and justly directed against the traditional solution. My thesis is that the addressees of Hebrews are Judaising because of their dependence on the Old Testament, especially in its LXX form. The author's presentation shows that he ascribes to them a comprehensive knowledge of the Old Testament. Their study of scripture may well have led to unwanted consequences. The readers mostly belonged to a generation that had not experienced the founding period, when questions such as the relationship between Jewish and Christian, synagogue and church, law and gospel, old and new covenants were dis-

---

20 E. Käsemann, *Das wandernde Gottesvolk*. FRLANT. NF 37 (Göttingen: Vandenhoeck & Ruprecht, 1939; 4. Aufl. 1961). The conception of Käsemann is developed by Gräßer, *Hebräer*.
21 Michel, *Hebräer*, 48, 56. C. Spicq, *L'Épître aux Hebreux II*. Études bibliques (Paris: Gabalda,1953) ad 5:11-6:1.
22 G. Theißen, *Untersuchungen zum Hebräerbrief*. SNT 2 (Gütersloh: Gütersloher Verlagshaus. Gerd Mohn 1969), 76ff., 110ff.
23 Übelacker, *Hebräerbrief*, 124ff.

cussed and settled. Their ideas about the old and new revelations may have been unclear and confusing, leading to uncertainty with regard to Christian belief and praxis. One can, for instance, easily imagine that the biblical prescriptions about sacrifices can have created difficulties and led to doubts regarding the Christian neglect of the sacrificial cult. This becomes even more probable, if one may assume that the congregation is living in a Hellenistic environment where sacrifices were regarded as natural expressions of religious belief (cf. 1 Cor 8; 10:19ff.). My assumption therefore is that the exhortations of Hebrews are directed to a situation characterised by spiritual paralysis and uncertainty, caused by the addressees' erroneous understanding of the Old Testament.[24]

If one presupposes such a situation, the majestic opening of Hebrews becomes even more meaningful as an introduction to the letter as a whole (1:1-4). The author proclaims his fundamental message at the very beginning: the old revelation given by God, when he spoke through the prophets, is now superseded by his speaking through the Son. This theme then forms the basis of the paraenesis and of their "dogmatic" foundations throughout the letter, which he designates at 13:22 as ὁ λόγος τῆς παρακλήσεως. The motif of superseding does not mean that the word spoken through the Son simply replaces God's previous speaking: the new revelation is a fulfilment of the old.

The same dialectic lies behind the comparison between the Son and the angels in 1:5-14. Many attempts at an interpretation of this parallel have been made, but these cannot be discussed here. I wish to observe only that one can scarcely find any basis in the text for interpretations which affirm that the author uses this comparison to fight against worship of angels,[25] that he refutes speculations concerning angels,[26] or that he is rebutting tendencies to an angelic christology.[27] The comparison is most probably to be seen as an expression of the dialectic between the old revelation and the new. This becomes apparent in the first admonition, 2:14, where the importance of the word spoken by angels is empha-

---

[24] The environment of the addressees cannot be identified. The letter does not indicate that they are living in Palestinian surroundings rather than in a Hellenistic milieu. The question is dealt with by most commentators. See, for instance, the short overview by F. F. Bruce, *Commentary on the Epistle to the Hebrews* (London – Edinburgh: Marshall, Morgan and Scott 1964), XXXIff.

[25] So, for instance, H. Windisch, *Der Hebräerbrief*. HNT 14 (Tübingen: Mohr [Siebeck] 1931), 17; Bruce, *Commentary*, 9. Bruce is, however, cautious regarding the idea of angel-worship.

[26] See the discussion by O. Kuß, *Der Brief an die Hebräer*. RNT 8:1 (Regensburg: Friedrich Pustet 1966; 2. Aufl.), 47.

sised and then compared to the even greater importance attached to the word spoken by the Son. Behind the statement about the angels stands the primitive Christian and Jewish notion that angels mediated God's word to Moses at Mount Sinai. Thus the angels were associated with the Old Testament revelation, especially the law.[28] New Testament parallels to Heb 2:2 are Gal 3:19 and Acts 7:53 (cf. 7:38). In my view, the whole comparison in Heb 1-2 is to be understood as a demonstration of the superiority of the new revelation over the old. The relationship between the angels and the Old Testament is the very reason why the author discusses their position at all.[29]

In my previous exposition, I have attempted to show that the comparison between the Son and the angels aims at a clarification of the relationship between the word mediated by angels and the word spoken through the Son.[30] Interpreted in this way, the parallel naturally fits into the total conception of Hebrews. This is not the case, if one understands the analogy as a polemic against the worship of angels, speculations concerning angels, etc. This becomes even more clear if one notes how Hebrews continues. In 3:1ff., we find a new comparison, which also concerns the old and the new revelations. Moses, who received and mediated the law, is compared to Christ: the author claims that Christ is superior in every respect (3:2ff.). The decisive argument is that Christ is son (υἱός, v. 6), while Moses is servant (θεράπων, v. 5f.). The point of comparison is that they both were faithful. If one asks what Moses' faithfulness consists in, one is led via the LXX quotation to Num 12:7f., where Moses is depicted as πιστός, i.e. faithful to God. But he is πιστός in another sense too, as one "entrusted". This becomes apparent in the fact

---

[27] Michel, *Hebräer*, 131 discusses such a solution without deciding in favour of it. — It should be added that many scholars regard the comparison Son – angels as a theological discussion without connection with concrete problems. See O. Hofius, *Der Christushymnus Philipper 2, 6-11*. WUNT 17 (Tübingen: Mohr [Siebeck] 1976), 75-92; A. Strobel, *Der Brief an die Hebräer*. NTD 9 (Göttingen: Vandenhoeck & Ruprecht 1975), 98. These attempts at a solution fail, according to my view, to do justice to the intensity and urgency that characterize the author's exposition. These traits are more explicable, if he discusses a concrete problem.

[28] The LXX's rendering of Deuteronomy 33:2 has probably inspired many of these ideas in Jewish writings: angels were with him on his right hand (ἐκ δεξιῶν αὐτοῦ ἄγγελοι μετ' αὐτοῦ); cf. Ps. 57:18 (LXX). The motif is expressed in many Jewish writings, for instance, in Josephus, *Ant.* 15:5.3, Philo, *Som.* 1:141ff., *Jub.* 1:27ff.

[29] This view is further substantiated in my studies referred to in note 10.

[30] "The word spoken through the Son" has to be taken in a rather inclusive sense, meaning words from the incarnate as well as the preexistent Christ.

that God has spoken to him in a unique manner. He speaks to him "face to face, plainly and not in riddles", while prophets in general have to be content with visions and dreams (v. 6). The author of Hebrews thus depicts Moses as the most prominent human representative of the old revelation. Here too, the intention is to show that the new revelation through the Son completely surpasses God's previous word which was spoken through Moses.

Christ is superior to the angels and to Moses. Consequently, his revelation supersedes the old one. This motif is employed in many different ways as the exposition continues. In the immediate context of 3:1ff., it functions as a warning against disobedience towards God's calling. The superiority of the new revelation is emphasised most clearly in chs. 7-10, where Christ is described as representing a priesthood higher than the Levitical priesthood. He mediates a covenant greater than the old one, and including a superior worship. He has offered a sacrifice which in all respects is superior to the sacrifices prescribed in the Mosaic law.

Let us now return to the supposed situation of the addressees of Hebrews. The assumption was that their situation was characterised by spiritual weakness and confusion, because of their defective understanding of the Old Testament. The author tries to help his readers out of this uncertainty, through exhortations which are undergirded by christological explanations. These serve to show that the Old Testament prescriptions concerning sacrifices, priesthood, temple etc. have reached their fulfilment in Christ. This means that all regulations are of no consequence to the readers' present situation. Through his exhortations, the author thus intervenes in the unclear situation of the addressees. Through his "doctrinal" explanations he seeks to eliminate the real cause of their confusion, viz. their erroneous understanding of the Old Testament and its role in the Christian era.

The validity of this thesis can of course be tested only by a thorough analysis of the letter as a whole. Some points seem, however, to speak in favour of this view:

1. If the addressees had become Judaising through study and use of the Old Testament, their attitude had nothing to do with their origin. This explains the author's lack of interest in this question. The readers were Judaising, without being Jews.

2. If the thesis is correct, it seems quite natural that Hebrews does not contain any explicit anti-Jewish polemic. The "Judaising" attitude of the readers is then due to literary influences. It has not arisen because of Jewish missionary propaganda.

3. If the thesis is valid, we can explain the somewhat "literary" argumentation concerning the temple. What the author and the addresses know of the temple would then be based on the study of scripture: there is no need to assume that he or they had been in any immediate contact with the Herodian temple.[31]

How "mighty" was the mighty minority? The influence of Jewish Christianity in the early church was no doubt very far-reaching. It represented the continuity with the old covenant as well as the connection with the beginnings of the church. This gave Jewish Christianity a powerful position, regardless of its numerical strength. Like other Israelites, they too (as the apostle puts it) were "adopted as children, the glory was theirs and the covenants, to them were given the Law and the worship of God and the promises. To them belong the fathers and out of them, as far as physical descent is concerned, came Christ who is above all" (Rom 9:4f.). Entrusted with such a position, Jewish Christianity necessarily became a powerfully influential group. Jervell has rightly drawn attention to this somewhat neglected fact.

I have maintained in this article that the legalistic-"Judaising" development in the period from 70 to 100 is not necessarily due to Jewish Christianity. There are also other possible explanations. I have pointed to the possibility of political pressure from radical Jewish groups, which might have compelled the church to make an unintended accommodation to Judaism. In dealing with central themes in Hebrews, I have reached the conclusion that the emphasis on Old Testament and Jewish issues in this letter is independent of Jewish Christianity. The stress on such matters is due to the addressees' inadequate understanding and use of the Old Testament. This lack of insight into the real significance of their scriptures made them "Judaising" in spite of their not being Jews.

Having made these reservations, I am still aware of the important role of the mighty minority in the early church. It seems appropriate to me to conclude by referring to the apostle Paul and his profound insight that Jewish Christianity is sustaining the church as a whole (Rom 11:18).

---

31 The date of Hebrews is uncertain. A first-century date is required because of its being alluded to in the first epistle of Clemens Romanus (ca. AD 96). There is reason to assume that Hebrews was written some few years before the epistle of Clement. By that time the temple was destructed, which may have affected the author's knowledge of it. In any case he is dealing more with the Old Testament tabernacle than with the Jerusalem temple.

"He saw that the city was full of idols" (Acts 17:16)

Visualizing the World of the First Christians

Halvor Moxnes

Among Jacob Jervell's finest achievements as a theological teacher for popular audiences are his programmes on Paul's travels in Asia Minor and Greece, produced on the spot and transmitted through Norwegian Broadcasting. With great enthusiasm he described the present sites and succeeded in bringing alive the ancient cities as visual, cultural, religious and social environments for Paul and his first followers.

For those of us who have followed in the literal as well as figurative footsteps of Jervell, it is easy to share his enthusiasm. Texts from the New testament come alive in a special way when read in places where they had their first audiences. It is an experience of suddenly becoming more fully aware of the context of the lives of Paul and his addresses, not of finding memories or traces that they left behind.

Seeing the major cities where the first Christians lived, such as Ephesus, Pergamon and Corinth, we become fully aware that they were not "Christian cities". The first Christians did not live in a "Christian" world. Their minority status is reflected in the lack of visible remains they left in the physical structures of human-made environments. It was well into the third century before we can speak of anything like a "Christian architecture", of special buildings set up for worship and community use. Likewise, examples of Christian works of art from the first two centuries CE are very rare. Thus, there are few possibilities to establish a specific Christian identity reflected in art and architecture, e.g. in terms of the interrelationship between Christian writings, liturgy and architecture and art that we find in later periods. What we find when we study the cities that hosted the first Christian communities is the world that influenced them every day.

In what ways did it influence them, and in what ways did they react against this influence from the city? Apart from the gospels, New Testament writings give very little in terms of descriptions of their environment. It is not a type of literature where such descriptions are important. But if we know more about their environment, we may also be able to understand references to that environment better.

The goal of this article is to point to some of the studies of urban structures and mentalities that will help us to understand the urban context of the first Christians, and to read parts of one text, the Acts of the Apostles, as an example of early Christian reaction to their urban environment.

1. Urban Studies of the World of Early Christianity

Recently there has been an increasing number of studies that locate early Christians groups or authors in the context of city life. The most prominent example is Wayne A. Meeks, *The First Urban Christians*.[1] Meeks places the formation of early Christian groups within the setting of the ancient city, above all in the Greek cities of Greece and Asia Minor and their social structures and groups. Likewise, two recent studies to Luke-Acts are relevant. The first is Philip F. Esler, *Community and Gospel in Luke-Acts*. Esler says that "the conclusion that Luke wrote in a city of the Roman empire where Hellenistic culture was strong or even dominant is of great assistance in reaching an understanding of the social and political world in which his community found itself."[2] A collection of studies edited by J. H. Neyrey, *The Social World of Luke-Acts*,[3] uses models from social anthropology. In this interpretation of the social world of Luke and his audience both the city and the countryside are relevant settings.[4]

These authors do not see the first Christians as passive recipients of impressions from their urban world. Rather, they were actively engaged in responding to, criticizing and interpreting it. In order to grasp the totality of this urban context, i.e. not just the physical and social context, but also the ideological one, New Testament students employ a term

---

1 W. A. Meeks, *The First Urban Christians*, New Haven, CT: Yale University Press, 1983.
2 P. F. Esler, *Community and Gospel in Luke-Acts*. SNTSMS 57 (Cambridge: Cambridge University Press, 1987), 30.
3 J. H. Neyrey, *The Social World of Luke-Acts*, Peabody, MA: Hendrickson, 1991.
4 Cf. therein Richard L. Rohrbaugh, "The Pre-Industrial City in Luke-Acts," 125-49; Douglas E. Oakman, "The Countryside in Luke-Acts," 151-79.

coined by social anthropologists: "social world." Wayne A. Meeks has described the term "social world" in this way: "it has a double meaning, referring not only to the environment of the Early Christian groups, but also to the world as they perceived it and to which they gave form and significance through their special language and other meaningful actions."[5]

This perspective, viewing early Christianity within its social setting, represents a significant advance over a mere "history of ideas" point of view. Important progress is made through the use of methods and models from social sciences within historical and literary studies. There is one problem, however. As a result of this type of interdisciplinary studies the world of the first Christians has been reconstructed primarily in terms of social, economic and political relations. What is lacking, it seems, is a more conscious attitude towards the place of the community, towards its physical and symbolic space. We need to develop methods to study the interrelations between urban structures, architecture and art and the social and ideological world of the community.

1.1. New Trends—Cities as Meaning

Developments within disciplines like archaeology, geography, history of art and architecture show some of the same trends we find in biblical and social science studies. Archaeology plays a particularly important role since we know ancient cities now only as archaeological sites. S. Dyson describes the most important aspect of the new trend in archaeology as "the importance of theoretical debate and the development of new models which combine archaeological data and innovative intellectual paradigms."[6] He refers to the attempts to use methods and models from social sciences, and thus to move archaeology from the collection and interpretation of single artifacts to an interpretation of social development. To Dyson, it is this discussion of method and intellectual models within the field that makes it possible for classical archaeology to "assume its rightful role in the reconstruction of ancient society." In particular, archaeology can throw light upon large, little known segments of that society: "Archaeology is the most valuable tool at our command if we want to understand the life-experience of those millions of Greeks

---

5 Meeks, *First Urban Christians*, 8.
6 S. Dyson, "The relevance for Romanists of recent approaches to archaeology in Greece," in *Journal of Roman Archaeology* 2 (1989), 143-46.

and Romans who were outside the narrow intellectual circle covered by the literary and even epigraphic sources."[7]

This development within archaeology appears immediately relevant to the study of early Christians in an urban context and the attempts to reconstruct the world of "ordinary Christians," which Wayne A. Meeks describes in this way: "To write social history it is necessary to pay more attention than has been customary to the ordinary patterns of life in the immediate environment within which the Christian movement was born ... the task of the social historian is to describe the life of the ordinary Christian within the environment—not just the ideas or the self-understanding of the leaders and writers."[8]

A recent attempt to encourage the study of past cultures both from geographical and archaeological points of view describes the situation and the changes in a similar way. The title of the book signifies the new approach: *Landscape and Culture*.[9] Until recently, both geography and archaeology were disinterested in theoretical development: "Although geography and archaeology dealt with the results of human activity, social theory was poorly developed and both subjects remained detached from the developing social sciences."[10] Now, there is a change underway: "In both disciplines, questions of the subjective individual, mind, meaning and symbolism have played a central role in this reaction ... Heightened theoretical awareness in the two disciplines has led to the common discovery of central debates in philosophy and social theory which affect all who work in the social and human sciences."[11]

With the convergence between geography and archaeology, there is also a renewed interest in the relationship between town and countryside, between human environment and its physical setting.[12] Classical archaeology and history have often been very urban oriented. Now a number of studies focus on the interrelationship between the urban centre and the countryside, and show how dependent cities were upon their

---

7 S. Dyson, "Relevance," 146. Kevin Greene, in *The Archaeology of the Roman Economy* (London: Batsford, 1986, 9-13) points to some of the same changes and to new forms of cooperation between various disciplines.
8 Meeks, *First Urban Christians*, 2.
9 J. M. Wagstaff (ed.), *Landscape and Culture*, Oxford: Blackwells, 1987.
10 Wagstaff, "Introduction," *Landscape and Culture*, 2.
11 I. Hodder, "Converging Traditions: The Search for Symbolic Meaning in Archaeology and Geography," in *Landscape and Culture*, 135.
12 Cf. Fernand Braudel, *The Mediterranean and the Mediterranean World in the Age of Philip II* (New York: Harper & Row, 1976).

countryside.[13] The classical historian Moses I. Finley has dominated the discussion with his paradigm of the ancient consumer-city, and of a "primitive" economy without a market-economy. The peasants were dominated by the urban centre and lived a subsistence existence.[14] In criticism of that dominant view, Donald Engels has put forward an alternative model, based on Corinth, of ancient cities as "service cities" with a more equal relationship between peasants and cities.[15]

This discussion is immediately relevant to studies of the economic and social structures in Palestine as they are described in the Gospels.[16] Even if such relations are not emphasized in Acts and in the letters, they are important for our understanding of town life and town mentality, so as not to construct them in our idea of a modern city with sharp distinctions from the rural countryside.

Another issue that becomes central within this new development is the relationship between ideology and space. This is not a simple one-to-one relationship, rather, the situation may be that "not all members of society share the dominant ideology or accept it with equal conviction. Subordinate groups may have different perspectives on material symbols and spatial relationships." In line with this development, the individual, not just the totality becomes important. Hodder says that "by re-centering the individual in geographical and archaeological theory, we can begin to see individuals making choices, interacting, negotiating different and opposing interests, using strategies to manipulate the spatial and temporal world around them, with its varied contexts and meanings."[17]

---

13 E.g. Kevin Greene, *The Archeology of the Roman Empire*; Robin Osborne, *Classical Landscape with Figures. The Ancient Greek City and its Countryside* (New York: Sheridan, 1987); T. W. Potter, *Roman Italy* (Berkeley, CA.: Californian University Press, 1987).

14 Cf. especially M. I. Finley, *The Ancient Economy* (London: Chatto and Windus, 1973) and *Economy and Society in Ancient Greece*, ed. with introd. by B.D. Shaw and R. P. Saller (New York: Viking, 1981).

15 D. Engels, *Roman Corinth. An Alternative model for the Classical City* (Chicago: University of Chicago Press, 1990). See also the discussion in Greene, *Archeology of the Roman Empire*, 14-16.

16 Several recent studies build on the "Finley model", see e.g. Rohrbaugh, "The Pre-Industrial City", and Halvor Moxnes, *The Economy of the Kingdom. Social Conflict and Economic Relations in Luke's Gospel* (Philadelphia, PA: Fortress, 1988), 22-47.

17 Hodder, "Converging Traditions," 142, 143.

1.2. City Space and Social Control

The physical layout of a town reflected social concerns, e.g. the need to create a controlled urban environment and one where order could be maintained. Dominic Perring has pointed out two ways in which that can be achieved.[18] In the first "space is structured to encourage public use; social cohesion is promoted by developing activities attached to specific and identifiable locations. In such an approach, a strategy of inclusion, social order is encouraged by the identification of community interest in urban space which is supervised through public use. In contrast it is possible to develop strategies of exclusion where space can be structured to exclude or deter unwanted peoples and activities, and thereby reserve it for uses deemed more acceptable." All towns have some elements that invite involvement, e.g. piazzas, porticoes and broad avenues, while others exclude it, like town walls.

These elements of towns and town planning have been studied by William L. MacDonald, in his investigations of public open spaces in Roman towns.[19] Towns are not just buildings; other important elements are gates (in the city walls), "thoroughfares", main streets that connect gates and the third important element, plazas, agoras, marketplaces. Gates, meeting points and way stations (e.g. fountains, exedras [seats]) are often marked by arches. MacDonald sees Roman towns formed around a "path-like core of thoroughfares and plazas" which he call an "armature." Through a large building programme the Romans made alterations and additions to older Hellenistic cities also, e.g. through colonnaded streets that created visual and spatial foci at routes into towns. In addition to an older single centre, e.g. an agora/forum, additional foci could develop as the town grew, most commonly outside the gates.

The result was to draw visitors to these towns into public open spaces and into paths leading to the centre of town. Public life was concentrated in a single core, or in a series of spaces linked to this core. A steady flow of people in daily activities, and community participation in rituals and festivals that took place in these spaces, outside of buildings, ensured a supervision or control. These public spaces were not empty, but filled by statues and small monuments, that functioned both to enliven the space,

---

18 D. Perring, "Spatial Organisation and social change in Roman Towns," in *City and Country in the Ancient World* (eds. J. Rich and A. Wallace-Hadril, London: Routledge, 1991), 273-93, citations from 274.

19 W. L. MacDonald, *The Architecture of the Roman Empire. II. An Urban Appraisal* (New Haven: Yale University Press, 1986), 32-110.

and to reinforce the "ideologies which promoted social cohesion."[20] Relevant examples from the cities of the first Christians are e.g. the agora in Athens, the Curetes-street in Ephesus and the street leading up to the Asclepeion in Pergamon.

It seems that over time there were changes in approach to open space, in particular the agora. In its earlier form it was an open space, surrounded by public and commercial buildings, but later developments created a more formal space. In Hellenistic times (about the middle of the second century BC) the Agora in Athens was formally structured by the building of several stoas.[21] The early imperial period is another example of such a development. In Rome one can mention the imperial fora, and in the Hellenistic cities in the east, the stoa in the state agora in Ephesus. This stoa linked various public buildings at the state agora into a harmonious unity.[22] While the earlier open fora allowed a free flow of people and made control difficult, the newer enclosed fora with gateways could be more easily controlled and closed. Also, enclosed temple precincts could serve to control public activities, similarly amphitheatres with different sections assigned to different social groups. This gradual process of changes from open to more closed and controlled space may have served to reinforce awareness of social divisions, and made it easier for the town elites to control public activities that were seen as undesirable or threatening.

Town walls were important elements of social control and represented a clear boundary to an urban area. The drawing of boundaries was the first act of establishing a Roman town, the area inside these boundaries being regarded as sacred. This concept was important to control of the town (e.g. what was impure did not belong within the walls, so that the necropolis was outside the walls) but it also helped to form social behaviour. Consequently, not only the walls, but also the entryways into the town were important. As a result, gates and arches were often impressive structures.

Housing in ancient cities was often mixed, with accommodation for rich and poor close together. It has been suggested that this represents the social structure of a clan-like society, with ties of *familia* or *clientela*. Again, from the early imperial period there may have been changes in

---

20 Perring, "Spatial Organisation," 276.
21 John M. Camp, *The Athenian Agora* (London: Thames and Hudson, 1986), 172-80.
22 Ekrem Akurgal, *Ancient Civilizations and Ruins of Turkey*, 5. ed. (Istanbul: Haset Kitabevi, 1983), 166-68.

this structure, so that styles and distributions of buildings reflected a more hierarchical structure and more concern for social distinctions.[23]

Thus, there was a process of change in city planning and architecture that reflected social changes. Originally, city space was organized around institutions and ceremonies, e.g. processions, festivals and sacrifices that made citizens identify themselves with the town. In late republic and early imperial times there started a process of change, especially in wealth and social complexity, that created more of a segmentary and divided society. The new urban designs and town planning changed the city so that it became easier to oversee and to control social interaction in the community.

1.3. Cities as Culture—Honour and Shame

One of the strongest visual impressions made by ancient cities was the large amount of statues of citizens in public spaces: at the market squares, along major streets, outside public buildings like temples and theatres. Many of these statues are now lost, but a large number of statue bases with inscriptions remain and witness to this extraordinary eagerness to honour people. A similar impression is rendered by extensive collections of epigraphic material, often on walls of theatres or other public buildings centrally located in the city. In theatres themselves we often find seats of honour with inscriptions on them.

These are all visible remains of one of the most pervasive elements of Greco-Roman culture, a quest for honour that led to a constant competition in all areas of life. In Homeric society the warrior was the ideal in an often violent quest for honour.[24] The concern for honour remained a dominant element in later Greek and Hellenistic periods, but in a less aggressive form. Competition for honour turned to peaceful means.[25] Members of the city elites competed with one another to win honour, i.e. status and power in the city, primarily through their benevolence to the city. Although this was a game within the powerful elite, it is also possible to see some advantages for "ordinary" people in the city. In order to win political power and honour, rich citizens had to contribute towards the common goods, i.e. by financing public buildings like baths, stoas and theatres, or public festivals, food distributions etc.[26]

---

23 Perring, "Spatial Organisation," 284-87.
24 Moses I. Finley, *The World of Odysseus* (London: Penguin Books, 1962).
25 A. W. H. Adkins, *Merit and Responsibility* (Oxford: Clarendon, 1960).
26 P. Veyne, *Bread and Circuses: Historical Sociology and Political Pluralism* (London: Penguin, 1990).

This culture of benefactions and honours met with criticism from philosophers. In the latter part of the first century CE, i.e. at the time of Luke, the most outspoken critic was Dio Chrysostom.[27] He was a member of a wealthy family of the provincial aristocracy in Bithynia, with links to several emperors. But for parts of his life he was exiled, and lived as a wandering philosopher, influenced by Cynic philosophy. In several of his orations he criticizes the benefaction and honour system, and urges a competition towards the common good of the city, not for visible honours. In his criticism he also provides a full list of various types of honour, from common honours like statues and seats of honour, to exceptional honours like "a portrait statue of beaten gold" (*Or.* 44.1-2).

The quest for honour was not confined to the area of benefactions; it was rather a mentality that pervaded society and culture. As such it has been studied as part of a typical Mediterranean culture.[28] The most important aspect of honour was the recognition by one's peers or "significant others" in society, from whom one was in constant need of reassurance. In this way all social interaction was characterized by a competition for recognition. One had at all times to be ready to defend one's honour. Thus, interactions often took the form of challenge and riposte. A challenge that could not be rebutted resulted in loss of face; it incurred shame, the opposite of honour. Many aspects of honour and shame culture are similar in different societies. The most characteristic aspect of Mediterranean honour and shame culture appears to be the way it is associated with sexuality and gender roles. That is an aspect that comes strongly to the fore in Paul's writings, but in general the honour-shame paradigm is of thematic and even structural importance in many New Testament writings, thus witnessing to its pervasiveness in Hellenistic culture.[29]

---

27 H. Moxnes, "The Quest for Honour and the Unity of the Community in Romans 12 and in the Orations of Dio Chrysostom," in *Paul in His Hellenistic Context* (ed. T. Engberg-Pedersen, Minneapolis, MN: Fortress, 1995), 203-30.

28 The most relevant collection of studies are J. G. Peristiany (ed.), *Honour and Shame: The Values of Mediterranean Society* (London: Weidenfeldt & Nicholson, 1966); D. G. Gilmore (ed.), *Honor and Shame and the Unity of the Mediterranean* (Washington: American Anthropological Association, 1987); J. G. Peristiany and J. Pitt-Rivers (eds.), *Honor and Grace in Anthropology* (Cambridge: Cambridge University Press, 1992).

29 See e.g. B. J. Malina and J. H. Neyrey, "Honor and Shame in Luke-Acts: Pivotal Values in the Mediterranean World," in *Social World of Luke-Acts*, 26-65; and the review article by H. Moxnes, "Honor and Shame," *BTB* 23 (1993), 167-76.

1.4. "The Power of Images"

Large number of statues honouring citizens contributed to the upholding of a public ideology of benefactions as well as to a visible structuring of society into honourable and less honourable members. This is an example of the principle that art and architecture always convey meaning. Without going into details in this large area of study, it suffices to point to the early imperial period as a time with a heightened emphasis on art and architecture as "propaganda." Several studies have been devoted to the question of the relationship between Roman art and propaganda, most successfully Paul Zanker, The Power of Images in the Age of Augustus.[30] His premiss is that art and architecture are mirrors of society, that reflect the state of values, especially in a period of transition. Augustus came to power in a period where much of Rome's traditional cultural identity was lost, and he attempted a total moral and spiritual revival.

Zanker's starting-point is that to do that, Augustus needed a new visual language. His observations here are relevant to the question of the importance of the visual for a contemporary experience of a society, and thus for the importance for us of the study of visual art. Zanker is interested "in the totality of images that a contemporary would have experienced. This includes not only 'works of art,' buildings, and poetic imagery, but also religious ritual, clothing, state ceremony, the emperor's conduct and forms of social intercourse, insofar as these created a visual impression. I am concerned with the contexts of these images and with the effect of this tapestry of images on the viewer. 'Visual imagery,' understood in this sense, reflects a society's inner life and gives insight into people's values and imagination that often cannot be apprehended in literary sources."[31]

At the centre of this revival was the image of Augustus himself, often depicted as an example of piety, as priest with covered head (togatus). Apart from the image of Augustus, representing the state, a conscious use of the Classical Greek tradition in an extensive building programme was an important element in Augustus' plan. Whereas in earlier Hellenistic time the Romans had been mere recipients of Greek art, now Augus-

---

30 P. Zanker, *The Power of Images in the Age of Augustus*, Ann Arbor, MI: University of Michigan Press, 1988. For a review article on other relevant studies by i.a. N. Hannestad and T. Hölscher, see R. Brilliant, "Roman Art and Roman Imperial Policy," in *Journal of Roman Archeology* 1 (1988) 110-14.

31 P. Zanker, *Power of Images*, 3.

tus introduced a conscious use of it to emphasize traditional values. Among these private simplicity and generosity towards the public good (publica magnificentia) held prominent place. Zanker points out how this made it possible to create an integrated system of shared values within the empire, which had not been possible in previous periods. The emperor become the ideal for every individual, and the classical moral ideals impressed themselves on all inhabitants through the revival of classical buildings. One example of this is the rebuilding of the Agora in Athens by M. V. Agrippa, the son-in-law of Augustus.[32] The large Odeon erected in front of the existing stoas had as its main purpose to present the great classical literature. Moreover, Agrippa emphasized the links between the emperor and the classical gods by moving a temple dedicated to the war god, Ares, into the agora, and by dedicating a statue to the emperor's son as the "new Ares."

In his study of Roman architecture, William L. MacDonald reaches similar conclusions.[33] A great building programme took place all over the empire, and created a great impact and dominated the urban scene. Much emphasis was put upon connecting streets, especially the impressive colonnaded streets, in agoras smaller, classical buildings were connected into an impressive unity through large stoas. MacDonald emphasizes especially the structural and symbolic importance of the new architectonic device, the vault. It made large arches, aqueducts, and large vaulted buildings possible. The vaulted style, MacDonald argues, expresses the imperial ambitions in a unique way, to order and to organize their world. It has the same hortatory qualities as in official statues, coinage and panegyric literature. Built on axis and symmetry, the vaulted style reflected "the balance and order, the almost choreographic clarity, of Roman ritual and liturgy." When looked upon as expressions of "meaning", "all the great vaulted buildings were charged with the property of expressing unity. ... the architecture of Rome, like that of Egypt and Greece, spoke of a particular way of life and the institution it fostered rather than the independent opportunity and taste of any single individual."[34]

It is time to sum up this brief review. Recent studies of cities show a broader range of perspectives than before. Thus, studies of city planning,

---

32 Zanker, *The Power of images*, 261-63; Camp, *Athenian Agora*, 184-87.
33 W. L. MacDonald, *The Architecture of the Roman Empire I. An Introductory Study*. Rev.ed (New Haven: Yale University Press, 1982), 167-83.
34 MacDonald, *Architecture I*, 181.

political and social institutions are combined with studies of cities within the landscape or of control of space in the city.[35] Last but not least, the visual impact of the city, its architecture and its images, contributes to the create the totality of meaning that is the city. It is of particular interest that several studies point to the early imperial period, i.e. the first century CE, as a period where visual and political impressions are very strong to create a unified ideology. This is the time when the first urban Christian communities were established as small groups in most urban centres of the Empire. Can we imagine that they were not influenced by this visual context within which they lived?

2. Luke as an Urban Writer in the Hellenistic City

2.1. Luke as an Urban Writer

It is commonly held that Luke and his audience were located outside of Palestine, most likely in one of the Hellenistic cities in the Eastern part of the Mediterranean.[36] However, there are various ways to argue for Luke's location. Vernon Robbins looks primarily at the various groups of people that appear to be the implied addressees of Luke in his Gospel and in Acts. He finds that "the social location of thought appears to lie among a cosmopolitan population mixture somewhere between the western coast of Asia Minor and Syria."[37] Luke's descriptions of authorities appear to be located not in Jerusalem but in the Hellenistic diaspora. Philip Esler suggests that Luke was located in Ephesus, a suggestion based on the immediate character of Paul's farewell address to the Ephesians in Acts 20, where he addresses them as his "flock".[38] In a forthcoming study, Peter Lampe undertakes a very thorough examination of all the evidence that points towards Ephesus as Luke's location.[39] Another argument for the provenance of Luke-Acts in an Hellenistic city is found

---

35 Examples of such studies are O. Murray and S. Price (eds.), *The Greek City from Homer to Alexander* (Oxford: Clarendon Press, 1990), and *City and Country in the Ancient World*. These collections can serve as models for the study of the first Christians within a city context.
36 This suggestion does not exclude the possibility that Luke was primarily addressing Jewish Christians.
37 V. Robins, "The Social Location of the Implied Author in Luke-Acts," in *Social World of Luke-Acts*, 318.
38 Esler, *Community and Gospel in Luke-Acts*, 27.
39 P. Lampe, *Lokalisation der Lukas-Leser* (forthcoming from J. C. B. Mohr [Paul Siebeck], Tübingen and Fortress Press, Minneapolis, MN).

in the total picture of social structures and relations found in these books.[40] It has been suggested that whereas the description of the house built on rock in Matt 7:24-27 reflects building styles and rain seasons in Palestine, Luke's version in 6:47-49 is more at home in a large river valley, e.g. that of Orontes near Antioch in Syria.[41] But apart from this suggestion scant attention has been paid to the visual, urban environment in Luke-Acts.[42]

If Luke lived in a Hellenistic city, he knew not only its social and political structure, but also of course its physical structure, its visual impressions, its temples, monuments, its festivals, processions and rituals. We would expect him to use this knowledge in his descriptions of Paul's missions to the cities of the eastern Mediterranean. I shall therefore look at a few of his descriptions for traces of such knowledge. From discussions of the purpose of Luke's writing, be it directed primarily towards a Jewish Christian community, or towards the Roman world as an apologetic writing, or for some other purpose, it is obvious that Luke is a resourceful writer and an astute observer. He has a strategic purpose for the way in which he tells the story of Paul's mission.

Can we see Luke as a writer who is engaged in interpreting the social and symbolic world that surrounds him in such a way that he sets up a "counter-interpretation" to the dominant ideology? And does his strategy also include the way he sets the story within the environment of the city, the way in which he uses different spaces in the city? Where do we find the Christians in Luke's presentation of the cities in Acts, i.e. in what sort of places or space? What are the implications of that particular space, i.e. what connotations does this space carry, and to what degree do the Christians actively engage in manipulating this spatial world?

2.2. "He saw that the city was full of idols" (Acts 17:16). Pausanias and Luke in Athens

The phrase "the power of images" comes to mind when one reads the introduction to Luke's description of Paul's visit to Athens: "Now while Paul was waiting for them in Athens, his spirit was provoked within him

---

40 H. Moxnes, "The Social Context of Luke's Community," *Int* 48 (1994) 379-89.
41 Joseph A. Fitzmyer, *The Gospel according to Luke* (AB 28/1; Garden City, NY: Doubleday & Co, 1979), 644.
42 But see the attempt by Vernon Robbins to read Luke-Acts in light of "human geography" or "territoriality" in "Luke-Acts: A Mixed Population seeks a Home in the Roman Empire," in *Images of Empire* (ed. L. Alexander; JSNTSup 122; Sheffield: JSOT Press, 1991), 202-21.

as he saw that the city was full of idols" (17:16). This theme is picked up again in v. 23: "for as I passed along, and observed the objects of your worship, I found also an altar with the inscription: to an unknown god." What we see here is the typical motif of "sightseeing," *periegesis*.[43] There is a puzzling contrast in attitude between Paul's strong reaction in v. 16 and the much more conciliatory one in v. 22, but there is no doubt that Luke describes a situation in which the images make a great impact upon Paul. It may be said that they had "power."

We are here dealing with Luke's narrative, not with the "historical Paul" or with questions whether this is an eyewitness report or a literary piece.[44] Therefore it is of limited value to raise the historical question "what did Paul see? What were the statues and monuments in Athens of his time?"[45] This type of knowledge would only be helpful together with an interpretation of their meaning for the viewers, of the myths and stories that made up the religious history of Athenians. Such a combination is found in the most important source for an historical reconstruction, Pausanias, *Guide to Greece*.[46] In Book 1, 1-19 he describes Athens and the statues of gods found in particular on the Agora. Although his work dates from the second half of the second century CE, that is, a few generations after Luke, most of the buildings and monuments at the Agora dated from classical and Hellenistic times. Moreover, Pausanias paid special attention to older monuments. His book is a typical example of periegetic, i.e. guide literature.[47] It was a type of literature that was popular in Hellenistic times. It had similarities with other well known types of description such as geography and art history. But in contrast to geography, periegesis concentrates not on topography, but on the cultural

---

43 Hans Conzelmann, "The Address of Paul on the Areopagus," in *Studies in Luke-Acts. Essays Presented in Honor of Paul Schubert* (eds. L. E. Keck and J. L. Martyn; London: SPCK, 1968), 219.

44 Colin J. Hemer argues that the description is based on actual observation rather than based on literature, *The Book of Acts in the Setting of Hellenistic History* (WUNT 49; Tübingen: J. C. B. Mohr [Paul Siebeck] 1989), 116.

45 These questions are competently dealt with by Oscar Browneer, "Athens. 'City of Idol Worship'," *BA* 21 (1958), 2-28.

46 *Guide to Greece. I. Central Greece*. Transl. with an Introd. by P. Levi, S.J.; Harmondsworth: Penguin Books, 1971. Greek text from Pausaniae, *Graecia descriptio*, 1 (ed. M. H. Rocha-Pereira; 2nd ed., Leipzig: Teubner, 1989).

47 Jostein Børtnes, "Pausanias som perieget," in *I Hellas med Pausanias* (eds. Øyvind Andersen og Tormod Eide; Skrifter utgitt av Det norske instituttet i Aten 3; Bergen: Klassisk institutt, 1992), 9-19.

monuments in an area. And in contrast to art history, it is not the aesthetic, but the historical and cultural importance of monuments that are in focus.

Pausanias gives a broad and detailed picture of buildings, monuments and statues in and around the Agora. We get a vivid impression of the presence of the major Olympic gods, such as Apollo, Zeus, Athena, Aphrodite, often represented by more than one statue. There are also temples and statues of ancient gods, e.g. the "Mother of Gods" (1.3.5), Ares, the war god (1.8.5), and Demeter (1.14.1), as well as of numerous heroes. He also mentions several herms that according to him were an Athenian invention (1.24.3).[48]

As part of the genre, periegesis, information about myths associated with the monuments, about cultic functions, or about their worshippers is added to the description of the monuments themselves. Here Pausanias often adds information he has received from local guides or cult personnel.[49] In his description of the way from Pireus to Athens, he also mentions altars of "unknown gods" (1.1.4.), a reference that is discussed as a plausible background for the altar "to an unknown god" mentioned in Acts 17:23. But this reference does not have additional comments or information. But there is another passage that combines an observation of sights and an evaluation of the piety of the Athenians in a similar way to Paul in Acts 17:22-23.[50] That is his comments on the "altar of piety", probably the old altar of "twelve gods" that once was the central public sanctuary of Athens.[51] He remarks that it was not well known to everyone, and continues: "The Athenians are the only Greeks who pay honours to this very important god in human life and human reverses. It is not only that love of the human race is in their institutions, but they worship gods more than other people, ..." (1.17.1).

Pausanias himself is well aware that his text consists of these two elements: his own description as an eyewitness, and the narratives, myths etc. that are interpolated. He describes this as a combination of θεωρήματα and λόγοι (1.39.3).[52] Thus we find two levels of texts interacting

---

48 Herms are a simple sculpture, a rectangular shaft with a set of male genitalia halfway up and a portrait of the god Hermes on top. Their function was to guard entrances; J. M. Camp, *The Athenian Agora*, 74-77.
49 A. Hultgård, "Pausanias och religionen," in *I Hellas med Pausanias*, 139-40.
50 Bertil Gärtner, *The Areopagus Speech and Natural Revelation* (Acta Seminarii Neotestamentici Upsaliensis 21; Lund: Gleerup, 1955), 242-47.
51 Camp, *Athenian Agora*, 40-42.
52 Børtnes, "Pausanias som perieget," in *I Hellas med Pausanias*, 16-18.

with each other. When the narratives and myths he has received from others are added, a new dimension is added to the visual observation of monuments: they are put not only within a spatial frame of reference, but also within an historic one. Pausanias may describe monuments within a causal framework, narrating the relation between a monument and its creator. But he can also put it within a framework of parallels, emphasizing similarities between monuments and the myths associated with them. It is through this process that the monuments receive *meaning* in Pausanias. The monuments themselves have no fixed meaning without the context provided by e.g. inscriptions, myths and rituals.

In Luke's description of Paul in Acts 17 we find a construction similar to that of the θεωρήματα and λόγοι in Pausanias. Paul also started by *seeing* (θεωροῦντος [16] ἀναθεωρῶν [23]) the statues. His interpretative task started at once; by naming them εἴδωλα[53] or σεβάσματα, and by discussing (διελέγετο, 17). Finally, he puts what he has seen within the context of his own narrative, his proclamation (καταγγέλλω, 23). The characterization in 17:16 of the images as "idols", implies a negative judgment. Luke Johnson has observed that it "reflects a Jewish judgment on Greek piety,"[54] that is, a minority viewpoint vis-à-vis the dominant culture of Athens.

There is a contrast between Paul's reaction to "idols" in v. 16: "his spirit was provoked within him", and the tone when the *periegesis* is continued in his speech and he narrates what he saw in Athens: "for as I passed along and observed the objects of your worship, I found also an altar with this inscription: 'To an unknown god'. This description is prefaced by his address to the Athenians: "I perceive that in every way you are very religious." Of course, this is the *captatio benevolentiae* of the rhetorical address,[55] and the speech continues with Paul's proclamation of the true God. He is here narrating important myths of his own religious tradition combined with other important elements of Jewish tradition about God, e.g. that he does not live in shrines made by man, and that he

---

53 It is a brief account, employing a rare word, κατείδωλος. Some translations used the form "wholly given to idolatry," but it is better translated with terms indicating the visual impression, and not referring to the character of the inhabitants. It has been suggested, based on comparisons with other words construed with "κατά", that the term had associations like "a forest of idols," see Büchsel, "εἴδωλον", in *TDNT* 2 (1973), 379.

54 L. Johnson, *The Acts of the Apostles* (Sacra Pagina Series 5; Collegeville, MN: Liturgical Press, 1992), 312.

55 Johnson, *Acts of the Apostles*, 314.

is not like a sculpture made from gold, silver or stone. It is well known, however, that these ideas about God correspond to a large degree with philosophical ideas. David Balch has pointed out how this focus on images in the discussion is reminiscent of a similar discussion by Dio Chrysostom in *Oratio* 12.[56]

A comparison with Pausanias makes us more aware of Luke's position as belonging to a minority in the Graeco-Roman cities. His picture of Paul wandering around among cult statues for a large number of gods describes a typical situation for his audience, be it in Athens, Ephesus, Corinth, Antioch or any of the other cities in the Eastern Mediterranean. The reactions attributed to Paul show a variety of possibilities. One is the emotional disgust typical of a minority as a "sect." Another is the attempt to find some positive elements in discussion with members of the majority. And finally Luke engages in an intellectual discussion of "images" skilfully combining Jewish theology and Hellenistic philosophy. The first reaction is that of "insiders" among themselves. It has the function of drawing boundaries against the outside (cf. 15:29). If we compare this reaction in Acts 17:16 with Stephen's speech in Acts 7, we notice how it can draw upon similar reactions in central myths from Jewish history that make absolute the distinction between the one true God and "idols" (7:41). This is an important motif in early Christian missionary preaching, particularly preaching to recent converts (1 Thess 1:9).

The other reactions to Greek cult images in Acts 17 indicate a different position: that of a minority which desires to engage in discussion with the majority, wants to position itself within the city and in the discussion of the meaning of images and of what myths should be the foundation of the community.

2.3. Christian Missionaries in City Space: Who is in Control?

What is Luke's strategy in terms of urban space and the buildings in which Paul and his co-Christians are found when he describes Paul in Hellenistic towns? Since Luke obviously knows towns very well, it is interesting to start by seeing what part of the urban "repertoire" of space and buildings he actually employs.

We have given an outline of urban space above, but it is useful also to

---

56 D. L. Balch, "The Areopagus Speech: An Appeal to the Stoic Historian Posidonius against later Stoics and the Epicureans," in *Greeks, Romans and Christians. Essays in Honor of Abraham J. Malherbe* (eds. D. L. Balch, E. Ferguson and W. A. Meeks; Minneapolis, MN: Fortress), 72-79.

remind ourselves of what type of buildings we may expect to find in Hellenistic towns. Let us first hear Pausanias' description of what we should minimally expect to find in a town (πόλις), when he speaks of Panopeus in Phokis: "if you can call it a city when it has no state buildings, no training-ground, no theatre, and no market-square, when it has no running water at a water-head and they live on the edge of a torrent in hovels like mountain huts" (X.4.1).

Full scale cities had buildings that covered various functions:[57]

(1) administrative (basilica, senate house);
(2) commercial (market, ship, storehouse);
(3) cultural (odeum, library, theatre, sometimes bath and amphitheatre);
(4) hydraulic/hygienic (bath, cistern, latrine;
(5) recreational (amphitheatre, bath, circus, stadium);
(6) religious (capitolium, other temple, cult building).

Many of these buildings were open for all for public use in the town, and many were recreational and cultural, built for non-commercial purposes. Smaller cities did not have all these buildings, e.g. they often lacked amphitheatre, odeum or library. Towns with particular tasks had other significant structures, e.g. garrison towns had military barracks, administrative centres had palaces, harbours had lighthouses etc.[58]

What are the structures that Luke describes in his presentation of the hellenistic towns in Asia Minor and Greece?

Buildings:
prisons (16:23-40);
synagogues (13:5, 14; 14:1; 15:21; 17:1,10,17; 18:4, 7, 19, 26; 19:8);
temples (14:13; 19:27);
theatre (19:29-41);
private houses or homes (16:15, 34; 18:7; 20:7-12).

Public spaces:
agora (market square) (16:19; 17:7);
bema, judges' seat (18:12-17).

---

57 MacDonald, *Architecture* II, 111.
58 MacDonald, *Architecture* II, 125-30.

Passage structures:
   city gates (9:24; 14:13; 16:12);
   gates for temple precinct (3:2, 10; 21:30);
   prison gate (12:10).

We will now investigate where we find Christians within these structures in a selected sample of Luke's city scenes in Acts.[59]

LYSTRA: ACTS 14:6-23

The locations in this scene are a) at the city gate, close to the Zeus temple, 14:13-18. and b) outside the city 14:19. The scene of a sacrificial procession in front of the Zeus temple in Lystra evokes strong visual impressions. There are many alter reliefs, miniatures etc. that depict similar scenes. At the outset of the story the crowds want to proclaim Paul and Barnabas to be gods in human forms, because of their healing of a crippled man. No specific space for this incident is mentioned, but from what follows, it is most likely inside the town walls. The rest of the drama is played out with the boundaries between "inside" and "outside" the city playing a prominent role. The space in front of the Zeus temple just outside the town gate obviously is an important public space in the town (cf. above). Luke's description here is vivid, his audience would easily be able to imagine a sacrificial procession with oxen and garlands leading up to the town gates (πυλῶνες, 14:13). The identification of Barnabas with Zeus makes their visit an important event in the city that the citizens want to celebrate. With their missionary speech Paul and Barnabas are only just able to prevent the crowd (ὄχλοι) from sacrificing oxen in their honour (14:18).

The scene changes quickly, however. Jews from Antioch and Iconium persuade the crowd to stone Paul. Paul's opponents are described as another "minority group" of outsiders who were able to form an alliance with the majority population of Zeus worshippers. This summary execution is presented as a mob murder, without any legal procedure. There is

---

   59 Not treated in detail are the narratives set in Thessalonica and Corinth, which share elements with the Lystra and Ephesus episodes. The Jews, in an alliance with city crowds (Lystra), bring Paul or other believers instead of him before the authorities, but are rebuked (Ephesus). *Thessalonica*, Acts 17: 1-9: The localities in this narrative are: (a) The Jewish synagogue, with Jews, god-fearers, and women of the leading groups in the town; (b) the house of Jason; (c) the city court, with the city judges. *Corinth*, Acts 18:1-17: The localities are: (a) the house of Aquila and Priscilla, 18:2-3; (b) the Jewish synagogue, 18:4-6; (c) the house of Titius Justus, a Jew, 18:7-11.

no intervention by any town authority, this may be Luke's strategy to say that it is "the town" as a unity that performs the execution.

The fate of Paul is reflected in his position in relation to the boundaries of the town. Believing that he is dead, his enemies drag him along to the outside of the city, i.e. to the place of the dead, the unclean that cannot remain within the boundaries (14:19). Here Paul was left supposedly dead, isolated and alone. But when his disciples gathered around him, he rose, and went into (εἰσῆλθεν εἰς) the town again (14:20). That is, not only was his life restored, but also human fellowship, and finally he re-entered the town. The attempt by his Jewish opponents to throw him out of the community did not succeed. We may read Luke's story as an emphasis on the place of the Christians within the town.

But there is more to Luke's story than Paul's re-entry into the town, which he quickly leaves again. The same phrase, εἰσέρχομαι εἰς, turns up again in the next section. In a short summary statement he describes how Paul, after a missionary journey, returns to Lystra, Iconium and Antioch and strengthens the disciples by saying that "through many tribulations we must enter (εἰσῆλθεν εἰς) the kingdom of God" (14:22). Thus, his re-entry into Lystra after being stoned is also an example of the tribulations Christians must undergo before they can enter the Kingdom.

PHILIPPI: ACTS 16:11-40

There are several different localities in this story: a) outside the city gates (16:13) (a synagogue and) a place of prayer at the river, frequented by women; b) the house of a wealthy woman and her household (16:15,40); c) the market place (agora) with the judges's seat (19-22), with judges, accusers, and a city mob; d) the city prison (16:23- 32) with a jailer; e) the house of the jailer and his family (16:33-34).

Philippi is introduced as a Roman colony and a leading city in Macedonia. In this way Luke emphasizes the importance of its Roman character, an aspect that is of great importance to the narrative.[60] Apparently it does not have a synagogue within the city, and so Paul and his companions on the Sabbath went outside the gates (the impressive arches found at excavations) to a "place of prayer", or most likely, a synagogue (13-15).[61] At the synagogue, or on their way there, they met a group of women, including Lydia, who became the first European Christian. She

---

[60] A. N. Sherwin-White, *Roman Society and Roman Law in the New Testament* (Repr., Grand Rapids, MI: Baker, 1981), 92-95.

[61] Johnson, *Acts of the Apostles*, 292.

entreated them to come to her house and enjoy her hospitality. There is here a shift from the open space outside the gates, to a private house in the city.

The road to the synagogue is the scene for another dramatic encounter (16-18): Paul and his companions were followed by a female slave with a prophesying spirit, who revealed their identity. When Paul drove the spirit out, and the woman lost her gift, her owners turned on Paul and Silas. They brought them by force to the agora, which then is the scene for the following events (19-24). The agora is also the seat of the city magistrates. There, in the public centre of the town, Paul and Silas were accused of disturbing the town, and of being Jews. The accusers were joined by the crowds gathered in the market square. Moreover, the magistrates (στρατηγοί) bowed to the accusers and had them beaten in a show of public punishment. Finally, the magistrates completed the humiliation by throwing them into the city prison.

While this scene has been set in the most public place of the city where free men gather, the securely closed prison is a place for those who have lost their freedom. Here follows, however, the miraculous salvation through an earthquake, which in a "symbolic gesture" brought the prison doors to open (26-27). The jailer, who became a convert and was baptized, did as Lydia did: he brought Paul and Silas to his house and entertained them with a meal.

In another unexpected turn of events the next morning the magistrates send word that Paul may leave. Now comes, however, Luke's masterful conclusion of the story: Paul, who entered Philippi, the Roman colony, so to speak incognito (16:12) reveals himself to be a Roman citizen (16:37)! Moreover, Paul's reply interprets the events in the agora within the context of a Mediterranean paradigm of honour and shame:[62] he had, illegally, been publicly (δημοσίᾳ) beaten, i.e. he had been exposed to shame in front of everybody in the agora. When, in contrast, the magistrates now wanted to send him away secretly (λάθρᾳ), that meant that his shame would remain and that they would not be held responsible for their truly shameful behaviour. As a result of Paul's demands, a reversal of fortunes follows:[63] the magistrates arrived to apologize, that is, to humiliate themselves and restore honour to Paul. And Paul could not be thrown out of the city; he again visited the house of Lydia, before he left.

---

62 Johnson, *Acts of the Apostles*, 301.
63 For the significance of "reversal" in Luke, see John O. York, *The Last Shall be First. The Rhetoric of Reversal in Luke* (JSNTSup 46; Sheffield: JSOT Press, 1991).

In this narrative the synagogue does not play a separate role. Paul is only on his way to the synagogue. Nevertheless, he and Silas are identified as Jews and the conflict turns on the status of the Jews in Roman eyes. In this narrative the agora, a public place that welcomes all people who are inside the city walls, turns into a mob scene, where the crowds and the authorities join together to humiliate Paul. The city prison, where the authorities takes the outmost precautions to lock up Paul, turns out to be outside their control: a divine miracle makes the doors spring open. In this way the prison, the stronghold of the city, turns out to be the scene of the power of God. The public sphere which includes the agora and the magistrates, is an arena of conflict over honour and power. And it is Paul who restores order to the city. The fact that he is a Roman citizen forces the magistrates to reverse their shameful behaviour. Finally, in contrast to public spaces, private houses are meeting places for the believers and places of nourishment (16:15,34) and encouragement for them (16:40).[64]

EPHESUS: ACTS 19:23-41

The primary scene of this dramatic narrative is the imposing theatre in Ephesus, with a seating capacity of 24000, in a prominent position in the hill facing Arcadiane, the harbour road. A large Hellenistic structure, it was enlarged under the Roman emperors from 40 CE onwards. Theatres and amphitheatres illustrate more than many other buildings the question of city space and social control. Here large crowds of people of different sections or communities in the city met together, and at times the structural control imposed by the division into different seating sections could be broken. Conflicts between Jews and citizens could break out into the open in theatres.[65] The fragile line between control and chaos could easily be broken, and it is this that appears to happen in Luke's account of the scene in the theatre in Ephesus. It was in the theatre that the throng led by the silversmith Demetrius, running through the streets, gathered and forced two of Paul's fellow travellers to come along with them (19:29). The theatre was a likely place to meet, since it was also the

---

64 This contrast between "public scenes" and "private homes" has structural similarities to the contrast between temple and household, see John H. Elliott, "Temple versus Household in Luke-Acts: A Contrast in Social Institutions," in *Social World of Luke-Acts*, 211-40.

65 Robert F. Stoops, Jr., "Riot and Assembly: The Social Context of Acts 19:23-41," in *JBL* 108 (1989), 84.

meeting place for the people's assembly, the ἐκκλησία in Ephesus.[66] But what is described was not a legal assembly (ἔννομος ἐκκλησία); rather, Luke's description characterizes it as a "disturbance" (συστροφή) and a riot (στάσις, 19:40).

The statement directed to the unruly crowd by the city clerk of Ephesus that "We are in danger of being charged with rioting today" (19:40) is an accurate description of the worst fear of the elite in the Eastern Hellenistic cities: that they should lose control over the city population, so that the Romans would move in and establish direct rule. This is a fear that is illustrated by John 11:47-48 and also by many Hellenistic writers, e.g. by Dio Chrysostom. One of his main concerns was the fear of strife and contention that threatened the unity of the city.[67]

In his speech the city clerk pointed in two directions to calm down the unruly crowd. First, he points towards the pride of Ephesus, the enormous temple of Artemis, of which Ephesus was protector, (νεωκόρος), just outside the city. He said that its cult statue had fallen down from heaven, i.e. its authority was unquestioned, and therefore any rash action was unneccessary (19:35-36).

Secondly, he pointed towards the state agora, where court days (ἀγοραῖοι) were held with the proconsuls (19:38). The proper place for a court case was not the theatre, with its agitated mob, but the dignified state agora, which was separate from the commercial agora, and stood at the end of the long Curetes street with its rows of statues and monuments. The gateway at the end of street was guarded by Hermes; then followed the dignified state agora. The long stoa, built in the late Augustean time, united into an impressive structure the main administrative buildings of the city: the council hall (βουλευτήριον), the town hall (πρυτανεῖον), and the temple of Roma and Julius Caesar (Price, 254).

The city clerk argued for an orderly procedure. That was a procedure that took the accusations out of the hands of the city mob, who could take control of the theatre with their shouts (19:34), and put it into the hands of elected officials and Roman administrators, in the calm and controlled surroundings of the state agora. And if there were any issues left to be discussed by the people, they had to do so through a legal meeting of the δῆμος.

With his descriptions of accusations against Christian missionaries, Luke shows that he knew the fears of the city elites and that they were

---

66 Sherwin-White, *Roman Society*, 87.
67 Moxnes, "Quest for Honor," 207-11.

concerned with unity and therefore with the control of the city. With his narrative of the scene in the theatre in Ephesus, Luke has ironically reversed the charges of the Christians' enemies by putting the silversmiths, who are filled with greed, and the crowds in the position of the disturbers of civic order. The popular arenas, like the theatre and streets, are described as dangerous for the Christians, but they are protected by the bearers of authority and power.

3. Conclusion

Luke presents the Christian missionaries within a spatial vision of the city. The scenes chosen for each individual city are described with attention to characteristic aspects of structures or buildings of that city, but also with attention to their social and symbolic function.

Part of the drama is the way in which the Christian missionaries move from one type of space to another. Luke portrays them as existing in locations that are socially marginal, i.e. shameful and also as being totally insecure, existing without rights, in the city's *prisons*. This is the visible manifestation of their status as a minority, at the margins of city life. This marginal position is also illustrated by a portrayal of them in liminal positions in the city's *gates*, i.e. betwixt and between, where identities are insecure. Their marginal position is further indicated by the fact that there are large areas of city life that is not described: we do not find Christians in buildings with cultural or recreational functions, like baths, libraries, odeums. They walk among the large number of images of gods with great reserve and describe them, at least among themselves, as 'idols'. Thus, there is in Luke's description clear indications of the minority status that his addressees experienced.

This being so obvious, Luke's strategy in presenting the Christian missionaries as defending their right to space in the city is all the more remarkable. This strategy can be seen in the way they are portrayed in the central public spaces of the cities, above all the *agora*. It is not the commercial activities in the agora that interest Luke, he focuses on its position as centre of public life and place for judicial authority. Be it in discussions with philosophers or with city crowds or before the judge's seat, the Christians are in challenged positions. Most often, the cause of the challenge is that the Christian mission brings the Christians into conflict with non-elite groups, which sometimes succeed and sometimes fail in associating themselves with the elite in marginalizing the Christians. Most often, however, they do not succeed. The elite dismisses the charges. The Christian missionaries are presented as cleverly playing their cards, or, their opponents are presented as "market rabble" whose stupidity causes them to fail. Thus, the Christians defend their rights to exist in the city, and even position themselves as defenders of control over public space. According to Luke, they were not a cause of riots and schisms that threatened the peace and stability of the city, thus there was no reason to exclude their missionary activity from the agoras and the streets.

We may see Luke as a witness to conflicts that went on in the cities of the Roman empire in the latter part of the first century CE, conflicts that often resulted in questions of control of public space within the city. When Luke defends the rights of the Christians to public space, he strategically positions the minority to which he belongs in the midst of city life.

Israel als integrierter Teil der christlichen Hoffnung

(Matthäus 23)

Sigfred Pedersen

I. Methodologischer und forschungsgeschichtlicher Auftakt

In einem früheren Artikel habe ich das erste Kapitel als einen Teil des Prologs zum Matthäusevangelium aus der allgemeinen Erwägung heraus analysiert, daß der Weg zu einer historisch tragfähigen Interpretation der einzelnen neutestamentlichen Schriften, *in casu* der Evangelien, über eine genaue Bestimmung sowohl ihres Prologs als auch ihres Epilogs führt[1]. Aufgrund ihrer Funktion als Prolog bzw. Epilog stellen sich diese umrahmenden Abschnitte als hermeneutische Arsenale für die Interpretation der theologischen Eigenart und des aktuellen Anliegens des jeweiligen Evangeliums dar. Hinter dieser *methodologischen* Bemerkung liegt eine implizite Erfahrung – mit ihrer Wurzel in der antiken Rhetorik –, daß nämlich der Schlüssel zum Inhalt der neutestamentlichen Schriften in der Komposition und damit auch in der Reihenfolge der einzelnen Perikopen liegt[2].

Als *forschungsgeschichtlicher* Ausgangspunkt für die folgende Analyse soll uns Jacob Jervells Arbeit zu den "Testamenten der zwölf Patriarchen" aus dem Jahre 1969 dienen. In einer kritischen Stellungnahme zu M. de Jonge, nach dem sich der christliche *Verfasser* von Test XII haupt-

---

1 In: "Kristustydning og kirketanke i Mattæusevangeliet" [Christusdeutung und Kirchengedanke im M.], *Teologi og kirke* [Theologie und Kirche]. FS P. Nepper–Christensen (Hgg. J. Nissen – H. Simonsen; København: Unitas, 1986), 25–42. Ferner D. Dormeyer: "Mt 1,1 als Überschrift zur Gattung und Christologie des Matthäusevangeliums", *The Four Gospels 1992*. FS F. Neirynck (Hgg. F. Van Segbroeck et al.; Leuven: University Press, 1992) II, 1361–83.

2 S. auch die relevante Unterscheidung zwischen "the vertical approach" und "the horisontal approach" bei P. F. Ellis, *Matthew: his mind and his message* (Collegeville, MN: Liturgical Press, 1974), v–vi; 8–16.

sächlich für den paränetisch anwendbaren jüdischen Stoff interessierte, und zu M. Philonenko, demzufolge nahezu alle universalistischen Elemente in Test XII als Interpolationen aus Qumran zu betrachten sind, schließt Jervell sich der entgegengesetzten Auffassung bei F. Schnapp und S. Aalen an, wonach die universellen Züge in Test XII primär auf die christliche *Bearbeitung* zurückzuführen sind[3]. Das, was bei Jacob Jervell weiterführt, ist demzufolge eine umfassende Argumentation dafür, daß Test XII durch ihre heilsgeschichtliche (im Zusammenhang mit der christologischen) Bearbeitung der prophetischen Elemente in der jüdischen Vorlage eine Sonderstellung in der Auffassung der soteriologischen Beziehungen zwischen Juden und Heiden einnehmen.

Das hat wesentliche Bedeutung für die Beurteilung dieser ersten, nach Jacob Jervell judenchristlichen Bearbeitung von Test XII in zweierlei Hinsicht. Zum einen läßt sich die Bearbeitung chronologisch so früh wie auf das Ende des 1. nachchristlichen Jahrh.s datieren[4]. Zum andern kann man sie betrachten als eine neu-interpretierende Übertragung der biblischen Traditionen von Israels wiederholtem, Strafe herabrufenden Abfall vom Gesetz (mit anschließender Umkehr gefolgt von Gottes erlösendem Eingreifen) auf Israels aktuell vorliegende Ablehnung der christlichen Verkündigung Jesu als des messianischen Erneuerers und Wiedererrichters des Gesetzes. Die judenchristliche Bearbeitung von Test XII erhält so den Charakter einer Bußverkündigung gegenüber dem gleichzeitigen Israel über das Bekenntnis zu Jesus als dem Erlöser sowohl der Juden als auch der Heiden – wobei das Interesse ganz und gar auf die eschatologische Zukunft Israels konzentriert ist (TestSeb 9,5–9; TestDan 5–6).

Nach meinem Urteil enthält die christliche Bearbeitung von Test XII somit zentrale Elemente, die – mit oder ohne Akzept des Jubilars – von

---

3   J. Jervell, "Ein Interpolator interpretiert. Zu der christlichen Bearbeitung der Testamente der zwölf Patriarchen", in C. Burchard – J. Jervell – J. Thomas, *Studien zu den Testamenten der Zwölf Patriarchen* (BZNW 36, Hg. W. Eltester; Berlin: A. Töpelmann, 1969), 30–61.

4   Obwohl de Jonge an seiner Ablehnung der Interpolationshypothese festhält und die christliche Bearbeitung von Test XII auf die 2. Hälfte des 2. Jahrh.s datiert, erkennt er die Bedeutung von Jervells Abhandlung an: "... because it shows that the future destiny of Israel can remain the concern of an author or authors who have accepted Jesus Christ as saviour of the world" ("The Main Issues in the Study of the Testaments of the Twelve Patriarchs", *Jewish Eschatology, Early Christian Christology, and the Testaments of the Twelve Patriarchs* [NT.S 63; Leiden: Brill, 1991], 163).

wesentlicher Bedeutung für die Interpretation des Matth. und nicht zuletzt von Kap. 23 sein können[5].

II. Kap. 23 als Teil einer kompositorischen Einheit

Kap. 23 ist Teil einer größeren kompositorischen Einheit, die sich als eine weitere Bearbeitung der Überlieferung in Mk 11–13 darstellt. Durch seinen bedeutenden Umfang läßt die Bearbeitung des Evangelisten die Kapitel 21–25 als eine *jerusalemische* Komposition erscheinen, die überlieferungsgeschichtlich und theologisch mit der ebenfalls langen, *galiläischen* Komposition in Kap. 5–7 auf einer Ebene steht. G. Lohfink möchte annehmen, daß Kap. 23–25 mit der kurzen Adressatenangabe (V. 1) im Verhältnis zu den übrigen Redekompositionen des Evangelisten eine Ausnahme darstelle[6]. Tatsache ist indessen, daß der gesamte vorangehende Komplex von Traditionen über Jesu Aufenthalt in Jerusalems Tempel (strukturell gleich wie 4,23–5,2) als Hintergrund dient für Jesu "Tempelrede" Kap. 23–25 mit ihrem unmittelbar bevorstehenden Auftakt in der resümierenden Feststellung, daß das Gespräch mit den offiziellen Vertretern der jüdischen Gruppierungen vorbei sei (22,46). Hierauf folgt Kap. 23 als eine prophetische Strafpredigt, die primär an die jüdischen Scharen gerichtet ist, in einer Erklärung der markinischen Feststellung, daß "viel Volks ihn gern hörte" (Mk 12,37b). Während die Bergpredigt in Kap. 5–7 differenzierend an dieselben beiden Gruppen gerichtet ist, die Jünger bzw. die Scharen, ist die Tempelrede in Kap. 23 zu den Scharen und zu den Jüngern (in dieser Reihenfolge) gesprochen, wobei sich Kap. 24–25 ausschließlich an die Jünger wenden. Außerdem gilt das Eigentümliche für Kap. 23, daß es, während es sich direkt an die Scharen und an die Jünger wendet, zugleich den direkten Ausfall gegen die

---

5   Als Beispiel einer christlichen Bearbeitung pseudepigraphischen Stoffes, die eindeutig von der Ablösung des verworfenen Volkes Israel durch ein "kommendes Volk" spricht, nennt Jacob Jervell die Schrift V Esra (1,35. 37–38), die er mit dem Barnabasbrief gleichstellt (Anm. 20; 95). Dagegen will G. N. Stanton hier (sowie in Apoc. Pet.) nicht nur Bruch, sondern auch Zusammenhang entdecken ("5 Ezra and Matthean Christianity in the Second Century", *JThS* 28 (1977), 67–83).

6   G. Lohfink, "Wem gilt die Bergpredigt?" *ThQ* 163 (1983), 269. Von positiver Relevanz für das Verständnis von Kap. 23 ist der Nachweis, daß die Einleitung zu Kap. 5–7 (sowie Kap. 8–9) die Verse 4,23–5,2 umfaßt (mit der schriftgemäßen Voraussetzung im Jesaia-Zitat in 4,12–17), mit der Konsequenz, daß "die Scharen" als Adressaten hier "Israel" meinen (ὁ λαός; "Gesamt-Israel") (267–281).

Schriftgelehrten und Pharisäer, die als eine zusammengehörige Gruppierung gesehen sind, enthält[7].

Von diesem Befund aus glaube ich, der traditionsgeschichtlich und theologisch interessanten Tatsache gegenüberzustehen, daß Kap. 23 in seiner Kombination mit Kap. 24–25 dieselben Elemente enthält wie diejenigen, die – wie gesagt – die christliche Bearbeitung von TestXII kennzeichnen sollen. Eine solche Parallelisierung setzt natürlich voraus, daß die Frage nach dem eschatologischen Heil des jüdischen Volkes für den Evangelisten überhaupt ein positives Anliegen ist. Genau dies werden viele Forscher bestreiten wollen. Es stellt sich also die Aufgabe, eine angemessene Argumentation für folgende These vorzulegen: Die Tatsache, daß Matthäus in Kap. 23 die kurzen polemischen Anweisungen von Mk 12,37b–40 und 12,41–44 zu einer umfassenden und prinzipiellen Belehrung von sowohl Scharen als auch Jüngern entwickelt hat, ist als ein theologisch notwendiger Ausdruck dafür anzusehen, daß die Hoffnung auf Israels eschatologisches Heil als ein christologisch integrierter Bestandteil der christlichen Hoffnung auch im Matthäusevangelium ihren Platz hat[8].

III. Die einzelnen Abschnitte innerhalb von Kap. 23

a) V. 1–12

Innerhalb des ersten Hauptabschnittes des Kapitels (V. 1–12) stellen V. 2–3 eine *crux interpretum* dar, die man gewöhnlich auf traditionsgeschichtlichem Wege zu lösen versucht[9]. Man wird aber zu beachten haben, daß diese Verse[10] und damit das gesamte Kapitel kontextuell gesehen eine Weiterführung der Diskussion über die rechte Schriftauslegung darstel-

---

7   Hierzu bes. H.-J. Becker, *Auf der Kathedra des Mose* (ANTZ 4; Berlin: Institut Kirche und Judentum, 1990), 17–23; 219–220 ("... als Bezeichnung der Chakhamim zu verstehen ..."; vgl. σοφοί Mt 23,34).

8   Oder stehen wir mit einer religionsgeschichtlichen Betrachtung bloß vor dem polemisch destruktiven "zweier einander entgegengesetzter Gesichter" bei Matthäus – nämlich dem ersten, dem feindliebenden in der Bergpredigt? (A. J. Saldarini, "Delegitimation of Leaders in Matthew 23", *CBQ* 54 [1992], 659–680).

9   Oft wird V. 3 als übernommene judenchristliche Tradition beurteilt. Eine ausführliche überlieferungsgeschichtliche Analyse des ganzen Kapitels u.a. bei H. Schürmann, "Die Redekomposition wider 'dieses Geschlecht' und seine Führung in der Redenquelle (vgl. Mt. 23,1–39 par Lk. 11,37–54)", *Studien zum Neuen Testament und seiner Umwelt* 11 (Hg. A. Fuchs; Linz 1986), 33–81 (Lit.); ferner D. Kosch, [s. unten Anm. 17].

10 St. Mason argumentiert dafür, die Aussage auf Jesus selbst zurückzuführen ("Pharisaic Dominance before 70 CE and the Gospels' Hypocrisy Charge (Matt 23:2–3)", *HTR* 83 [1990], 361–381).

len, die damit eingeleitet wird, daß ein pharisäischer Schriftgelehrter[11] Jesus vor die Frage stellt, welches Gebot er als das "große" und damit als im Gesetz als Ganzem hermeneutisch richtungsweisend ansehe. Diese Frage beantwortet Jesus, indem er Dtn 6,5 und Lev 19,18 als *gleichgestellte Gebote in der angegebenen Reihenfolge* zitiert. Das geschieht speziell im Matth. mit der nachfolgenden Präzisierung, daß "das ganze Gesetz und die Propheten" auf diesen beiden Geboten beruhen (22,34–40). Die Antwort ist also in einem absoluten Sprachgebrauch formuliert, was als ein indirekter Hinweis darauf zu verstehen ist, daß quantitative Angaben keine Frage des äußeren Umfangs, sondern zusammenfassender Interpretation sind. Ebenso wie es innerhalb von Mt 5,17–48 der Fall ist, wo die Gerechtigkeit des Reiches Gottes, die als die Erfüllung von "Gesetz und Propheten" diejenige der Schriftgelehrten und Pharisäer übertrifft (V. 20), abschließend in dem doppelten Liebesgebot zusammengefaßt wird (V. 43–48)[12].

Das impliziert notwendigerweise die Frage nach dem autoritativen Interpreten, und eben darauf gibt die dann folgende Diskussion über den Messias als "Sohn Davids" oder als "Kyrios" Antwort (22,41–45). Die christologische Diskussion enthält also ein schrifttheologisches Anliegen. Aufgrund der zitierten Stelle Ps 110,1 befinden wir uns damit *situationell in einem urkirchlichen Zusammenhang*, wo der Jesus, der als Folge seiner Schriftauslegung den Tod erlitt, als der erhöhte Christus sich jetzt als der hermeneutische Herr der Schrift erweist, so wie dies in dem zuvor genannten doppelten Liebesgebot als dem Deutungsschlüssel sowohl für die biblische Überlieferung als auch für die Jesusüberlieferung in ihrer Ganzheit beschlossen liegt[13].

Man hat die auf den ersten Blick auffälligen Aussagen in V. 2–3 primär als ein allgemeines Bekenntnis zur gemeinsamen biblischen Tradition anzusehen, abgelegt als Einleitung zu einem urkirchlichen Plädoyer

---

11 νομικός, das nur hier im Matth. auftritt, ist jedoch textkritisch unsicher (B. M. Metzger, *A Textual Commentary on the Greek New Testament* [London–New York: United Bible Societies, 1971], 59).

12 U.a. H.–W. Kuhn, "Das Liebesgebot Jesu als Tora und als Evangelium", *Vom Urchristentum zu Jesus. FS J. Gnilka* (Hgg. H. Frankemölle – K. Kertelge; Freiburg: Herder, 1989), bes. 204–220; D. Marguerat, "Jésus et la Loi dans la mémoire des premiers chrétiens", *La mémoire et le temps. FS P. Bonnard* (Hgg. D. Marguerat – J. Zumstein; Paris: Labor et Fides 1991), bes. 67–74.

13 Mein Verständnis der fundamentalen Rolle, die das doppelte Liebesgebot im Neuen Testament spielt, habe ich dargelegt in: "Det paulinske menneskesyn" [Die paulinische Menschenauffassung], *Menneskesynet* (Hg. S. Pedersen: København: Gad, 1989), 71–98.

für ihre speziell mit Christus gegebene Interpretation (V. 10–12). Unmittelbar vorher hat Jesus in 22,34–40 unwidersprochen die "prüfende" Frage nach der Interpretation dieser gemeinsamen biblischen Tradition beantwortet, worauf der Wortwechsel zwischen Jesus und den Pharisäern in 22,41–45 anklingen läßt, daß die eigentliche Kontroverse in ihrer theologisch–anthropologischen Deutung liegt. Diese schrifttheologische Spannung liegt in der Aufforderung, daß die Jünger einerseits "alles tun und halten sollen", was die pharisäischen Schriftgelehrten als Träger der biblischen Tradition zu ihnen sagen, und daß sie andererseits "nicht nach ihren Werken tun sollen".

Es gilt bekanntlich für die jüdische wie für die christliche Position (7,1–23), daß es eben die theologisch–anthropologischen Konsequenzen ("Früchte") sind, welche die Wahrheit über die divergierenden Interpretationen der vorliegenden Traditionen enthüllen. Die anklagende Formulierung, "sie reden wohl, doch tun sie's nicht", deutet also nicht an, daß nicht gehandelt würde[14], sondern daß im Widerspruch zu den konkreten Konsequenzen gehandelt wird, die Matthäus seinerseits glaubt, aus seiner Schriftauslegung ziehen zu müssen[15]. Dementsprechend umfaßt der Ausdruck "Gesetzlosigkeit" (ἡ ἀνομία; 7,23; 23,28) keine Anklage der Anarchie, sondern im Gegenteil eine vielleicht sogar minutiöse Einhaltung des Gesetzes, die der Evangelist als eine in Wirklichkeit existentielle Absage an das Gesetz betrachtet[16].

Die entscheidende und weiterführende Frage ist danach, was mit "schweren Bürden" (φορτία βαρέα) gemeint ist, die die pharisäischen Schriftgelehrten "binden und auf die Schultern der Menschen legen", während sie selbst – polemisch karikiert – mit den liturgisch nach außen gewandten und sozial ehrenvollen Seiten der Gottesverehrung beschäf-

---

14 Obwohl diese Problemstellung, "daß gelehrt, aber nicht gehandelt wird," auch als interne jüdische Kritik bekannt ist, yBer 3b (Ch. Horowitz, *Der Jerusalemer Talmud in deutscher Übersetzung*, I [Tübingen: Mohr, 1975], 23–24). Ferner H.–J. Becker, *Auf der Kathedra des Mose*, 85–120.

15 Relevant ist hier L. Gastons Hinweis auf entsprechende Anklagen von jüdischer Seite gegen die Christen, zwar an der Schrift festzuhalten, nicht aber nach ihrem Gebot zu leben ("Retrospect", *Anti–Judaism in Early Christianity* [Hg. St. G. Wilson; Waterloo: W. Laurier University Press, 1986], 167).

16 Beachte die Definition von "Gesetzlosigkeit" bei W. Trilling: "Gemeint ist keine prinzipielle oder theoretische Leugnung des Gesetzes, sondern eine praktische Mißachtung, die zur durchgängigen Einstellung geworden ist" (*Der zweite Brief an die Thessalonicher* [EKK; Neukirchen–Vlyun: Neukirchener Verlag, 1980], 83). Ferner J. E. Davidson, "*Anomia* and the Question of an Antinomian Polemic", *JBL* 104 (1985), 617–635.

tigt sind? Die eigene Antwort des Evangelisten darauf ist in V. 23 gegeben, wo "die schwereren Dinge des Gesetzes" (τὰ βαρύτερα τοῦ νόμου) als "das Gericht" (ἡ κρίσις), "die Barmherzigkeit" (τὸ ἔλεος) und "der Glaube" (ἡ πίστις) bestimmt werden. Und als eine selbständig geformte Version der zugehörigen Formulierung in Lk 11,42 (... τὴν κρίσιν καὶ τὴν ἀγάπην τοῦ θεοῦ)[17] leitet diese Antwort über zu einer anderen umstrittene Matthäus–Kontexte betreffenden Schriftauslegung, zum Verhältnis von Kult und Ethik sowie zum eschatologischen Schicksal von Juden und Heiden. "Schwerer" ist eine hermeneutische, keine psychologische Bestimmung!

In Kap. 12 endet so der erste Sabbatstreit mit den Pharisäern (als Sondergut) damit, daß Jesus "Barmherzigkeit" (τὸ ἔλεος) über Tempel und Sabbatvorschriften stellt – und zwar, indem er direkt Hos 6,6 zitiert: "Barmherzigkeit will ich und nicht Opfer" (12,1–8). Es ist ein kultkritisches Prophetenwort (I Sam 15,22), das zuvor in 9,13 als Begründung dafür dient, daß Jesus bei seinem Umgang mit Zöllnern und Sündern von den Reinheitsvorschriften absieht[18]. Der zweite Sabbatstreit endet damit, daß die Pharisäer darüber beraten, wie Jesus entfernt werden könne (12,9–14). Das lange Zitat aus Jes 42,1–4 prophezeit demgegenüber (als Sondergut) u.a., daß der auserwählte Diener als Messias "den Völkern (τοῖς ἔθνεσιν) das Gericht (κρίσις)" verkünden und "das Gericht zum Sieg (... εἰς νῖκος τὴν κρίσιν)" führen werde und "daß Völker (ἔθνη) auf seinen Namen hoffen werden" (12,18–21)[19]. Was das dritte Element der "schwereren Teile des Gesetzes" angeht, so betrachtet Matthäus auf urkirchliche Weise (Act 11,17; 15,9) eben den Glauben (ἡ πίστις) als die existentielle Gegenantwort, die auch den Heiden Anteil an dem biblisch verheißenen Heil gibt, – mit einer Spitze gegen das abweisende Israel (8,10–13 par.; vgl. 21,28–32). Dieses ganze Spektrum zusammengehören-

---

17 D. Kosch bezieht die Lukas–Version auf das doppelte Liebesgebot (*Die eschatologische Tora des Menschensohnes* [NTOA 12; Freiburg (Schweiz)–Göttingen: Universitätsverlag/Vandenhoeck & Ruprecht, 1989], 115).

18 K. R. Snodgrass spricht von einer "prophetischen" Schriftauslegung mit einem Paradigmenwechsel, indem das Hauptgewicht von Reinheit auf Liebe, Barmherzigkeit und Gerechtigkeit verschoben wird ("Matthew's Understanding of the Law", *Interp* 46 (1992), 368–378). Zu R. Johanan b. Zakkai's Deutung von Hos 6,6 in Bezug auf die Zerstörung des Tempels s. J. Neusner, *First Century Judaism in Crisis* (New York: KTAV, 1982), 165–172.

19 U. Luz: "Durch dieses, den Kontext sprengende, überlange Erfüllungszitat öffnet Matthäus seinen Lesern die Augen für das Ganze der Geschichte Jesu ..." (*Das Evangelium nach Matthäus* [EKK, 2. Aufl.; Neukirchen–Vluyn: Neukirchener Verlag, 1989], 250).

der Elemente wird dann in Mt 15,1–28 wieder aufgerollt mit der Heuchelei–Anklage in seiner schrifttheologischen Untermauerung als dem polemischen Signal.

Es sind diese "schwereren Dinge" – das Gericht, die Barmherzigkeit, der Glaube –, von denen das Gesetz nach der Auffassung des Matthäus grundlegend handelt und die die Schriftgelehrten und Pharisäer als Verwalter der mosaischen Tradition damit den Menschen auferlegen, während sie selbst aufgrund ihrer eigenen Interpretation dieser Tradition das Hauptgewicht auf andere Dinge legen, die sozial gesehen mit größerem Prestige verbunden sind. Diese vielleicht unerwartete Deutung von anscheinend widersprüchlichen Aussagen wird noch dadurch unterstützt, daß sich die "schwereren Dinge" des Gesetzes in V. 23 als eine für Matthäus eigentümliche Ausgabe der urchristlichen Triade: Glaube, Liebe und Hoffnung auffassen lassen, die allgemein in der Urkirche als Wiedergabe des zweiten Teils des doppelten Liebesgebotes diente (I Kor 13; vgl. Mt 19,19)[20]. Die etwas abweichende Wortwahl: ἔλεος für ἀγάπη (wie Lk 11,42)[21] und κρίσις für ἐλπίς kann aus dem Einfluß der Zitate Hos 6,6 und Jes 42,1–4 erklärt werden.

Wenn wir so die "schweren" Aussagen des Gesetzes auf das doppelte Liebesgebot beziehen, sind wir zugleich auf der Spur einer kontextuellen Erklärung des Inhalts von V. 8–10, der als Alternative zu V. 3–7 geformt ist. Diese Verse sind möglicherweise als ein Midrash über Jes 54,13 und Jer 31,33–34 zu betrachten[22]. Das darf allerdings nicht den Blick dafür verstellen, daß sie namentlich als eine Zusammenfassung dessen angesehen werden können, worauf wir schon bei Matthäus in 5,43–48 und 12,15–21 gestoßen sind und wozu sich 20,20–28 fügen läßt. Vor allem ist bemerkenswert, daß das erste Glied des jüdischen Glaubensbekenntnisses: das Bekenntnis zu Gottes Einheit, das Matthäus in Kap. 22,34–40 nicht hat (im Unterschied zu Mk 12,29), hier auftaucht.

Die trotz ihres polemischen Anlasses einzigartige Charakteristik Got-

---

20 Hierzu: "Agape – der eschatologische Hauptbegriff bei Paulus", *Die Paulinische Literatur und Theologie* (Hg. S. Pedersen; Århus–Göttingen: Aros/Vandenhoeck & Ruprecht, 1980), 159–186; sowie S. Pedersen, *Om at være menneske* (København: Anis, 1992), 98–103.

21 Ἀγάπη kommt im Mt nur in 24,12 vor; hier dafür aber in einem Zusammenspiel mit "Gesetzlosigkeit" (ἀνομία), die den Gedanken der "Nächstenliebe", des zweiten Gliedes in dem doppelten Liebesgebot, als der manifestierten Verpflichtung des Gesetzes voraussetzt. Ferner D. Hill, "On the Use and Meaning of Hosea vi. 6 in Matthew's Gospel", *NTS* 24 (1978), 107–119.

22 U.a. J. D. M. Derrett, "Mt 23:8–10 a Midrash on Is. 54:13 and Jer. 31:33–34", *Studies in the New Testament* III (Leiden: Brill, 1982), 215–229.

tes als "des einen Lehrers" (εἷς ... διδάσκαλος) in V. 8, woraus die folgende Charakteristik "aller" als "Brüder" entspringt, läßt sprachlich und theologisch Matth. 5,43–48 sowie 1. Thess. 4,9–10 assoziieren – Kontexte, die gleichermaßen nach dem doppelten Liebesgebot strukturiert sind. Die "vollkommene Liebe", über die die unterschiedlose Güte des himmlischen Vaters belehrt, schließt ein, daß unter den Kindern dieses Vaters Brüder implizit "alle" Brüder umfassen. Zugleich wird uns verdeutlicht – adversativ kulminierend, daß Christus als der Herr (κύριος) der christlichen Schriftauslegung der Lehrer (ὁ καθηγητής) ist, dessen Tod als des apokalyptischen Menschensohnes eine Identifikation des Herr und Richter Seins mit dem Dienen für die Befreiung der "Vielen" bedeutete (Mt 20,24–28).

b) V. 13–33
Um die religiöse Anklage "Heuchler", die mit der tragischen Geschichte so vieler Jahrhunderte zwischen Juden und Christen verbunden ist, zu entdramatisieren, mag es angebracht sein, hier einleitungsweise auf Gal 2,11–16 zu verweisen. Nicht zuletzt ist es wesentlich, daß uns hier in V. 16 demonstriert wird, daß eine solche Anklage Einigkeit in der gemeinsamen basalen Tradition voraussetzt (vgl. Mt 23,2–3).

Ebenso wie für die paulinischen Briefe gilt auch für das Matthäusevangelium, daß externe Polemik und interne Polemik neben einander stehen. So gesehen schließt Kap. 7 im Verhältnis zu Kap. 5–6 ab und bildet zugleich eine christliche Parallele zu der jüdischen Auseinandersetzung in Kap. 23. Dementsprechend wird die Bezeichnung "Heuchler" für den jüdischen Gegner in 6,2. 5. 16 nun in 7,5 auf den christlichen übertragen, der im Widerspruch zu seinem eigenen Bewußtsein darüber, daß der Balken in seinem eigenen Auge sitzt, seinem Bruder anbietet, ihm mit dem Splitter in dessen Auge zu helfen (7,3–5). Später folgt dann eine Warnung vor den "falschen Propheten", die an "ihren Früchten" zu erkennen sind (7,15–20), – wie das nach 23,3 ganz genauso für die Schriftgelehrten und Pharisäer gilt. Und wie diese heuchlerischen Christen in Kap. 7 als "Wölfe in Schafspelzen" (V. 15) charakterisiert werden, so wird die Heuchelei in Kap. 23 mit dem Bilde der "weiß gekalkten Gräber, die von Totengebeinen und allem möglichen Unrat starren" beschrieben[23]. Zugleich wird deutlich gemacht, daß sich die Heuchelei primär auf die schismatische Spannung bezieht, was "Gerechtigkeit" beinhaltet.

---

23 S. auch die Definition der "Heuchelei" in Act 23,3.

Die allgemeine Anklage der Heuchelei, die die spezielle Kennzeichnung der jüdischen Führer (die Weherufe (5) finden sich auch in Lk 11,37–52) durch den Evangelisten ist, ist hier vor allem eine schrifttheologische Bestimmung[24]. Der Gebrauch der Bezeichnung Heuchler besonders in Bezug auf das Gesetz (23,23) ist innerhalb der LXX–Überlieferung bekannt seit Hiob 34,30[25]. Ferner ist das heuchlerische Auftreten gegenüber dem Gesetz in Sir 1,25–30; 32,14–24; 33,1–3 beschrieben. Und in dem Bericht, wie der Schriftgelehrte Eleazar unter der Verfolgung durch Antiochus IV. wohlgemeinte Ratschläge, öffentlich den Anschein zu erwecken, er esse Schweinefleisch, ablehnte, werden die beiden zusammengehörigen Aspekte direkt angeführt: daß nämlich Heuchelei Andere zum Abfall vom Gesetz bewegen und daß die religiöse Gesetzlosigkeit vor dem Allmächtigen nicht verborgen bleiben könne (II Makk 6,21–26; vgl. IV Makk 6,15–19). In den Psalmen Salomos kommt die Verbindung der Heuchelei mit der Einhaltung des Gesetzes darin zum Ausdruck, daß der "den Menschen Behagende" durch den Heuchler definiert wird, der trügerisch über das Gesetz spricht (4,6–8).

In der Damaskusschrift werden die Pharisäer der Zeit unter Bezugnahme auf Ez 13,10 mit den falschen Propheten identifiziert, die sich damit begnügen, die unfertige Mauer mit Tünche zu verputzen (CD 4,19; 8,12; 19,24–33), d.h. sie werden angeklagt, "nach glatten Dingen zu suchen" und nach Löchern im Gesetz zu fahnden, so daß der Gesetzlose für Gerecht erklärt wird, während der Gerechte für Gesetzlos erklärt und ihm nach dem Leben getrachtet wird (CD 1,13–21)[26]. Im Kommentar zum Buche Nahum sind "diejenigen, die nach glatten Dingen suchen" wahrscheinlich mit den Pharisäern gleichzusetzen, die Demetrios III. gegen Alexander Jannaios zu Hilfe riefen (4QpNah 1,2. 7)[27]. Der Weheruf über Ninive in Nah 3,1 wird auf die Stadt Ephraims (= Jerusalem) bezogen, d.h. auf die, "die nach glatten Dingen suchen am Ende der Tage". Deren Schriftauslegung wird als charakteristisch für "die, die in Lug und Trügereien wandeln" bezeichnet. Und Nah 3,4 wird folgendermaßen kommentiert: "… bezieht sich auf die, die Ephraim verführen, die durch trügerische Lehre und ihre lügnerische Zunge und falsche Lippe viele verführen … Städte und Stämme werden zugrunde gehen

---

24 In seinem griechischen Ursprung hatte ὁ ὑποκριτής positiv einen hermeneutischen Grundton, in LXX wird der Begriff überwiegend negativ verwandt synonym mit gottlos, gesetzlos (U. Wilckens, *ThWNT* 8 [1969], 558–563). Ferner D. E. Garland, *The Intention of Matthew 23* (NT.S 52; Leiden: Brill, 1979), 96–117.

25 Sj. van Tilborg, *The Jewish Leaders in Matthew* (Leiden: Brill, 1972), 17–26.

26 Hierzu A. I. Baumgarten, "The Names of the Pharisees", *JBL* 102 (1983), bes. 420–428 (Lit.). Andre Gegner sowie Anhänger verbanden übrigens die pharisäische Gruppe mit Genauigkeit (ἀκρίβεια) in der Einhaltung der Gesetze (Jos. Bell 1,108. 110; Ant 17,41–45; vgl. 20,200–201; Act 22,3; 26,5). Aufgrund bes. von Bell 2,162 und Vita 191 schließt Baumgarten auf die Vorstellung von "Pharisäern" als einer Selbstbezeichnung: "die Genauen" (413–417).

27 Vgl. Jos. Bell 1,92–97; Ant 13,376–383.

durch ihren Rat" (4QpNah 2,1–10; vgl. 3,1–8; 4,1–6). Man beachte auch den Weheruf in I Hen 99,2 und das Vokabular in PsSal 12,1–4.

Ein synonymer Ausdruck für die Anklage wegen Gesetzlosigkeit, wie sie die Gemeinschaft von Qumran formuliert hat, ist nun aber gerade, daß sich der Gegenpart der Heuchelei schuldig macht (1QH 4,13; 7,34; vgl. Ps 26,4–5)[28]. Und die einleitende Anklage wegen Heuchelei in Mt 23,13 hat ihr Gegenstück in 1QH 4,11: "... sie verschlossen den Trank der Erkenntnis vor den Dürstenden, und gegen ihren Durst gaben sie ihnen Essig zu trinken". Ebenso wird man sich zu merken haben, daß die abweichenden Auslegungen der gemeinsamen mosaischen Tradition auch hier in ihren eschatologischen Konsequenzen alternativ sind[29]. So wird in der Damaskusschrift behauptet, daß Gott als Antwort auf den Treubruch Israels sein Angesicht vor dem Volk und dessen Heiligtum verborgen habe (CD 1,3–4; vgl. Jer 23,39; Mt 23,38).

Im Mekilta–Kommentar zu Ex 19,8 heißt es, das einstimmige Ja der Israeliten zum Sinaipakt sei nicht durch Heuchelei gekennzeichnet gewesen[30]. Was die rabbinische Überlieferung im übrigen betrifft, so verwies schon G. Dalman darauf, daß das hebräische Wort für "gottlos" (*ḥanef*), das LXX für Hiob 34,30 und 36,13 mit "Heuchler" (ὑποκριτής) wiedergibt, gewöhnlicher Sprachgebrauch war für Juden, die als heimliche Gesetzesübertreter auftraten (tYom 5,12; bYom 86b). Nicht weniger relevant ist der Hinweis G. Dalmans, daß die Bezeichnung "farbig" zur Charakterisierung eines Heuchlers verwandt wird (bSot 22b), da wir ja sowohl in den Qumrantexten als auch in Mt 23 den Ausdruck "mit Tünche verputzen" als Metapher für einen Heuchler angetroffen haben[31].

Die Heuchelei–Anklage mußte natürlich auch den jüdischen Proselyten treffen[32].

---

28 Cl. Thoma behauptet, daß seit der Mitte des 2. Jh. v. Chr. Heuchler "ein stereotyper polemischer Ausdruck aus dem Vokabular der Apokalyptiker" gewesen sei ("Der Pharisäismus", *Literatur und Religion des Frühchristentums* (Hgg. J. Maier – J. Schreiner; Würzburg: Echter, 1973), 262). Wie auch E. Kosmala meinte, der Kampf gegen das heuchlerische Verhalten lasse sich vom Exil (z.B. Ez 33,31) bis zu den Essenern verfolgen ("Gottvertrauen und Zukunftshoffnung", *Hebräer–Essener–Christen* [St PB 1; Leiden: Brill, 1969], 306).

29 Außer mSan 10,1 auch die Aussage von Av 3,15 (3,11) verbunden mit dem gleichzeitigen R. Eleazar von Modiim, das sich nach Travers Herford einer pharisäischen Ketzer–Definition nähert: "He who ... gives interpretations of Torah which are not according to Halachah, even though he possesses Torah and good deeds he has no portion in the world to come" (*The Ethics of the Talmud: Sayings of the Fathers* [New York, 3. Ed.: Schocken, 1966], 80–82). E. E. Urbach sieht die Aussage als gegen Paulus in Röm 2,28–29 gerichtet (*The Sages* [Jerusalem: Magnes, 1975], 295–296).

30 J. Z. Lauterbach, *Mekilta de–Rabbi Ishmael* (Philadelphia, PA: Jew. Publ. Soc., 1962), 207.

31 G. Dalman, *Die Worte Jesu* (Leipzig: Hinrichs'sche Buchh.; 2. Aufl., 1930), 284.

32 Vgl. *Pesikta Rabbati* (übersetzt von W. G. Braude; New Haven, CT–London: Yale University Press, 1969), 459–460 (Piska 22).

Von Epiktet kennen wir die antike Redeweise "er ist kein Jude, aber er heuchelt, es zu sein"[33]. Im christlichen Kontext kann Irenäus anti–markionitisch versichern, daß die Apostel mit der Rede vom Gott des Herrn Jesu Christi als dem Vater und Schöpfer nicht sophistisch heuchelten (Adv. haer. 3,5,1–2).

Angesichts des vorgelegten Materials kann es nicht verwundern, daß das angefochtene Gesetzesverständnis in dem abschließenden siebten Weheruf in heilsgeschichtliche Perspektive gesetzt wird. Die aktuell angegriffene Heuchelei besteht nach der Auffassung des Evangelisten darin, daß die Schriftgelehrten und Pharisäer auf der einen Seite – anscheinend im Unterschied zu den Generationen vor ihnen – dem in der Verkündigung der Propheten enthaltenen Gesetzesverständnis durch Respekt vor dem Nachruhm der Propheten ihren Tribut zollen und zugleich auf der anderen Seite nichtsdestoweniger das mit Jesus gegebene, just von denselben Propheten bezeugte Gesetzesverständnis ablehnen. Ihr existentielles Söhne–Väter–Verhältnis zu denjenigen, die seinerzeit diesen biblischen Propheten ein gewaltsames Nein entgegenhielten, ist also jetztzeitig durch ihre konkreten geschichtlichen Taten bezeugt (V. 31–32). Und das muß unwillkürlich die Frage nach ihrem kommenden eschatologischen Schicksal aufwerfen (V. 33)[34].

c) V. 34–39

Zwei Sachverhalte sind für das Verständnis der dieses Kapitel abschließenden Verse 34–39 und damit des gesamten Kap. 23 von Wichtigkeit. Erstens ist die gewaltsame Ablehnung, auf die auch die christliche Verkündigung der Jünger gestoßen ist (10,16–42), in eine schöpfungstheologische Perspektive gebracht, so wie wir das ebenfalls von Röm 4 (Abraham) bis Röm 5,12–19 (Adam) kennen. Die aktuell ablehnende Generation wird somit nicht allein als Söhne derer bestimmt, die die Propheten erschlugen, sondern auch als Glied im Geschlecht bis zurück zu Kain, der als der erste Mörder Abels, des ersten Gerechten, unschuldiges Blut auf Erden vergoß. Es ist also für nichts Geringeres als das fortgesetzte Vergießen unschuldigen Blutes durch eine gesamte Menschheit Rechenschaft abzulegen. In V. 35–36 ist dieser Sachverhalt durch die verbreitete Verantwortungsformel ausgedrückt, die sonst vor allem aus 27,25 – und zwar dort im Verhältnis zum "ganzen Volk" – bekannt ist[35].

Zum zweiten findet diese Verantwortungsformel hier Eingang in eine

---

33 Epiktet, Disc. 2,9,19–21 (LCL I, London–Cambridge, MA 1946).
34 Zu "Otterngezücht" (vgl. 3,7 par.; 12,37) siehe J. D. Kingsbury, "The Developing Conflict between Jesus and the Jewish Leaders in Matthew's Gospel: A Literary–Critical Study", CBQ 49 (1987), bes. 60–64.

Untermauerung der prophetischen Gerichtsverkündigung des Evangelisten. Dadurch werden wir daran erinnert, daß dieses futurisch–eschatologische Gerichtsmotiv offensichtlich weit größere Bedeutung für sein Verständnis der Heilsgeschichte in ihrer Ganzheit hatte als die Zerstörung der Stadt und des Tempels im Jahre 70[36]. Das hat natürlich entscheidende Bedeutung für die Interpretation von V. 37–39.

Während die Verwendung des Zitates aus Ps 118,26: "Gelobt sei, der da kommt im Namen des Herrn!" der Schilderung des Einzugs in Jerusalem in allen vier Evangelien gemeinsam ist, ist seine Wiederholung bei dem Abschied Jesu eine Besonderheit des Matthäusevangeliums. Diese Aussage ist daher als der interpretierende Rahmen für das gesamte Wirken Jesu in Jerusalem anzusehen. Den drei synoptischen Evangelien ist ferner gemeinsam, daß die symbolische Tat Jesu in Jerusalem: die Reinigung des Tempels, auf dem Hintergrund einer Kombination von Jes 56,7 und Jer 7,11 gedeutet ist[37]. Im Mt kann man den Bezug auf Jer 7,11 als Ausdruck für die Verbindung zum Jeremiasbuch betrachten, die in dieser Schrift besonders ausgebaut ist (2,17–18; 16,14; 27,9)[38]. Dies gilt auch von der toposartigen Formulierung über die Verfolgung der Propheten als der Diener des Herrn (21,36; 22,6–7)[39].

Als Sondergut läßt Matthäus die "Scharen", die Jesus mit den Worten aus Ps 118,26 huldigen, auf Anfrage der Stadt den Einziehenden als den Propheten Jesus von Nazareth in Galiläa (21,11; vgl. 21,46) bestimmen. Dem entspricht, daß diese Aussage "kommen im Namen des Herrn" vor allem im Jeremiasbuch präzisiert ist (bes. 11,21–23; 14,14–16; 23,9–40; 29,8–9; 44,16–18). Dieses Kriterium tritt Jer 26,7–19 dadurch als Todeskri-

---

35 Ferner: Sigfred Pedersen, "Antijudaisme og antisemitisme i evangelierne?" [Antijudaismus und Antisemitismus in den Evangelien?], *Judendom och kristendom under de första århundradena* [Judentum und Christentum während der ersten Jahrhunderte], I (Hg. T. Kronholm, Oslo: Universitetsforlaget, 1986), 193–198. Sowie G. M. Smiga, *Pain and Polemic* (New York: Paulist, 1992), bes. 60; 86–90.
36 Dagegen z.B. bei Hippolyt, C.Jud. 7; ferner R. Goldenberg, "Early Rabbinic Explanations of the Destruction of Jerusalem" (FS Y. Yadin; *Jud.* 33 [1982], 517–525).
37 Ich kann unmittelbar keine Erklärung dafür geben, daß Matthäus im Unterschied zu Mk 11,17, aber übereinstimmend mit Lk "für alle Völker" aus Jes 56,7 nicht hat. Ferner R. Gram, "The Temple Conflict Scene: A Rhetorical Analysis of Matthew 21–23", *Persuasive Artistry.* FS G. A. *Kennedy* (Hg. D. F. Watson, JSNT.S 50; Sheffield: Academic Press, 1991), 49 n. 2.
38 D. J. Zucker, "Jesus and Jeremiah in the Matthean Tradition", *JES* 27 (1990), 288–305; bes. M. Knowles, *Jeremiah in Matthew's Gospel* (JSNT.S 68; Sheffield: Academic Press, 1993), Kap. 6 (Lit.).
39 Entwickelt in: Sigfred Pedersen, "Zum Problem der vaticinia ex eventu", *StTh* 19 (1965), 167–188.

terium auf, daß ein Prophet, der unrechtmäßig im Namen des Herrn auftritt, den Tod erleiden soll (Dtn 18,20) und daß diejenigen, die einen Propheten, der rechtmäßig im Namen des Herrn auftritt, hinrichten, Blutschuld auf sich nehmen, indem sie unschuldiges Blut vergießen (beachte auch Jer 2,34; 7,6; 22,3). Dem letzten Teil dieses Gedankenganges stehen wir in Mt 23,35–36; 27,3–5; 27,25 gegenüber; der erste Teil entspricht Mt 26,60–66.

Im Jeremiasbuch erhält dieses Kriterium seine Akzentuierung im Zusammenhang mit Jeremias' Prophetie über Jerusalem und seinen Tempel. Die prophetische Anklage der "Falschheit" ist hier Teil einer Gerichtsverkündigung, die auf die Bekehrung des Volkes abzielt, nicht auf seine definitive Verurteilung. Von einer kontextuellen Analyse aus ist dasselbe der Fall in Mt 23. Man muß sich nämlich vor Augen halten, daß V. 39 nicht von V. 37–38 aus, sondern umgekehrt V. 37–38 von V. 39 aus inhaltsmäßig zu bestimmen ist, so daß die Gerichtsverkündigung *offen* gehalten wird wie eine Verkündigung der Umkehr hinsichtlich des Bekenntnisses zu Jesus als dem, "der da kommt im Namen des Herrn" und damit auch als Israels "Messias und Herr" (22,41–45; vgl. Act 2,34–36)[40].

In diesem Zusammenhang wäre es ein sowohl historisches als auch methodisches Mißverständnis, wenn man den offenen Inhalt von 23,39 als durch die Aussage in 27,24–26 aufgehoben betrachten wollte[41]. Erstens: Sollte das jüdische Volk durch die Tradition in 27,24–26 endgültig verworfen sein, dann müßte dasselbe nach Mt 26,31–58. 69–75 auch von den flüchtenden und verleugnenden Jüngern gelten. Deshalb hatte die folgende Auferstehungsverkündigung denn auch allgemein den Charakter von Gerichts- und Umkehrverkündigung, so wie das noch in den ersten Missionsreden in der Apg. festgehalten ist[42]. Zweitens: das quellenkritisch Basale, daß die Evangelientradition die Auferstehungsverkündigung zur Voraussetzung hat, schließt nicht aus, daß sie sich auf zwei historischen Ebenen innerhalb derselben Überlieferung bewegt,

---

40 G. N. Stanton möchte den schroffen Übergang vom Gericht zur Verheißung durch das namentlich von M. de Jonge auf der Basis von Test XII nachgewiesene S–E–R–Muster nachweisen (Anm. 4), 385–389. Ferner eine positive Schlußfolgerung bei D. Patte, *The Gospel According to Matthew* (Philadelphia, PA: Fortress, 1987), 320.

41 T. L. Donaldson warnt denn auch davor, von einer "Verwerfung Israels" im Mt zu sprechen (*Jesus on the Mountain. A Study in Matthean Theology* [Sheffield: Academic Press, 1985], 205–208).

42 Näheres: Sigfred Pedersen, "Antijudaisme og antisemitisme i evangelierne?" 195–198.

d.h. sowohl vor als auch nach Ostern. Ein Sachverhalt, den der Evangelist selbst nicht verheimlicht (24,15; 27,8; 28,15) und den die Perikope in 22,41–46 vergegenwärtigt.

IV. Kap. 23 als Teil der Ganzheit des Matthäusevangeliums
Die theologische Bedeutung und die kompositorische Reichweite dieser synoptischen Perikope ist indessen weit schwerer zu gewichten, als es bisher der Fall gewesen ist. Sie macht nämlich zusammen mit der Cäsarea–Philippi–Perikope (Mt 16,13–23 parr.) die beiden Texte aus, in denen die Messianität Jesu zur Debatte steht, und zwar in beiden Fällen auf Jesu eigene Initiative hin als Ausdruck ihrer überlieferungsgeschichtlichen und theologischen Parität. Im ersten Text wird das basale Element des Leidens in der jesuanischen Messianität erörtert, gegen das sich die Jünger wenden; im zweiten Text wird das ebenso basale Element der Erhöhung erörtert, gegen das sich die jüdischen Anführer wenden. Beide Elemente machen in ihrer hermeneutisch–existentiellen Integration eben das Einzigartige in der jesuanischen Messianität in deren umkehrenden Charakter einer δοῦλος–κύριος–Messianität aus.

Die überlieferungsgeschichtliche und theologische Parität zwischen den beiden Texten hat ferner eine wesentlich kompositorische Seite. Es ist allgemein anerkannt, daß die synoptische Darstellung von der Cäsarea–Philippi–Erörterung an (einschließlich) ein Grundgepräge von Jesu Leidensweg von Galiläa nach Jerusalem erhält, sichtbar gemacht u.a. durch die summarischen Leidensverkündigungen und den Reisebericht des Lukas. Nicht minder wesentlich ist es, sich klar zu machen, daß die synoptische Schilderung von der Erörterung der Davidsaussage aus Ps 110,1 an (wieder einschließlich) einen Grundzug von apokalyptischer Endzeitvision erhält, wie er nicht zuletzt im Matthäusevangelium breit entfaltet ist. Was hier seinen Ausgangspunkt in 22,41–46 mit der Kyrios–Christologie nimmt, erhält seinen Abschluß mit der Gerichtsszene in 25,31–46. Hieraus lassen sich eine Reihe zentraler Tatbestände ableiten, die hier aus Platzgründen nur angedeutet werden können.

Zum ersten haben wir hiermit eine relevante Erklärung für die nachfolgende Einfügung des apokalyptischen Stoffes innerhalb der synoptischen Überlieferung, da ja Ps 110,1 in der Urkirche nicht nur als eine Auferstehungsaussage, sondern auch als eine der apokalyptischen Hauptaussagen diente (I Kor 15,20–28).

Zum zweiten tragen diese Kapitel kraft ihres apokalyptischen Inhalts in dessen jesuanischer Auslegung dazu bei, den literär–theologischen Charakter der Schrift als einer "dritten" Gattung in der damaligen Zeit zu zeichnen, welche weder einem jüdischen Midrash noch einem hellenistischen Geschichtswerk entspricht, sondern in ihrer Mischung aus beiden Teilen eine jesuanisch–christologisch gedeutete Darstellung dessen ist, wie sich der biblische Schöpfungsglaube entwickelte: von einer exklusiven Zentrierung um die Heilsgeschichte eines bestimmten Volkes hin zu einem Glauben, der implizit das eschatologische Heil aller geschichtlichen Völker umfaßt (Mt 5,13–16; 24,9.14: ... ἐν ὅλῃ τῇ οἰκουμένῃ ...). *Innerhalb dieses übergeordneten christlichen Gattungs–Horizonts sind die einzelnen Abschnitte definitiv zu interpretieren.* So ist es also nichts Geringeres als die jesuanisch–christologische Fundierung der schöpfungstheologischen Sprengung der partikulär ethnisch–orientierten Heilserwartung, welche in der Erörterung des Gesalbten als des Sohnes Davids oder als des Herrn Davids in 22,41–46 auf dem Spiele steht (25,34). Als Ausgangspunkt für Kap. 23–25 trägt diese zentrale Perikope dazu bei, die Wechselwirkung dieser "Abschieds"–Kapitel mit dem Prolog und dem Epilog der Schrift zu bestimmen.

Zum dritten wird in diesen Kapiteln festgestellt, welche "Gerechtigkeit" die "Gerechtigkeit der Schriftgelehrten und Pharisäer" übertrifft, d.h. welche "Gerechtigkeit des Reiches Gottes" im eigentlichsten Sinne Ausdruck des "Willens Gottes" ist. So ist es schon bei der Schilderung der erwarteten apokalyptischen Ereignisse in Kap. 24 auffallend, daß die Bewahrung der Hoffnung an das Festhalten am Glauben an Christus (V. 4–5. 9–11. 23) und an das Festhalten an der gegenseitigen Liebe der Menschen (V. 12) geknüpft ist. Daß dieser Glaube und diese Hoffnung diese Liebe als ihre konkrete gegenwärtige Manifestation haben, ist genau das, was die abschließende Gerichtsszene klar macht in einer endgültigen Enthüllung, wer die "Gerechten" sind (οἱ δίκαιοι, 25,37. 46; vgl. 1,19). Diese Gerichtsszene verrät somit auch, was unter den "schwereren Dingen des Gesetzes" (23,23) zu verstehen sei.

Was war denn das damals kontroversiell Trennende an den Forderungen der Gerichtsszene – analysiert innerhalb der Ganzheit des Matthäusevangeliums? Die traditionelle komparative Analyse der verschiedenen Einzelaussagen vermag ja viele nicht–christliche Parallelen aufzuzeigen. *Das kontroversiell Trennende ist die unbedingte Universalität der Forderungen*[43]. Wir stehen nämlich hier vor einer schöpfungstheologischen Interpretation der apokalyptischen Gerichtsvorstellungen, die sich in

---

43 Ferner U. Wilckens, "Gottes geringste Brüder – zu Mt 25,31–46", *Jesus und Paulus. FS W. G. Kümmel* (Hgg. E. E. Ellis – E. Gräßer; Göttingen: Vandenhoeck & Ruprecht, 1975), 363–383; A. Wouters, "... *wer den Willen meines Vaters tut*" (BU 23; Regensburg: Pustet, 1992), bes. 142–151.

Übereinstimmung mit dem Ganzheitsgepräge der Schrift – signalisiert durch die Entwicklung von Prolog bis Epilog – befindet. Diese schöpfungstheologische Deutung der Gesetzesforderungen ist uns indessen schon im ersten Kapitel der Bergpredigt begegnet. Schon dort wurde uns klar gemacht – nicht nur, was das trennende "Überschießende" (περισσεύειν, περισσόν, 5,20. 47) umfaßt, sondern auch, was es heißt, "vollkommen" (τέλειος, 5,48) zu sein, nämlich das Universelle im Unterschied zum Partikulären im Verhältnis zu anderen Menschen, so wie der himmlische Vater als der Schöpfer im Verhältnis zu seinen Geschöpfen universell ist[44].

Zum vierten wird in der abschließenden Gerichtsszene enthüllt, was das eschatologische Gottesvolk (τὸ ἔθνος/τὰ ἔθνη) qualifiziert (25,32; 28,19). Das tut weder ethnische Herkunft im jüdischen Sinne, noch theologisches Bekenntnis im christlichen Sinne, sondern vielmehr aktuell paränetisch: "alles zu halten, was Jesus befohlen hat" (28,19), d.h. "würdige Früchte der Umkehr" zu tun (3,8; 4,17), "die Früchte darzubringen, die dem Reich Gottes gehören" (21,43!)[45].

Es finden sich also Elemente in den Zukunftserwartungen des Matthäusevangeliums, die es nicht nur mit Test XII, sondern auch mit Paulus im Römerbrief verbinden. Dies gilt auch von der offenbar überraschenden Tatsache, daß jeglicher menschlicher Versuch, dem eschatologischen Gericht vorzugreifen, mit Jesus Christus als Herrn und Weltenrichter sowohl illegitim als auch unmöglich geworden ist (Röm 8,28–39; 11,33–36; 15,7–13). Sein himmlischer Vater, der im Verborgenen sieht, wird im Verborgenen bezahlen (6,4. 6. 18). Es ist nicht nur der Zeitpunkt des Gerichts (24,36. 42–44), den zu kennen dem Menschen nicht gegeben ist; er kennt auch nicht den Ausgang des Gerichts (24,40–41; 25,34–40. 44–45). Der Richter jedoch ist bekannt – und damit auch die Kriterien des Urteils. Dieser übergeordnete Sachverhalt gilt auch für die Interpretation von Kap. 23.

Aus dem Dänischen übersetzt von Dietrich Harbsmeier.

---

44 Hier – wie allgemein im Neuen Testament – ist die Forderung an den Menschen nicht inhaltsbestimmt kultisch im Verhältnis zu Gott, dem Schöpfer, der vielmehr als *das wesensbestimmende Subjekt* der Forderung angesehen wird, sondern anthropologisch im Verhältnis zum Menschen als Mitgeschöpf. Anders J. D. Kingsbury, *Matthew as Story*, (Philadelphia, PA: Fortress, 1986), 19.
45 Ferner Kun–Chun Wong, *Interkulturelle Theologie und multikulturelle Gemeinde im Matthäusevangelium* (NTOA 22; Freiburg [Schweiz]–Göttingen: Universitätsverlag/Vandenhoeck & Ruprecht 1992), 98–108; 144–154.

The Clash Between Christian Styles of Life in the Book of Revelation

Heikki Räisänen

On the Issue of "Majority" and "Minority"

The seer of Revelation implies that he speaks for a world-wide community. Not only does he behold a multitude of 144 000, who have the name of the Lamb and his Father on their foreheads, standing with the Lamb on Mount Zion (14:1-5; obviously the same group as those "sealed" from the twelve tribes of Israel in 7:4-8). He also sees "a great multitude which no man could number, from every nation, from all tribes and peoples and tongues," standing before God's throne and praising him (7:9-10).

Commentators discuss at length how these multitudes relate to each other (are they the same or are they different?) and whether the one beyond numbering refers to all Christians or to martyrs only.[1] But they fail to express surprise at the size of the multitude(s) which is stupendous, given the actual paucity of Christians at that time. How can John conceive of a multitude which cannot even be numbered, from all nations of the earth, one which must amount to millions?[2] Certainly, the mission to the Gentiles had had some remarkable successes by John's

---

1 For a short account of the discussion see H. Ulfgard, *Feast and Future: Revelation 7:9-17 and the Feast of Tabernacles* (ConBNT 22, Uppsala: Almqvist & Wiksell, 1989), 70-79.

2 Those expositors who think that John has Christian *martyrs* in view must presuppose that John reckons with myriads of martyrs during the short period of time left before the parousia. Even in the old view, now increasingly open to doubt (see below), that John lived in the midst of severe persecution, this is odd enough. E. Schüssler Fiorenza, *Revelation: Vision of a Just World* (Edinburgh: T. & T. Clark, 1993), 68, avoids some of these problems in thinking that the great multitude does not consist of Christians only, "but could include all those who have suffered the violence of the great tribulation, war, hunger, pestilence, death, and persecution." This, however, is a strange interpretation of "washing one's clothes in the blood of the Lamb."

time, but while figures are impossible to come by, the actual number of Gentile Christians toward the end of the century can hardly have exceeded a few thousand.[3]

There would be no problem if we could assume that John foresaw some of the future developments; no doubt the total number of Gentile Christians of all times would be hard to count. Yet for John, the time was short; the Lord was coming soon. Was he counting on a last-minute mass conversion, in response, say, to the flying angel's call to repentance (14:6-7)? Such an expectation would be akin to Paul's trust in Rom 11, likewise against all odds, that "all Israel" would still be converted—though to envision the conversion of more or less the whole world would entail a confidence more extreme than even Paul's.

This issue of "imagined majority" (as it might be termed) cannot be further explored here. But when trying to locate the seer in his actual environment, one is bound to ask whether he does in reality speak for a group of any size worth mentioning at all? Does he side with the majority even in those congregations to which he is appealing?

In his messages to the seven churches in Asia Minor John mounts an attack against those who "eat idol meat and practise immorality" in Pergamum (2:14; cf. 2:20) and pursue the "deep things of Satan" in Thyatira (2:24). In 2:6,15 (in Ephesus and Pergamum) they are called "Nicolaitans". One generally conceives of John's adversaries as a minority group, a "sect" within the larger Christian community. This is not self-evident, however.

In a classic work which turned the issue of majorities and minorities upside down, Walter Bauer concluded that the congregations of Pergamum, Thyatira, Sardes and Laodicea were actually led by those whom John considered heretics; οἱ λοιποί in 2:24 suggests that John's party was in the minority in Thyatira.[4] "There is also room for doubt as to whether the apocalypticist, with his extremely confused religious outlook ... can be regarded in any sense as an intellectual and spiritual leader of an

---

3 As late as around AD 200 the much-travelled Origen assessed the number of Christians in proportion to the whole population as quite small; cf. A. von Harnack, *Die Mission und Ausbreitung des Christentums in den ersten drei Jahrhunderten* (Wiesbaden: VMA-Verlag, s.a., Nachdruck der 4. Aufl.), 548, 948. According to R. L. Fox, *Pagans and Christians* (New York: Alfred A. Knopf, 1989), 317, as late as around AD 250 the total membership of the Christian faith "was still small in absolute terms, perhaps (at a guess) only 2 percent of the Empire's total population."

4 W. Bauer, *Orthodoxy and Heresy in Earliest Christianity* (Philadelphia, PA: Fortress 1971), 79-80.

important band of Christians in western Asia Minor. To what extent was he really an influential figure ...? To what extent might this have been only wishful thinking? ... Unqualified confidence that his recipients would follow his lead is not exactly the impression left ...."[5]

Bauer conjectured that John chose as the receivers of his messages those seven congregations where some influence still seemed possible (instead of, for example, Colossae or Hierapolis).[6] A somewhat similar line is now taken by several prominent interpreters of Revelation. Leonard L. Thompson considers Revelation to be "a minority report" which advocates "attitudes and styles of life *not* compatible with how most Christians were living in the cities of Asia." "Among the Christian groups at Ephesus *only* the writer of the Book of Revelation seems to be hostile towards urban culture and opposed to any Christian accommodation toward it."[7] The life style of "most Christians" in Asia minor is visible in the Pastoral epistles and 1 Peter, and probably in Luke-Acts as well.[8]

Elisabeth Schüssler Fiorenza also concludes that John argues "against rival Christian apostles and prophets who seem to have had greater influence than John in several of the communities in Asia Minor."[9] Hans-Josef Klauck admits that John gives the impression that the Nicolaitans constitute a heretical minority, rightly combatted by him; but he adds that this is a caricature, due to the subjective perspective of John. In reality, the Nicolaitans had been successful in the congregations, and this is still palpable in Rev 2-3.[10]

Bauer's psychological point is taken up as well. Fiorenza writes: "John's vilification of his prophetic rivals and his repeated rhetorical stress on Revelation's heavenly ratification and divine sanction evidence a great anxiety about the authority and influence of his work"[11] and characterize his discourse "as belonging to that of a cognitive minority

---

5 Ibid., 77-78.
6 Bauer, op. cit., 78. The number seven forced John to include some congregations which were not in themselves very "suitable" for his purposes.
7 L. L. Thompson, *The Book of Revelation: Apocalypse and Empire* (New York: Oxford UP, 1990), 132, 120 (emphasis mine).
8 P. Lampe, *Lokalisation der Lukas-Leser* (forthcoming) persuasively argues for the Ephesian provenance of Luke-Acts.
9 *Revelation*, 55.
10 H-J. Klauck, 'Das Sendschreiben nach Pergamon und der Kaiserkult in der Johannesoffenbarung', *Bib* 73 (1992), 170.
11 Cf. Klauck, op. cit., 181.

within the Christian community of Asia".[12] However, she constructs an impossible total picture, as she also holds that John "sides with the poor and oppressed *majority*" of people in the Roman empire.[13] For if that were the case, how could he possibly belong to "a cognitive minority within the Christian community of Asia"? According to Fiorenza, "the vast majority of the population" suffered from Roman colonialism, while only "some citizens ... enjoyed the benefits of Roman commerce and peace as well as the comforts and splendor of urban life."[14] If, then, John identified with the majority of the poor population but found himself in the minority in some Christian congregations, are we to conclude that the majority (!) of Asian Christians belonged to the privileged elite?

Actually different conditions may have prevailed in different congregations. In Ephesus the Nicolaitans have no foothold according to 2:6, yet Ephesian Christianity does not seem characterized by a Johannine life style either.[15] The word ὀλίγα in 2:14 (John's Christ only has "a few things" against the congregation, referring to their toleration of the Nicolaitans) indicates that in Pergamum the number of the Nicolaitans must have been small, and John could hardly have praised a congregation run by heretics as he praises Thyatira in 2:19. David Aune reasonably conjectures that many of the communities in question were dominated by a "centrist party" between the cultural and religious accommodation of the Nicolaitans and John's strict non-conformism.[16]

But if John represents a minority, this was—or in any case was to *become*—a mighty minority indeed. It became mighty in the course of history when the book exerted its influence, in particular on various millenarian groups within Christianity.

Whatever the numerical proportions between the various groups, the Book of Revelation reflects a clash between them and their styles of life.

John's Charges

To the church of Thyatira John's Christ has this to say (2:19-23):

> *I know your works, your love and faith and service and patient endurance ... But I have this against you, that you tolerate the woman Jezebel, who*

---

12 Fiorenza, *Revelation*, 138.
13 Ibid., 100.
14 Ibid., 127.
15 Cf. Thompson, *Revelation*, 120 (see above) and John's criticism of the congregation forsaking its "first love" — meaning eschatological fervour?
16 D. E. Aune, 'The Social Matrix of the Apocalypse of John,' *BR* 26 (1981), 29. Cf. Klauck, 'Sendschreiben,' 179.

calls herself a prophetess and is teaching and beguiling my servants to practise immorality and to eat food sacrificed to idols ... Behold, I will throw her on a sickbed, and those who commit adultery with her I will throw into great tribulation, unless they repent of her doings, and I will strike her children dead. And all the churches shall know that I am he who searches mind and heart, and I will give to each of you as your works deserve.

This is a strange picture of what is going on in a Christian congregation. A faction of it, at least, is ostensibly run by a promiscuous prophetess with a host of lovers—and of children, apparently the fruit of these affairs.[17] Scholars have taken John's insinuations at face value[18] and have condemned the prophetess along with the "immoral" Nicolaitans.[19] Today most would regard the Nicolaitans as licentious Gnostic libertines. The new Anchor Bible Dictionary is quite representative in telling us that they were "permissive about both eating meat offered to idols and immorality", the latter meaning "sexual license".[20]

It is inadvisable, however, to take religious polemic at face value. Luke T. Johnson demonstrates the universality of the "rhetoric of slander" both in the polemic between different Jewish groups and in that between ancient philosophical schools. In Hellenistic rhetoric, "certain standard categories of vice were automatically attributed to any opponent. They were all lovers of pleasure, lovers of money, and lovers of glory."[21] "The slander was not affected by facts."[22] On the Jewish side one may consult e.g. Wis 14:22-28 or 1 QS 4:9-14. "The Qumran rule of thumb is that you cannot say enough bad things about outsiders."[23] To

---

17 Some have even held, on the basis of a variant reading which adds "yours" to γυναῖκα that "Jezebel" was the local bishop's wife whom the poor husband did not manage to turn away from her profligate ways....

18 Cf. even Bauer, *Orthodoxy*, 100.

19 Some generations ago the Nicolaitans were largely regarded simply as Christians who were willing to accommodate to their environment. It was held that they might have appealed to Paul, and did *not* indulge in actual immorality; in the vein of the Tübingen school it was thought that John took an anti-Pauline stance. Some recent contributions show that the Tübingen view is now re-gaining ground, but it is still a minority position. For a full discussion see H. Räisänen, 'The Nicolaitans: Apoc. 2, Acta 6,' *ANRW* II, 26.2.

20 D. F. Watson, 'Nicolaitans,' *ABD* IV (New York: Doubleday 1992), cols. 1106-07.

21 L. T. Johnson, 'The New Testament's Anti-Jewish Slander and the Conventions of Ancient Polemic,' *JBL* 108 (1989), 432.

22 Ibid., 433.

23 Ibid., 439.

reconstruct the portrait of the Nicolaitans on the basis of John's attacks is rather like reconstructing the life and thought of the Pharisees on the basis of Matthew 23.

Eating Sacrificial Meat

John's first charge against the Nicolaitans is that they eat εἰδωλόθυτα, "idol meat" (2:14,20). This might refer either to participation in sacrificial meals in pagan shrines or to eating privately such meat as had been sacrificed to pagan gods before being sold, or both. Almost all available meat had, of course, first been sacrificed in a temple.

In view of the social circumstances in Thyatira, a prosperous trade centre, commentators have recognized the relevance of *guild-membership* to the issue of "idol meat". Thyatiran Christians who were also members of a trade guild were likely to be involved in social events which took place in pagan temples and included meals.

In 2:24, "Christ" promises not to lay upon the Thyatirans "any other burden" (βάρος). The wording recalls the "Apostolic Decree" (Acts 15:28) which liberates Gentile Christians from any "burden" except what is "indispensable"; this includes abstinence from "idol meat" and "fornication". A connection between Revelation and Luke's tradition is probable. It is difficult to make any sense at all of the "burden" of Rev 2:24, unless it refers to some well-known stipulation. On the other hand, the standpoint of the seer is clear, if the Decree stands in the background.

If it is the Apostolic Decree that constitutes the backdrop of John's criticism, then it is likely that he is not only offended by meals held at pagan temples, but also by the consumption by Christians of meat purchased in the market-place, for "idol meat" in any form seems to be prohibited by the Decree.

Practising Immorality

The Nicolaitans are said to practise fornication (2:14,20-21) or adultery (2:22). It is not self-evident that the reference to Balaam is intended as an allusion to actual fornication. The Old Testament story (Num 25) tells of Israelite men sleeping with *foreign* (Moabite) women who enticed them to eat pagan meat. Balaam himself (a pagan seer) is portrayed as one who entices to idolatry, not as one who is himself involved in prohibited sex. Therefore, idolatry might be the point in the reference to him.

Jezebel, the foreign princess married to king Ahab, was remembered as a person who strongly favoured the cult of Baal. G. B. Caird notes that "nobody ever accused Ahab's wife of harlotry except in a metaphorical sense".[24] Of course, "fornication" is a standard Old Testament metaphor to describe Israel's apostasy from Yahweh.

Moreover, would a horrendous case of illicit behaviour really be a temptation for "all the congregations" (2:23)? The offence was not obvious to the Thyatirans themselves. It took the revelatory activity of the divine acumen "which searches mind and heart" to point out its depravity: God sees what men cannot. Martin Kiddle rightly pointed out that Jezebel and her associates are accused "not of open and scandalous immorality, but of hiding vice beneath a cloak of respectability. In punishing them openly, Christ will reveal the hidden viciousness of their doctrines ...."[25]

It seems unlikely that John could have praised the Thyatirans for their love and faith, service and endurance (2:19), if the congregation had been so blind to the immoral nature of the behaviour of a prominent prophetess. The seer would hardly have been so 'tolerant' of sexual deviation; "fornication" seems just another name for eating sacrificial meat.[26]

The words "harlot", "fornication" and "fornicate" are all used figuratively in chapters 17-19, where the great harlot Rome is portrayed. John seems to suggest a connection between the behaviour of the Nicolaitans, who eat sacrificial meat, and the Satanic figure of the emperor to whom they in reality pay homage. The "lovers" of "Jezebel" have committed adultery with her in the same sense in which the "kings of the earth" have "committed fornication" with the harlot Rome (17:2; 18:3); "Jezebel" "beguiles" people just as the false prophet, the second beast, does (2:20; 13:14).

Fiorenza's change of standpoint might be taken as symptomatic. In 1973 she drew a parallel between the Nicolaitans and the libertine group in Corinth which did not shy away from visits to brothels.[27] In her later

---

[24] G. B. Caird, *The Revelation of St. John the Divine* (BNTC, London: Black, 1966), 39.
[25] M. Kiddle, *The Revelation of St. John* (MNTC, London: Hodder and Stoughton, 1940), 41.
[26] Thompson, *Revelation*, 122.
[27] E. Schüssler Fiorenza, 'Apocalyptic and Gnosis in Revelation,' *JBL* 92 (1973), 567-74. The same parallel was suggested already by Bauer, *Orthodoxy*, 100. Cf. now J. T. Sanders, *Schismatics, Sectarians, Dissidents, Deviants: The First One Hundred Years of Jewish-Christian Relations* (London: SCM Press, 1993), 322 n. 129. However, the fornication condemned by Paul in 1 Cor 6 is a matter of Greek men visiting *hetaerae* who were hardly members of the congregation! This was a feature of their inherited culture which they had not dropped when becoming Christians. By contrast, with a literal interpretation of "adultery" in Rev 2 we would have in Thyatira a prostitute as a Christian prophetess.

work Fiorenza no longer speaks of "immoral acts" of the Nicolaitans,[28] but takes "fornication" as a metaphor.[29]

The probability, then, is overwhelming that the conduct attacked by John consists simply of eating sacrificial meat. If so, John may be opposed to any kind of contact with such meat. The harsh collective condemnation of the prophetess and her circle could indicate that these people sin *together*, i.e. they eat sacrificial meat also in their congregational gatherings. This would suggest that the Nicolaitans of Thyatira were relatively well-to-do members of the congregation who could afford to buy meat, a privilege few had in antiquity. This conclusion of the social standing of the Nicolaitans is required anyway, if the problem has to do with membership in trade-guilds.

Exploring the Deep Things of Satan

In Thyatira the Nicolaitans explore the "deep things of Satan" (2:24). "But to the rest of you in Thyatira ... who have not learned, as they say, the deep things of Satan, to you I say ..." On the face of it, "as they say" (ὡς λέγουσιν) suggests that John is taking up a phrase used by the Nicolaitans themselves. Yet "of Satan" (though awkwardly placed) should be taken as a commentary by John. The meaning is then: you have not learned "the deep things", as they call them, which are in reality "deep things" of Satan. For if a faction of the Thyatiran congregation had actually been known to be pursuing Satanic wisdom, this would have meant nothing less than some kind of Satan-worship; but then surely John "would have had more to say about it than a passing allusion."[30]

Does "deep things", understood as an expression used by the Nicolaitans themselves, suggest a Gnostic group?

Paul refers (1 Cor 2:10) to "the deep things of God". A "spiritual" person like Paul can know such things. "Deep things" is a term at home in any Jewish or Hellenistic environment where the notion of divine revelation is valued (cf. 2 Bar 14:8; 1 QS 11:19); it is used by a writer as un-Gnostic as Clement of Rome (40:1) who had been allowed to glance at "the deep things of the divine gnosis".

In Rom 11:33 Paul praises the *depth* of God's richness, wisdom and γνῶσις. God's "mystery" concerning Israel (11:25) has been revealed to him either through a prophetic oracle or through inspired reading of

---

28 Fiorenza, *Revelation*, 132-35.
29 Ibid., 14, 56.
30 A. Farrer, *The Revelation of St. John the Divine* (Oxford: University Press 1964), 77.

Scripture. The Nicolaitans' pursuit of the deep things is explicable in either way, too. The fact that "Jezebel" is called a prophetess suggests oracles.

Additional Information on the Nicolaitans?

Some church fathers made statements on a Gnostic sect of Nicolaitans. Its doctrine and practice were branded as immoral.

However, the fathers seem to have possessed no knowledge of actual Nicolaitans.[31] Their writings probably contain nothing but assertions based on Revelation and attempts to make sense of the connection with Nicolaus. Once it was inferred from Revelation that the Nicolaitans were Gnostics (in this the fathers anticipated modern scholars), the picture was complemented by attributing to them views known to be held by Gnostics.

Reference is often made to patristic information about libertine practices attributed to Gnostics. But generalizations about Gnostic immorality should be avoided after the Nag Hammadi discoveries.[32]

There is one feature, however, which is not immediately explicable on the basis of Revelation and of general prejudice. The sect is said to have traced its ideas back to Nicolaus of Antioch, one of the seven leaders of the "Hellenist" wing of the Jerusalem church (Acts 6:5). To be sure, the actual story told about this Nicolaus is fanciful: he had in the presence of the apostles abandoned his beautiful wife, offering her free to any man. But the deacon of Antioch would hardly have been given the dubious honour of being the patron of the Nicolaitans, had the church fathers been aware of any other candidate.

The Nicolaitans seem to have appealed to this Nicolaus, with or without justification. But if the connection is fictitious, it is surprising that they should have chosen a figure of so little prominence. A historical connection is therefore possible, *pace* the declaration of J. T. Sanders that, "as everyone (!) observes, there is nothing to connect him with the Nicolaus of Acts 6".[33]

---

31 For references see Räisänen, 'Nicolaitans,' section IV 1 with n. 123.
32 It now seems clear that some Gnostics were libertine, but most were not. Cf. K. Koschorke, *Die Polemik der Gnostiker gegen das kirchliche Christentum unter besonderer Berücksichtigung der Nag Hammadi-Traktate "Apokalypse des Petrus" (NHC VII,3) und "Testimonium Veritatis" (NHC IX,3)*. (NHS 12, Leiden: Brill, 1978), 123-24.
33 Sanders, *Schismatics*, 322 n. 133.

Possible Roots of the Nicolaitan Position

Paul deals with "idol meat" in 1 Cor 8 and 10. His clear decisions are these: participation in a pagan cult is impossible (10:14-22); meat sacrificed to gods but later sold in the market-place is allowed (10:25-26); eating "idol meat" at a private meal is all right, unless someone makes it a matter of conscience (10:27-11:1).

The case dealt with in ch. 8 is that of a Christian eating in the "idol's house". Since Paul strongly condemns actual participation in a pagan cult in ch. 10, he is probably considering something else here: a social meal, e.g. a feast of a trade guild or a family event. He concedes that what is eaten is not really "idol meat", since idols are not real. However, he stresses concern for the "weak". Participation in a pagan cult is idolatry and, as such, prohibited; outside of a cultic context, "idol meat" can be freely eaten. The problem is that drawing such a line is difficult. Paul's solution looks like a compromise between the interests of the strong and the weak. It is impossible to know whether the Nicolaitans would have agreed more with Paul or with the 'strong' at Corinth.[34]

Paul's view seems to be rooted in the attitude adopted in Antioch toward Jewish food laws. This, in turn, had its roots in the views of the "Hellenists" around Stephen (to whom Nicolaus of Antioch belonged). It is probably correct to trace back to Antioch the assertions that "nothing is unclean in itself" (Rom 14:14), "everything is clean" (Rom 14:20) and "the kingdom of God does not mean food and drink ..." (Rom 14:17). It is reasonable to assume that in the mixed congregation of Antioch some applied the same principle to "idol meat". A free attitude toward food was part of the Hellenist legacy.

In this context, a connection between the Nicolaitans and Nicolaus of Antioch makes sense. At least the Nicolaitans are heirs to the *position* once taken by Nicolaus and his Hellenist friends. In view of "Jezebel's" role in Thyatira, it is interesting that Philip, one of the Seven, had his prophetic daughters around him in Caesarea (Acts 21:8) and lived later in Asia Minor (Eusebius, *H.E.* 3:31.3-4, 3:39.9, 5:24.2).

For Paul, the issue of "idol meat" was a problem of personal counseling. For John, by contrast, eating or not eating is a question of life and death in the battle between Christ and the Beast. John is not of the opinion that the Lord may "make stand" him who eats (Rom 14:4). He

---

34 Thompson, *Revelation*, 123.

"would not have liked Paul's complicated solution"; "(i)t is the 'lukewarm', he believes, who make God vomit."[35]

The Clash Between Two Perspectives on Culture

Chapters 2-3 are probably more closely linked to the rest of the book than is apparent at first sight. In "engaging in trades and actions connected directly with pagan worship"[36] the Nicolaitans, in John's view, join those citizens who accept the mark of the Beast in order to be able "to take part in the economic and social life of the earth", refusing to take upon themselves captivity and death (13:10). Adela Yarbro Collins argues that "the inability to buy or sell", anticipated in 13:16-17, would be the result of the refusal to use Roman coins that bore the image and name of the emperor.[37]

John's counsel to the congregations seems to be that of social separation. Verse 18:4 puts this clearly: "Come out of her [the fallen Babylon], my people, lest you take part in her sins, lest you share in her plagues ...."[38] Probably "the Christian faith and life-style as John understood them were incompatible with ordinary participation in the economic and social life of the cities." John's strict position on "idol meat" does not seem "compatible with continued membership in a guild."[39] Klauck notes that John requires of the congregations that very attitude which Paul refuted in 1 Cor 5:9-10 as a misunderstanding.[40] He asks: "What options are left in a city like Pergamum? Going underground? Forming a ghetto? Moving to a rural community?"[41]

Yarbro Collins points out that John's stance tends "toward the formation of separate Christian trade associations and burial societies (or toward the congregations taking on these functions)". Even more: it tends "toward the establishment of Christians as a third race", preparing (paradoxically enough) for the formation of a Christian state.[42]

Thus what is at stake is the Christians' attitude to society at large.

---

35 W. Meeks, *The Moral World of the First Christians* (London: SPCK, 1987), 112, 147.
36 Fiorenza, 'Apocalyptic,' 580.
37 A. Yarbro Collins, 'The Political Perspective of the Revelation to John,' *JBL* 96 (1977), 253.
38 A. Yarbro Collins, 'Persecution and Vengeance in the Book of Revelation,' in *Apocalypticism in the Mediterranean World and the Near East* (ed. D. Hellholm, Tübingen: J. C. B. Mohr, ^{2}1989), 741; cf. Meeks, op. cit., 147; Klauck, 'Sendschreiben,' 178-79.
39 Collins, art. cit., 740-41.
40 Klauck, 'Sendschreiben,' 182.
41 Ibid., 179.
42 'Vilification and Self-Definition in the Book of Revelation', *HTR* 79 (1986), 317.

Two different perspectives on the relation between faith and culture are at odds. Some economic tensions within the community also make themselves felt, possibly because "opportunities for advancement were tied to acceptance of pagan religious rites."[43] To be sure, "the disparity of wealth and privilege between the provincial elite and the ordinary people"[44] may not have been a major problem in Asia Minor.[45] But to John "wealth itself ... seems a vice". Lydia the purple-seller, "if she were still alive and returned to her native Thyatira, would have to go begging if John had his way."[46] John represents the radical old ethos of "wandering charismatics".[47]

John, the Nicolaitans, and Persecution

If John seems to recommend harsh measures, the justification for this is universally found in the severe situation he faced. Scholarly literature is full of assertions to the effect that Revelation was composed during a time of severe persecution. But several scholars have persuasively argued that the situation under Domitian was rather different from the seer's perception of it. Thompson concludes that "the attempt to link the Book of Revelation with upheaval and crisis is wrongheaded".[48] He shows that the portrait of Domitian in standard post-Domitianic sources (Pliny, Tacitus, Suetonius) cannot be trusted, for it "does not square with literary, epigraphic, numismatic and prosopographical evidence from the Domitianic period".[49] When John wrote, "some persecution had been experienced, more was expected" but "there is no need to posit a widespread or recent outbreak of persecution".[50] John knows only one martyr (Antipas of Pergamum, 2:13). One receives the impression that the fate of Antipas was an individual case; executions were not the rule.[51] To be sure, something had happened. John himself had been banned. Presumably some local disturbances had taken place. But on the

---

43 Collins, 'Persecution,' 746.
44 Ibid.
45 Thompson, *Revelation*, 154-56, 164-67.
46 Meeks, *Moral World*, 147; cf. Klauck, 'Sendschreiben,' 178.
47 Klauck, 'Sendschreiben,' 179-80.
48 *Revelation*, 197.
49 Ibid., 171.
50 Collins, 'Persecution,' 746; cf. J. Ulrichsen, *Das eschatologische Zeitschema der Offenbarung des Johannes* (Oslo 1988), 44-47 (with references); Klauck, 'Sendschreiben,' 153-56, 160-64. Rev 6:9-11 (the souls of the martyrs under the heavenly altar) probably refers to events during Nero's reign.
51 Klauck, art. cit., 163-64.

whole, "Revelation was written at a time of comparative peace for the Christians"![52]

There is "no indication" that Domitian demanded "greater divine honours than either his predecessors or successors".[53] He was sometimes called *dominus et deus noster*, though he did not encourage such titles, but "there is no record that this precipitated a clash between him and the Christians".[54]

It is useful to distinguish between "hard" and "soft" forms of the imperial cult.[55] The "hard" form entailed sacrificing before the image of the emperor and cursing Christ, but this was not at all the rule. "It occurred more seldom than we think, and it was not the Roman authorities who were mainly responsible for it, but the local pagan population; the authorities only became active after a denunciation from their side. John regards the 'soft' cult of the emperor as much more dangerous, i.e. when someone joined a festive multitude or participated in a social guild meal with religious overtones ...."[56]

Thompson likewise shows that "(i)n Asia opposition to Christianity came primarily from local people, not from the imperial machinery." "The Pliny correspondence confirms that the imperial cult was *not* a central issue in either official or unofficial attitudes toward Christians." The Christians "could not sacrifice to any god on behalf of the emperor. That put Christians on a collision course with local religious activity."[57] The sacrifices in connection with imperial images were, like most sacrifices related to the emperor, "for the most part made on *behalf* of the image of the emperor, not to it".[58] "The importance of the imperial cult for early Christianity should not be inflated. The greater issue revolves around Christians' relation to adherents of traditional religious cults."[59]

The persecutions depicted in the book of Revelation are "a product of the seer's expectations." The prediction that the Beast was to make war on the saints and to conquer them (13:7) "did not come true any more than all the other pictures of horror."[60] John's expectation of a world-

---

52 J. Sweet, *Revelation* (Pelican Commentaries, London: SCM Press, 1979), 27.
53 Thompson, *Revelation*, 104-07.
54 J. A. T. Robinson, *Redating the New Testament* (London: SCM Press, [3]1978), 236.
55 Klauck, 'Sendschreiben,' 181ff.
56 Ibid., 181.
57 Thompson, op. cit., 130-31.
58 Ibid., 163, with reference to S. R. F. Price.
59 Ibid., 164.
60 Ulrichsen, *Zeitschema*, 44.

wide persecution is due to the impact of his apocalyptic "symbolic universe". In early Christian eschatology predictions of persecutions, modelled on the war of the eschatological enemy against the saints (Dan 7) are a fixed topos.[61] John's world view requires persecutions, for "there is a fixed number of martyrs who must meet their deaths before the end can arrive" (6:9-11).[62]

John's symbolic universe forces him to see other signals of the end as well: there is the beginning apostasy of the congregation. This, too, is a well-known topos (cf. Matt 24; 2 Thess 2).[63] John detected some small signs that were open to an apocalyptic reading and magnified them: "occasional and selective" persecution[64] anticipated huge massacres;[65] a broad-minded attitude to social communication with outsiders on the part of the Nicolaitans was expected to expand to the apostasy of the majority from faith. The Nicolaitans might well have found John guilty of paranoia (and, of course, of false prophecy, had they taken Deut 18:21-22 as a guideline). They might also have found that his was a suicidal attitude which contributed to the worsening of relations with their pagan neighbours and, in the long run, with the state.

Among interpreters of Revelation, John's black-and-white stance still tends to be glorified. Even a commentator who draws a quite positive picture of the Nicolaitans can state: "Like a true prophet (John) had seen the eternal principles governing the contest between good and evil ...." He is "a realist ... in his analysis of the real nature of the forces that were devastating the earth."[66]

At the very least one should realise that this implies that those Christian writers who adopted a very different attitude to the *same* Roman power were false prophets, or at least unrealistic: the authors of 1 Clement, 1 Peter and the Pastoral epistles, and Luke. The counterposition is taken by Paul Walaskay: Luke "deserves a special place of honor in the canon of saints" because of his "practicality". "It is with respect to survival that Luke was a clear-headed, practical theologian *sans égal*. With great skill he was able to blunt the apocalyptic appeal of the anti-Roman wing of the church which he wisely saw as the primary internal threat to the Christian movement."[67] On this reading, John the seer is part of the

---

61 Ibid., 46.
62 Collins, 'Perspective,' 249.
63 Cf. Ulrichsen, op. cit., 46-47.
64 Sweet, *Revelation*, 26.
65 Cf. Klauck, art. cit., 175.
66 Caird, *Revelation*, 289.

"threat". John's stance is helpful as a critical corrective, but the voice of the other side, speaking for open and fearless relations with culture and civilization, also deserves to be heard.[68]

John's animosity cannot be explained on the basis of the difficult situation of the oppressed.[69] John thirsts for vengeance on *all* "those who dwell upon the earth" (6:10), for slaves no less than for kings and generals (6:15; cf. 8:13; 9:4ff.; 11:10; 13:8 etc.). All non-Christians are demonized. John expects that eventually those who keep their faith intact will receive "power over the Gentiles" and "rule them with an iron rod" (2:26).

Rome is not blamed for oppressing the conquered peoples. Fiorenza claims that, for John, Rome is "the powerful incarnation of international oppression and murder", "intoxicated with the blood not only of the saints, but also of all those slaughtered on earth."[70] On the contrary, the other nations are attracted to the Beast and have voluntarily "given over their royal power" (17:17) to him; their kings have willingly fornicated with the harlot Rome. John's hatred of Rome stems not so much from social as from religious reasons, the rivalry between Caesar and Christ.[71]

It is an oversimplification to praise Revelation's vision of salvation as "liberation from oppressive ecclesiastical structures", as Fiorenza does.[72] The Book of Revelation may just as well tend toward creating and upholding such structures. Fiorenza notes herself that John's way of appealing to God's authority "has had dangerous consequences in the history of Christianity because in its doctrinal and institutionalized form it has silenced all critique of ecclesiastical and civil authority".[73]

John and the Nicolaitans represent two different types of Christians; they might be termed 'separationist' or 'sectarian', on one hand and 'lati-

---

67 P. W. Walaskay, *'And so we came to Rome': The Political Perspective of St Luke* (SNTSMS 49, Cambridge: CUP, 1983), 66-67.
68 Klauck, 'Sendschreiben,' 182.
69 Thus Fiorenza, *Revelation*, 126-27, 134.
70 Ibid., 98.
71 In paying homage to the emperor, the Romans may have come close to the deification of a human being. But what then did the Christians do in turning a Jewish prophet into a "Gentile God"? True, the man made divine in the Christians' symbolic universe was a person very different from any of the emperors. Yet the notion of enthronement assimilated him to the latter later on in Christendom. After Constantine's time he too became a "Caesar" who turned out to be far more dangerous to "others" than a Domitian had ever been.
72 Cf. *Revelation*, 128.
73 Ibid., 137.

tudinarian' on the other. Thompson's descriptions are apt: on one hand we have "a Christian community that sets up high boundaries between itself and the rest of the world and that holds to a concomitant 'separatist' definition of the church", seeing "both Judaism and Greco-Roman society as demonic"; on the other hand there is "a Christian community that is less concerned with sharp boundaries and exclusive self-definition and seems to have little conflict with either Judaism or Greco-Roman urban institutions."[74] The positions are coupled with different social situations and exemplify the religious and theological diversity of early Christianity.

---

74 Thompson, *Revelation*, 125.

A Superior Minority?

The Problem of Men's Headship in Ephesians 5

Turid Karlsen Seim

According to the common understanding, the household codes, including Eph 5:(21)22-6:9, are primarily concerned about the subordination of wives and the obedience of slaves and children. This article is an attempt at reading the household code in Ephesians 5:(21)22-6:9 one more time by twisting the perspective: the problem addressed in the major section of the Ephesian household code is not the subordination of potentially subversive women but rather the understanding and practice of men's headship. In this respect it differs from the other household codes in a way that is sometimes noticed but rarely commented on. In communities where "many small men"[1] often were not as many as the women and where the common ideal was one of unity through mutual submission, the author attempts to accommodate a conventional standard of household duties by affirming headship and thereby reinforcing a hierarchy of roles.

There is no attempt in this article at offering new exegetical solutions to much discussed particulars of the passage—even though the change of perspective may mean that some of the awkward pieces of the passage exegetically fall into place. Neither is there any presentation of comparative material that might throw new light on the mythological language in the extensive motivating sections of the Ephesian household code. It seems to me that the subtlety of the theological speculations in these sections, so potent with possible connotations, captures the atten-

---

1 Cf. W. A. Meeks, "In one Body: The Unity of Humankind in Colossians and Ephesians," in *God's Christ and His People. Studies in Honour of Nils Alstrup Dahl*. eds. J. Jervell and W. A. Meeks (Oslo – Bergen – Tromsø: Universitetsforlaget 1977), 209-21, in referring to Peter Brown on p. 209.

tion of the commentators—even theirs who insist that the ethical interest is the primary one.

The position taken by several commentators that the author reproduces mythological language in a fragmentary way to support a certain ethical standard—and sometimes gets carried away beyond what is needed for this purpose[2] is to me convincing. But the point I make, is valid regardless of which background material the theological language may refer to. Possible references to *hieros gamos*, wisdom speculations or prophetic interpretations of the relationship between God and the elected people in terms of marriage, are therefore not discussed in what follows—however interesting they may be and also crucial to a fuller interpretation of the passage than it is possible to give in a short article.

When this is an appropriate contribution to a Festschrift honouring a cherished teacher of New Testament, professor Jacob Jervell,—it is not because of any suggestions implied by the theme. It is rather because his amazing ability to gain new insights by an unexpected twist of the tail has been a constant challenging gift. It has helped me remain convinced that New Testament interpretation has a potential of surprise however grinded a text might be by a host of interpreters.

A Reversal of Proportion—A Male Minority in Early Christian Communities

Demographic evidence seems to indicate that throughout antiquity males outnumbered females regardless of social strata.[3] The disproportion may have been as drastic as two males to one female, and even a cautious estimation considering the probability that women were "undernumerated when living and undercommemorated after death",[4] does not reverse the figures. The reasons for the disproportionate sex ratio are multiple but follow a rather consistent pattern of assumed male superiority. Female infants were more frequently exposed than male, and girls had a shorter life expectancy than boys due to poor health and exhaustion from an inferior diet and child bearing beginning most often

---

2   J. P. Sampley, *'And the Two Shall Become One Flesh'. A Study of Traditions in Ephesians 5:21-33.* (Cambridge: The University Press 1971); M. Teobald, "Heilige Hochzeit. Motive des Mythos im Horizont von Eph. 5,21-33," *Metaphorik und Mythos im Neuen Testament.* Quaestiones disputatae 126, hrsg. K. Kertelge (Freiburg im Breisgau – Basel – Wien: Herder 1990), 220-54.

3   Cf. S. Pomeroy, *Goddesses, Whores, Wives and Slaves. Women in Classical Antiquity.* (New York: Schocken Books 1976, 3rd ed.), 68f., 164, 227ff.

4   Pomeroy, *Goddesses*, 227.

at a physically immature age.[5] This had as its result that, with few exceptions, women were invariably a minority in the population—but hardly a mighty one.

One of the remarkable features of early Christianity was the support it gained from women many of whom are said to be of high standing. How this attraction may be explained is a complex matter but the fact still remains that in some, and perhaps many, early Christian communities women have been in majority[6] —thus reversing the sex proportion of the larger society.

So far the scholarly interest has been to provide explanations of the attraction that Christianity exerted on women in particular, and the perspectives entailed for the role of women in early Christian communities. But another challenge is to explore how those features that were attractive to women, affected the role of men especially in a situation where the sex proportion had been reversed. How did this influence the definition and interaction between masculine and feminine roles—and particularly so in situations of potential conflict?

Household Duties and the Ethos of the Empire

The large number of women in the Christian communities at a time when women were more scarce than men, would mean that many of the Christian women belonged to non-Christian households. It is also likely that many women were attracted to ascetic renunciation as it was broadly preached and practised in the early church even from its very beginning and core.[7] Sheltered by the emerging "order of widows" women assumed an ascetic life style as an alternative to their conventional roles of marriage and motherhood.

The early Christian tradition is in its ethos highly ambiguous in these matters—as is evident from the case of Paul: He is the celibate preacher

---

5 Pomeroy, *Goddesses*, 228f.; L. Portefaix, *Sisters Rejoice. Paul's Letter to the Philippians and Luke-Acts as Received by First-Century Philippian Women*. ConBNT 20 (Stockholm: Almqvist & Wiksell International 1988), 9-14.

6 H. Gülzow, "Soziale Gegebenheiten der altkirchlichen Mission," *Kirchengeschichte als Missionsgeschichte I: Die alte Kirche*, hrsg. H. Frohnes/U. W. Knarr (München: Chr. Kaiser 1974), 189-226, 200; A. v. Harnack, *Die Mission und Ausbreitung des Christentums in den drei ersten Jahrhunderten*. (Wiesbaden: VMA-Verlag 1924), 598.

7 I have discussed this at length in "Ascetic Autonomy? New Perspectives on Single Women in the Early Church," *ST* 43 (1989), 125-40; and also in *The Double Message. Patterns of Gender in Luke-Acts*. Studies of the New Testament and its World (Edinburgh: T & T Clark 1994), 185-248, where I argue that Luke favours ascetic renunciation.

whose advice it is that others should follow his example provided they have the gift to do so, but yet the base of the Pauline communities is the urban household. This ambiguity later leads to a split of the tradition that claims the authority of Paul. On the one hand there are letters written in his name, such as Colossians, Ephesians and the Pastoral Letters,[8] reinforcing the traditional convention of the patriarchal household and adopting the imperial ideals of family restoration.[9] On the other hand there is the Lukan tradition of Paul[10] and further on the Apocryphal Acts of Paul and Thecla advocating an ascetic standard in defiance of the ruling ethos of the empire and threatening its social fabric.

The household codes should be read against the alternative option of ascetic renunciation of household obligations, even if this also has to be tested in each individual case. With regard to the Pastoral Letters it has been convincingly argued that the author represents an attempt towards the end of the first century to defend a code of behaviour that is an overfulfilment of official ideals and requirements while serving ecclesiological purposes as well.[11] In consistence with household regulations that evoke the silent submission of married women, the author tries to decimate the order of widows by defining proper "widowhood" in a way that is a glorification and a reward of the expected virtues of womanhood rather than an offence to them.

For the interpretation of the letter to the Ephesians and especially the household code in 5:(21)22-6:9 these observations have several implications. It means that it is part of an advocacy on Paul's behalf, defending one stream of Paulinism that with particular regard to the parenetic

---

8   This article is, in other words, written from the assumption that Colossians and Ephesians are not authentic Pauline letters but belong to a Pauline school.
9   Augustus' legislation concerning marriage (Lex Julia 18 SD, and Lex Papia 9 SC) involved a restoration of the old Roman family ideals and aimed particularly at an increased legitimate reproduction of the Roman aristocracy. The new element was that the responsibility and the supervision of this moral domain was transferred from the *pater familias* to the imperial and public power as *pater patriae*. For further discussion and a survey of literature, cf. *Double Message*, 192ff. This means that the officially ruling ethos not necessarily need be the common one, as S. J. Tanzer seems to assume, "Ephesians", in *Searching the Scriptures. Volume Two: A Feminist Commentary*, ed. by E. Schüssler Fiorenza (New York: Crossroad 1994), 325-48, 328f.
10 Cf. note 7 above.
11 Cf. J. Bassler, "The Widows' Tale: A Fresh Look at 1 Tim 5.3-16," in *JBL* 103 (1984), 23-41; D. Verner, *The Household of God. The Social World of the Pastoral Epistles*. SBLDS 71 (Chico, CA: Scholars Press 1983). For an updated survey see L. M. Maloney, "The Pastoral Epistles", in *Searching the Scriptures*, 361-80.

material opposes a competing ethos of ascetic abandonment. By the very way in which the author employs nuptial imagery and interprets Scripture (Gen 2:24) he questions and counteracts an ascetic position.[12]

There is, however, no striking or overt polemic flavour in the Ephesian household code. Neither is there any general agreement among commentators as to whether the Ephesians at all is concerned about the relationship to outsiders. In my view, a household code will somehow regulate the relationship to the world outside of the Christian community itself not only by accommodating to common standards but also because it is not likely that all the households to which the Christians addressed belong, need be Christian households.

The Reciprocity of the Household Codes

Especially from the household code in 1 Pet 2:13-3:7,[13] it is clear that the household codes are not exhortations addressed to Christian households but rather to Christians as they live in households even in an inferior minority position under non-Christian mastery. Within the formal framework of the household code the author of 1 Pet deals with issues such as the brutal treatment of slaves by injust pagan masters and the difficulties a woman has to face in a mixed marriage where the husband opposes her faith. Apparently the incongruity applies more frequently to wives and slaves than to men and masters. This supports the view that in the early Christian communities women and slaves were over-represented. It could, of course, happen that a Christian husband had a non-Christian wife but this has been more of a rare case.

The pairs by which the structure of the household code operates, are therefore not necessarily interrelated at an individual level. Wife and husband are not mutually instructed about how they should relate to each other in a truly Christian marriage. The wives addressed may be subject to other husbands than those to whom the author speaks, and the slaves may have other masters. Within the pairs there is a correspondence of attitude, but each group addressed is supposed to act as advised regardless of actual reciprocity. This might explain why in the case of the wives there is a possible emphasis on their submission to "their own" (τοῖς ἰδίοις) men. In Koine Greek this remains an open case grammati-

---

12 Cf. A. T. Lincoln, *Ephesians*. WBC 42 (Dallas, TX: Word Books, Publisher 1990), 363.
13 The interpretation of the household code in 1 Pet is based on my article "Hustavlen i 1 Pet 3.1-7 og dens tradisjonshistoriske sammenheng," in *NTT* 91 (1990), 101-14.

cally, but it might imply that Christian wives are not to withdraw from the rights of their lawfully wedded husbands, and conjugal obligations should not be suspended by a transfer of authority to any leading male in the community.

In this perspective the requirements are non-compromising and unconditional.[14] The household codes are not primarily a matter of establishing an ethos for Christian households or, for that sake, a Christian doctrine of marriage. The subordination and obedience are not dependent on the husband or master being loving, caring and subordinate to the God with whom there is no partiality. This curtails the argumentation common among commentators of good will, that even though the inferior partners are admonished to be subordinate (in the case of wives) or obedient (in the case of children and slaves) the corresponding request to the superior partner is never to rule or control. The expressions used rather qualify and soften the way in which authority and dominion should be exercised. "Liebespatriarkalismus", the term coined by Ernst Troeltsch, is an appropriate expression for this and may be pertinent for a vision of a Christian household as implied by the assumed pattern of the household codes. But the formal pattern of reciprocity does not necessarily cover the realities of the experiential circumstances in which many members of the early Christian communities lived.

The Ephesian Household Code: an Advocacy of Headship

The difference between the household codes shows the adaptability of the form. Even though the formal structure is recognisable in each case, it has a flexibility that allows for different emphases and concerns. In this way the parenetical pattern is made to meet the particularities of a certain situation. It works quantitatively by the distribution of material, the omission of pairs or even one partner of a pair, and qualitatively by amplifications and the theological arsenal mobilised to motivate and justify the exhortations.[15]

---

14 Against B. Witherington III, *Women in the Earliest Churches*. (Cambridge: Cambridge University Press 1988), 57, who insists that the christological amplification indicates that the submission "hinges on their being a Christian context" and that Paul here does not deal with couples of mixed religion.

15 For further review of the formal structure of the household code and its background material, cf. D. Aune, "Household Codes," in *Greco-Roman Literature and the New Testament: Selected Forms and Genres*. SBL Sources of Biblical Literature/Sources for Biblical Study 21, ed. by D. Aune (Atlanta, GA: Scholars Press 1988), 25-50; and D. Verner, *The Household of God* , 87f.

The structure is complete only in the earliest codes, Col 3:18-4:1 and Eph 5:(21)22-6.9, while 1 Pet 2:13-3:7 shows significant alterations both in terms of additions and omissions. An introductory exhortation is added about the subordination of the whole community, not to each other as in Ephesians, but πάσῃ ἀνθρωπίνῃ κτίσει. The pair of children and parents is completely absent, while the slaves have no correspondent masters. There is also a reversal of order since the section on slaves precedes the section on wives and husbands. These variations reflect the special concerns of the author of 1 Pet and also the composition of his presumed group of addressees as well as their social situation.

The same adaptability applies to the household code in Eph 5:(21)22-6:9. It has the same structural pattern and sequence of sections as the code in Col 3:18-4:1 on which most interpreters presume it originally relies. It is therefore not an independent witness to the existence of a "Haustafel tradition" but yet it displays a remarkable originality in the content matter. The core elements of the exhortations remain, however, the same as in Colossians: the wives are told to be subordinate and the husbands to show love; the children to obey and the fathers not to provoke; the slaves to obey wholeheartedly and the masters to treat their slaves well. Also many of the amplifications are similar, especially in the children–fathers and the slaves–masters examples. Even though there is a certain variety of wording in the rather elaborate amplification of the exhortation to the slaves, the elements do not differ in any substantial way. It is also interesting to observe that both in Colossians, Ephesians and I Peter the parenetic interest in slaves is more extensive than interest in masters. In Colossians and 1 Peter the slaves seem to receive major attention as is indicated by the amount of space allocated to them, and in 1 Peter also by a shift of sequence and the total omission of the masters.

The section on wives–husbands in Colossians is extremely brief. In comparison, all the other household codes substantially elaborate the exhortations at this point. Generally, the emphasis is on the women's part advocating subordination and conventional ideals of subdued behaviour. This corresponds to the fact that the exhortation to the slaves overshadows that to the masters. The conviction held by most commentators has therefore been that the household codes generally are intent on subordination and obedience. They serve primarily an apologetic function denying possible charges against the Christian community about subversive activity among women, slaves and minors thus threatening the social fabric of the empire. The household codes should be read against the backdrop of an imperial policy concerned about the restoration of traditional ideals.[16]

Regarding the household codes in Colossians and especially in 1 Pet and the Pastoral Letters, I find this apologetic and missionary perspective convincing. Neither does it compete but goes well together with a position confronting ascetic streams in the communities—which in the case of women have been particularly politically provocative. The household code in Ephesians may address partly the same problem as the other versions of this topos. In a situation where the official ideals of a proper household management is being challenged by unconventional behaviour and suspicions about potential subversive activities on the part of Christian women, also this household code represents an attempt at reinforcing among Christians a traditional division of gender roles.

In the Ephesian household code the section on the slaves still reflects the close connection to Colossians; with respect to this part there is, as mentioned above, no substantial change. Concerning the section on wives–husbands it has been expanded in a way that at first may appear to be similar to the expansion in the other codes at this point. However, in the Ephesian version it far outweighs everything else.

The parenetical thrust of the exhortations to wives–husbands in the Ephesian household code may serve partly the same purposes as the other versions. Implicitly it opposes an ascetic fervour by insisting on the traditional standard of conjugal obligations. Neither is there any doubt that the Ephesian household code shares the position commonly held by all the household codes that wives should be subject to their own husbands. But beyond this, the approach is different and the emphasis relocated.

The position of Eph 5:21 with regard to the subsequent household code has been much discussed. Does it function as a programmatic heading for what follows so that the whole of the code should be read in view of a claim to mutual submission?[17]

In grammatical terms the construction of v. 21 is not particularly difficult or ambiguous. It is a subordinate participial clause depending on the preceding imperative in v. 18: ἀλλὰ πληροῦσθε ἐν πνεύματι. The manifes-

---

16 Apart from references already mentioned, C. S. Keener, *Paul, Women & Wives. Marriage and Women's Ministry in the Letters of Paul.* (Peabody, MA: Hendrickson 1992) has this as the dominant perspective.
17 This is the position taken by most commentators. The more surprising is the proposal made by Tanzer, "Ephesians," 340f., that the household code is a later addition to the letter. Her argumentation is neither sufficient nor convincing for such a radical conclusion.

tation of the Spirit in the lives of the believers is spelled out in a threefold pattern: (1) their singing both among themselves and to the Lord, v. 19; (2) their thanksgiving to God, v. 20; and (3) their subordination to one another "out of the reverence for Christ", v. 21. Mutual submission is a sign of the Spirit, and everything which is said in the letter about submission cannot but be seen in light of this.

The connection between v. 21 and the following household code is made even more immediate by the lack of a verb in v. 22. The first exhortation about the wives is in fact not very explicit, as is clear from the attempts by early copyists to amend the text by providing the missing verb. Since these variants obviously are secondary attempts, the verb most likely should be implicitly borrowed from v. 21—thus marking a very close connection. V. 21 functions not as much as a heading as a transition and a sounding board for the household code. It also means that the exhortation to wives that they be subject to their husbands, serves as the primary example of the mutual submission which is required of all believers as a manifestation of their communal life in the Spirit.

In this perspective the household code is an application of the initial and general prerequisite of mutual subordination. It is not uncommon among commentators to infer that this initial and programmatic emphasis on mutual submission is why the power of the superior partners (husbands, fathers and masters) is being so carefully defined and modified. They are being told to treat their subordinates with love, care and consideration rather than to rule or control—other than themselves and their own temper. In the Christian appropriation dominion is modified, and patriarchy assumes the deceptive, friendly face of paternalism (cf. the previous reference to "Liebespatriarkalismus"). This is general for the household codes, and even if the verbs prescribing how wives and slaves should behave (ὑποτάσσω and ὑπακούω) are more of a constant than the corresponding term for husbands and masters, the usage of ἀγαπάω in the Ephesian code is not an original choice by this author. As indicated by Col 3:19, it is likely to have been the main verb in the exhortation to husbands already in the form in which it was received by the author of Ephesians. In other words, the christological/ecclesiological elaborations do not have an ethical emphasis on love as their conclusion. The opposite is more likely the case so that the traditional admonishment to love provided an occasion for the author to expound the nature of this love by introducing as a model for it the relationship between Christ and his church.

However, no one seems to question that the primary purpose of the household code is either to ensure political and social credibility by maintaining a rhetoric of domestic subordination of wives, children and slaves and thereby living up to standard, or to develop a theology of a Christian marriage in dialectic reciprocity between subordination and loving care. There might, of course, be added benefits as well—such as the construction of a Christian doctrine of marriage and household relationships that was able to compete on the larger market of religious and philosophical groups.[18] In my view, all these interpretations, despite their variations, tend to disregard that the problem with which the Ephesian household code primarily deals, is not subordination but superiority.

The all-dominant theme of the Letter to Ephesians is unity or rather reconciliation and unification both at a cosmic level and in the human community. The divine μυστήριον, is God's plan to gather up τὰ πάντα in Christ, both the things in heaven and the things on earth (1:10). This means that alienation is brought to an end, both the alienation between heaven and earth and the alienation between human beings as exemplified by the unification of Jews and Gentiles in one community. The readers of the letter are called upon to manifest unity on earth, and the unity of the community is a sign of the cosmic unification.[19]

It is possible that the enigmatic expression in 2:14 ὁ ποιήσας τὰ ἀμφότερα ἕν reflects a myth of reunion of male and female. It is an essential part of the universal unification, and is since ethically explicated or converted in the household code where elements of the same mythical language occur. This demonstrates that "the one body", "the new human" is defined in terms of morality and in the end in very conventional terms of morality. But neither immediately nor necessarily does it *per se* lead to a reinforcement of conventional social roles.

The notion of a unity entered by the ritual of baptism, had a potential of suspending traditional divisions between Jew and Gentile, slave and free, man and woman. Its primary ethical affinity would be to establish common ideals for the whole of the community, rather than to specify the role of each group. It is clear already from the letters of Paul that this constantly ongoing project of a liminal life, caused unrest and conflicts in many communities and rendered them vulnerable to criticism from the larger and polite society. With more or less ambivalence, conventional

---

18 Especially Teobald, "Heilige Hochzeit," has this competitive perspective.
19 Meeks, "In one body," 214ff.; Tanzer, "Ephesians," 326f.

ideals and definitions of social roles are reintroduced by New Testament writers as they explore the compromises of a life in this yet existing world. The almost ironical result is that Christian uniqueness is urged to manifest itself in common and broadly popular moral terms.[20]

An ethical ambivalence is also present in Ephesians. The rhetoric of reconciliation and unification makes it susceptible to an abolishment of dividing barriers of most kinds. Accordingly, the Christians have all the same Master in heaven with whom there is no partiality, and the Spirit is manifest among them as they all be subject to one another out of reverence for Christ. Mutual submission is the specific ethos of the whole community.

If there is to be any accommodation to a conventional order of domestic roles, a convenient path could, of course, be to define specific types of submission.[21] Far more urgent and difficult is, however, the opposite task which is the one the author undertakes: How may a role of superiority in human relationships be maintained in a way that still is concordant with the general mutuality of submission and with the dominant theme of unity of the Christians? This is the purpose of the household code and its major point. It represents an attempt at exploring an understanding of domination that does not violate the prerequisite of mutual submission. If mutual submission is a manifestation of the Spirit in the Christian community, how is it possible to maintain or remain faithful to the social order of the larger community where the submission and obedience of one group is nothing but an adequate acceptance of the given superiority of their lords and masters? The unique feature of the Ephesian version is its overwhelming and explicit interest in expounding the role of the man in a marriage relationship. The role at stake is not primarily that of the subordinate female partner, but the ruling role of the male.

---

20 Cf. Meeks, "In one Body," 215, indicating that the Christians "learned from the apologists of the synagogue to define their uniqueness vis a vis the larger society in terms familiar to the popular moralists".

21 Cf. Lincoln, *Ephesians*, 366, who criticises those who use v. 21 to completely relativise what follows and assume "that the ensuing household code contains a viewpoint with which the writer does not entirely agree". He insists that "justice has to be done *both* to the force of v. 21 *and* to the force of the specific types of submission in the household code". Keenan, *Paul*, 141, moves along the same lines when asking: "Why does Paul, who calls for mutual submission, deal more explicitly with the submission of wives than with that of husbands?" They are both good examples of interpretations assuming that subordination remains the focus of interest in the Ephesian code.

The change towards this emphasis in the Ephesian code is evident already from its special distribution of material. As I have pointed out before, there is, relatively speaking, in Ephesians less of a particular interest in slaves. The focus has been shifted to the first section on wives and husbands which is expanded disproportionately. Nearly 60% of the total bulk of the Ephesian household code goes into this section. But within that section comparatively little is said to the wives.[22] This is the more remarkable since in the other examples where the wife-husband relationship occupies a larger section (in 1 Peter and the Pastoral Letters), the wives receive more space and attention than the husbands. While in those cases the parenetical attention is on subordination, the focus in Ephesians both in terms of parenetical concretisation and in terms of theological elaboration and motivation, is on the role of the man. The ten words directed to husbands in the Colossian code have become one hundred and forty-three in Ephesians. It is also the first section that grammatically constitutes an independent communicative unit, addressing the group in question by an undoubtedly vocative form.[23]

The orientation towards the role of the man becomes clear already in 5:23. The slightly amputated exhortation to the wives in 5:22, has a sharpening alteration of the Christological reference available in the Colossian version ὡς ἀνῆκεν ἐν κυρίῳ (Col 3:18). In Ephesians it simply and harshly states ὡς τῷ κυρίῳ. The wives should be subject to their husbands as to the Lord. Their conjugal and domestic submission should take their primary subordination to the Lord as an example. This is in v. 23 motivated by a statement not about the wife, but about the husband being the head of the wife just as Christ is the head of the church.

The image of head[24] is the clue to the introduction of superiority and it is connected with the organic image of the church as body. In Paul's usage of the body image this connection is not made. From 1 Cor 11:3 it is clear that the idea of a man being the head of his wife was part of a conventional statement that included and defined this relationship within a hierarchy of relationships. But in 1 Cor 11 Christ is the head—not of the church—but of every man. The basic terminology is the same but it takes in Ephesians on a new dimension when the forceful combination of christology and ecclesiology (Christ as the head of his body, the church) is made ethically effective for the husband–wife relationship.

---

22 Sampley, *One Flesh*, 26. For more word statistics cf. Lincoln, *Ephesians*, 355.
23 Teobald, "Heilige Hochzeit," 231 n. 47.
24 Lincoln, *Ephesians*, 368f., provides a good discussion on this.

And there is no way that it here may mean "source". It clearly refers to supremacy; cf. also Eph 1:22.

Because of the husband's superior position, the wife's relationship to her husband should reflect the same total submission as the church owes to Christ. Correspondingly the husband should love his wife just as Christ loves the church. The image serves to introduce headship as the common prerogative of Christ and husbands, but it never makes any direct prototypical identification saying that the husband is like Christ or the wife is like the church. It may be true that the maleness of Christ is not incidental to this text and that the nuptial symbolism does not remain abstract.[25] But the similarities are not ontological but relational.[26] They are invoked rather by the transfer of relational terms indicating attitude and behaviour—more so from above to below than the opposite way.

On the one hand this differentiation leaves the author free to make christological statements that is not meant to be referred to the husband–wife relationship such as Christ himself being the saviour of the body. On the other hand, a one-sided identification of wives and church would be extremely difficult to maintain with any consistency since the husbands hardly could be excluded from being members of the church also perceived as the body of Christ. In the programmatic opening statement of the epistle in 1:14 the author sets over against one another the same dual characteristics that later dominate his concerns in 5:26-27.[27]

However, there is a shift of the image during the long and also straying exhortation to husbands in Eph 5:25-33, which partly may be due to this strain of the analogy. To love the wife as Christ loves the church and as the head loves the body leads to the final argument that loving the wife is for the husband to love himself and his own body since they, according to Scripture, are one flesh.[28] The wife becomes himself. It thereby becomes possible for the man to be both head and body at the same time. And the relationship to the wife is inescapably a reflection of his relationship to himself. The same dilemma may further explain the, in the context peculiar, usage of the inclusive pronoun "we" in what

---

25 Tanzer, "Ephesians," 333, with a reference to B. Brooten.
26 Cf. B. Witherington III, *Women in the Earliest Churches*. (Cambridge: Cambridge University Press 1988), 58.
27 Sampley, *One Flesh*, 74.
28 I find myself in agreement with those who see this as the argumentative significance of the citation from Genesis in the context; so both Lincoln, *Ephesians*, and Sampley, *One Flesh*.

appears to be an intrusion in v. 30: "because we are members of his body".

The image of a body as applied to social organisations or structures has in its parenetical effect an in-build resistance to fundamental change which accounts for its political usefulness.[29] The interdependence renders importance to each member in their specific function. However insignificant and subordinate it may feel or seem, even the most humble part is indispensable and has an effect on the totality. This inclusiveness is the strength of the image, as is clear when Paul in 1 Cor 12 warns the nobel parts like the head and the eye against the arrogant illusion of self-sufficiency. But it is also excellently suited to silence any objections to a present state of affairs: each should remain content in his or her allocated station. The image of the body defends that stratified differentiation into a hierarchy of roles need not compromise but promote the unity of the group. The combination of the body image with the image of the head strengthens this dimension.

It is, however, interesting that the introduction of ecclesiology into the motivating section of the household code, in Ephesians does not lead to an ecclesiology based on a household model like the one we see developing in the Pastoral Letters. The latter in the end entails a confusion of both the literary and ethical pattern of the household code itself.

The Ephesian household code struggles with how members of the Christian community should be brought to accept and even approve a hierarchy of roles in circumstances where many of them had no choice but to relate and submit to the power structures of the outside world. If they are not withdrawn into the shelter of ascetic renunciation, they have to remain and function as members of households and thereby under public attention and regulations.

The emphasis of the Ephesian code is on the wife–husband relationship, but it does not primarily call the wives to order by submission even if that is clearly also wanted. Its focus is on the exercise of headship which might seem to be contrary to the common ideals of Christian submission. The men are encouraged to observe their ruling role in marriage and household. It is to the author theologically acceptable provided that it is exercised according to the paradigm of Christ's love for the church. It is thereby restrained as well as maintained. The language of unifica-

---

29 Cf. the examples given by C. K. Barrett, *A Commentary on The First Epistle to the Corinthians*. (London: Black 1971, 2nd ed.), 287, and also W. A. Meeks, *The First Urban Christians. The Social World of the Apostle Paul*. (New Haven, CT/London: Yale University Press 1983), 89f.

tion is by means of the organic image of head and body converted into moral terms to ascertain what seems to have been the indisputable superiority of the male. Even in minority they remained representatives of the ruling majority in society, while the women are called to be the real exemplary Christians by their overfulfilment of the life in the Spirit. Therefore, in this compromise with the ethos of the world no one in the end comes out a winner.

Jünger als Gewalttäter
(Mt 11,12f.; Lk 16,16)

Der Stürmerspruch als Selbststigmatisierung einer Minorität

Gerd Theißen

Wie können Minoritäten auf die Gesamtgesellschaft einwirken? Wie können sie aus der Position der Ohnmacht heraus Macht ausüben? In direkter Konfrontation mit den Mächtigen müssen sie meist unterliegen. Aber ihnen bleibt ein anderer Weg. Minoritäten können durch Selbststigmatisierung, d.h. durch die demonstrative Übernahme sozialmoralisch verachteter Außenseiterrollen, bestehende Werte und Normen erschüttern[1]. Sie können durch ihr abweichendes Verhalten die Frage aufwerfen, ob sie, die nach den geltenden Werten und Normen verurteilt werden, nicht in Wirklichkeit positiven Wert haben, wohingegen die Normen, die sie verurteilen, fragwürdig sind. In Zeiten der Umorientierung können Minoritäten auf diesem Wege neue Werte oder Wertinterpretationen zur Geltung bringen. Ihr Stigma kann in Charisma umschlagen, ihr Defizit an Wert in die Fähigkeit, Werte neu zu interpretieren, neu zu definieren und durchzusetzen.

Die Jesusbewegung war eine Minorität mit sozial-abweichendem Verhalten. Wir finden in ihren Überlieferungen oft die demonstrative Uminterpretation von Stigmata in Vorzüge. Angesichts der hereinbrechenden Gottesherrschaft werden die Armen glücklich gepriesen (Mt

---

1 Das zugrunde liegende Konzept eines grundlegenden Zusammenhangs von Stigma und Charisma stammt von dem Soziologen W. Lipp. Vgl. dessen zusammenfassende Darstellung in: "Charisma – Schuld und Gnade. Soziale Konstruktion, Kulturdynamik, Handlungsdrama", in: W. Gebhardt / A. Zingerle / M. N. Ebertz (Hrsg.), *Charisma. Theorie – Religion – Politik* (Materiale Soziologie TB 3, Berlin/New York: de Gruyter 1993), 15-32. Zur Anwendung auf das Urchristentum vgl. M. N. Ebertz, *Das Charisma des Gekreuzigten. Zur Soziologie der Jesusbewegung* (WUNT 45, Tübingen: Mohr 1987) und H. Mödritzer, *Stigma und Charisma im Neuen Testament und seiner Umwelt. Zur Soziologie des Urchristentums* (NTOA 28, Freiburg Schweiz/Göttingen: Universitätsverlag/Vandenhoeck 1994).

5,3), wird den Kranken und Behinderten frohe Botschaft gebracht (Mt 11,2-6) und den Sanftmütigen das Land zugesprochen (Mt 5,5). Läßt sich auch der viel umrätselte Stürmerspruch als solch eine demonstrative Umwertung verstehen? Die Antwort ist nicht leicht. Denn bei der Auslegung des Stürmerspruchs ist fast alles umstritten, insbesondere aber das, was in unserem Zusammenhang entscheidend ist: die in ihm zum Ausdruck kommende Wertung[2].

Ein gewisser Konsens besteht nur hinsichtlich der Rekonstruktion der ursprünglichen Fassung des Spruches in Q. Die lk Version gilt allgemein als sekundäre Erleichterung: In ihr wird die Gottesherrschaft "verkündigt" und (nicht so direkt wie bei Mt) mit "Gewalttat" in Verbindung gebracht. Mt bringt hier die schwierigere Version. Umgekehrt wird oft damit gerechnet, daß die lk Reihenfolge der beiden Spruchhälften ursprünglicher ist[3]:

Mt 11,12f	Lk 16,16
	Das Gesetz und die Propheten reichen bis zu Johannes.
Aber von den Tagen Johannes des Täufers bis heute leidet das Himmelreich Gewalt, und Gewalttäter reißen es an sich. Denn alle Propheten und das Gesetz haben geweissagt bis hin zu Johannes.	*Von da an wird das Evangelium vom Reich Gottes gepredigt und jedermann drängt mit Gewalt hinein.*

Die Umstellung bot Mt die Gelegenheit, mit der Zeitbestimmung "von den Tagen Johannes des Täufers" an den vorhergehenden V. 11 anzuknüpfen, der den Täufer aus allen Menschen hervorhebt; der Täufer steht sowohl am Ende der vergangenen Zeit wie am Beginn der Gottesherrschaft. Das entspricht mt Theologie, die den Täufer als Vorläufer Jesu sieht, ihn aber zugleich an Jesus angleicht und beide die "Himmelsherrschaft" verkündigen läßt (Mt 3,2/3,17). Die nachgestellte Spruch-

---

2 Einen ausführlichen Forschungsbericht bringt P. S. Cameron, *Violence and Kingdom. The Interpretation of Matthew 11,12* (ANTI 5, Frankfurt/Bern/New York/Nancy: Lang 1984), 4-213. Im folgenden weise ich innerhalb der forschungsgeschichtlichen Übersicht manchmal auf dies Werk zurück, ohne die referierten Arbeiten voll bibliographisch aufzuführen.

3 Das ist kein allgemeiner Konsens. J. Weiß, *Die Predigt Jesu vom Reiche Gottes* (Göttingen: Vandenhoeck [2]1900), 192-197 und P. Hoffmann, *Studien zur Theologie der Logienquelle* (NTA 8, Münster: Aschendorff 1972; [3]1982), 51-60, verteidigen die mt Reihenfolge als ursprünglicher.

hälfte formuliert Mt in demselben Sinne um: "Propheten und Gesetz" (in dieser Reihenfolge) prophezeien auf den Täufer hin. Beide gehen dem Täufer voraus. Beide sind als Prophetie weiterhin gültig, so daß ein antinomistisches Verständnis des Spruches ausgeschlossen ist; auch das in Übereinstimmung mit mt Theologie, die in Jesus den Erfüller des Gesetzes sieht (Mt 5,17ff.). In Lk 16,16 liegt die Zäsur dagegen eher zwischen Täufer und Jesus. Das widerspricht lk Theologie, obwohl man das lange anders gesehen hat[4]. Denn Lk parallelisiert beide Gestalten in den Kindheitsgeschichten und faßt sie in der Act zusammen (Act 10,37-41). Die ursprüngliche Fassung des Stürmerspruchs hätte dann in Q so gelautet, wie er fast wörtlich bei Justin (dial. 51,3) erhalten ist[5].

ὁ νόμος καὶ οἱ προφῆται ἕως Ἰωάννου
ἀπὸ τότε ἡ βασιλεία τοῦ θεοῦ βιάζεται
καὶ βιασταὶ ἁρπάζουσιν αὐτήν.

Unabhängig davon aber ist die Deutung des Stürmerspruchs stark umstritten. Die entscheidenden Probleme ergeben sich daraus, daß 1. βιάζεται sowohl als Medium wie als Passiv gedeutet werden kann[6], daß 2. die βιασταί in bonam partem als auch in malam partem interpretiert werden können[7] und daß es 3. mehrere Möglichkeiten gibt, sie auf kon-

---

4   Vor allem H. Conzelmann, *Die Mitte der Zeit. Studien zur Theologie des Lukas* (Tübingen: Mohr 1954; [6]1977), 16f., 20, wollte in Lk 16,16 einen Beleg für seine These finden, daß Lk den Täufer scharf von der Zeit Jesu abgrenzt.
5   Nach P. S. Cameron, *Violence*, 199, ist diese Rekonstruktion "the most widely held opinion". Unabhängig von ihm gelangt auch D. Kosch, *Die Gottesherrschaft im Zeichen des Widerspruchs. Traditions- und redaktionsgeschichtliche Untersuchung von Lk 16,16/Mt 11,12f bei Jesus, Q und Lukas* (EHS XXIII, 257, Bern/Frankfurt/New York: Lang 1985), 18 u.ö., zu demselben Ergebnis. Vgl. u.a. A. Polag, *Fragmenta Q, Textheft zur Logienquelle* (Neukirchen-Vluyn: Neukirchener Verlag 1979), 74; S. Schulz, *Q. Die Spruchquelle der Evangelisten* (Zürich: Theologischer Verlag 1972), 262; J. Gnilka, *Das Matthäusevangelium* (HThK I, 1, Freiburg/Basel/Wien: Herder 1986), 413. Eine andere Rekonstruktion legt B. D. Chilton, *God in Strength. Jesus' Announcement of the Kingdom* (SNTU B, 1, Freistadt: Pöchl 1979), 205-230 vor. Er ersetzt die dritte Zeile durch die lk Version καὶ πᾶς εἰς αὐτὴν βιάζεται. Jedoch ist die mt Fassung eindeutig die lectio difficilior.
6   Die Deutung als Passiv dominiert in der alten Kirche, die mediale Deutung begegnet zuerst bei Melanchthon, dann bei J. A. Bengel, H. E. G. Paulus, Th. Zahn, A. v. Harnack, R. Otto u.a.; vgl. P. S. Cameron, *Violence*, 55f., 66, 67f., 122f., 123ff.
7   Die Deutung in bonam partem ist die allgemein herrschende bei den Kirchenvätern. Erst bei Karlstadt begegnet die Deutung in malam partem (P. S. Cameron, *Violence*, 48ff.). Sie wird von Alexander Schweizer 1836 neu begründet (ebd. 77ff. s. folgende Anm.) und hat seitdem die Überhand erhalten.

krete geschichtliche Gruppen zu deuten. Die folgende Übersicht soll die wichtigsten Alternativen verdeutlichen. Das Wort kann nach dieser Übersicht in der vermuteten Q-Fassung in vierfacher Weise verstanden werden:

Das Gesetz und die Propheten (sind) bis Johannes.
Von da ab

wird die Gottesherrschaft vergewaltigt (Passiv)	setzt sich die Gottesherrschaft gewaltsam durch (Medium)

| und feindliche Gewalttäter erbeuten sie (in malam partem)[8]. | und entschlossene Rebellen erbeuten sie (in bonam partem)[9]. | und feindliche Gewalttäter erbeuten sie (in malam partem)[10]. | und entschlossene Rebellen erbeuten sie (in bonam partem)[11]. |

Bei der inhaltlichen Deutung der "Gewalttäter" bzw. "Rebellen" lassen sich weiterhin drei Grundtypen unterscheiden: Die Gewalttäter gelten 1.

---

8 Die Deutung "Passiv + in malam partem" wird vertreten von A. Schweizer, "Ob in der Stelle Matth. xi,12 ein Lob oder ein Tadel erhalten sei?", in: *ThStKr* 9 (1836), 90-122; G. Schrenk, Art. βιάζομαι, in: *ThWNT* I, 608-613; P. S. Cameron, *Violence*, 214ff.

9 Die Deutung "Passiv + in bonam partem" war in der patristischen Exegese vorherrschend – was zeigt, daß sie nicht nur sprachlich möglich ist, sondern griechischem Sprachverständnis nahelag. Dabei faßten die Kirchenväter βιάζω durchaus negativ auf, verstanden aber den gesamten Spruch positiv, da βιάζω z.B. ein Bild für asketische Selbstdisziplin war. Unter den modernen Exegeten trat W. Haupt, *Worte Jesu und Gemeindeüberlieferung. Eine Untersuchung zur Quellengeschichte der Synopse* (Leipzig: Hinrichs 1913), 84ff., für diese Deutung ein: Heiden haben sich an die Stelle Israels in die Gottesherrschaft hineingedrängt.

10 Die Deutung "Medium + in malam partem" wird selten vertreten, so von O. Betz, "Jesu Heiliger Krieg", in: *NT* 2 (1958), 116-137 und D. Kosch, *Gottesherrschaft*, 23-27. Die meisten Exegeten, die ein mediales Verständnis von βιάζεται haben, deuten die "Gewalttäter" in bonam partem.

11 Für die Deutung "Medium + in bonam partem" treten ein: A. v. Harnack, *Zwei Worte Jesu (Mt 6,13 = Luk 11,4; Mt 11,12f. = Luk 16,16)* (Sitzungsberichte der Berliner Akademie 53/1907), 942-957; R. Otto, *Reich Gottes und Menschensohn. Ein religionsgeschichtlicher Versuch* (München: Beck 1934), 84ff.; E. Percy, *Die Botschaft Jesu. Eine traditionskritische und exegetische Untersuchung* (Lund: Gleerup 1953), 191-202; B. D. Chilton, *God in Strenght*, 229f. und zuletzt G. Häfner, "Gewalt gegen die Basileia? Zum Problem der Auslegung des 'Stürmerspruches' Mt 11,12," *ZNW* 83 (1992), 21-51.

als Feinde der Gottesherrschaft, 2. als Konkurrenten der Jesusbewegung oder 3. als Anhänger Jesu. Da jeweils politische oder nicht-politische Motive unterstellt werden können, erhalten wir sechs Deutungen, die in verschiedenen Varianten vertreten werden:

Zunächst seien die Deutungen in malam partem zusammengestellt, bei denen der Stürmerspruch als Kritik und Tadel verstanden wir:

Die "Gewalttäter" sind:	mit politischer Motivation	ohne politische Motivation
Feinde der Gottesherrschaft	antiherodianische Deutung: Sie sind Machthaber Palästinas[12].	antidämonische Deutung: Sie sind Dämonen und der Satan[13].
Konkurrenten um die Gottesherrschaft	antizelotische Deutung: Sie sind Widerstandskämpfer[14].	antipharisäische Deutung: Sie sind Schriftgelehrte wie in Mt 23,13[15].

---

12 P. S. Cameron, *Violence*, 64f., 70 nennt A. Calmet (1726) und C. G. Bretschneider (1824) als Vorläufer der antiherodianischen Deutung: Sie erwähnen die Gefangenschaft des Täufers als Beispiel für Gewalttat gegen das Gottesreich. A. Schlatter, *Johannes der Täufer* (ed. M. Michaelis) (Basel: Reinhardt 1956, 66-75) vertrat diese Deutung in seiner unveröffentlichten Dissertation. G. Schrenk, *ThWNT* I, 610 trat für sie ein. Ihr wichtigster Vertreter ist z.Zt. P. S. Cameron, *Violence*, 244, der in Lk 16,15b-18 eine antiherodäische Spruchsammlung sieht: V. 15b spiele auf Gewalttat und Ehescheidung des Herodes Antipas an, V. 16b kritisiere sein Vorgehen gegen den Täufer, V. 18 seine Ehescheidung. – Das Problem bleibt: Warum redet Jesus von dem Gottesreich, wenn er dessen Repräsentanten meint? Und warum redet er von mehreren "Gewalttätern", wenn er Herodes Antipas treffen will? Unmöglich ist die antiherodäische Deutung nicht, aber sie ist auf Zusatzannahmen angewiesen.

13 Die antidämonische Deutung wurde durch M. Dibelius, *Die urchristliche Überlieferung von Johannes dem Täufer* (FRLANT 15, Göttingen: Vandenhoeck 1911), 23ff. begründet. Ähnlich R. Otto, *Reich Gottes*, 84ff. O. Betz, *Jesu heiliger Krieg*, 116ff. kombiniert die antidämonische Deutung mit der Beziehung auf politische Machthaber: Hinter den feindlichen irdischen Herrschern stehe letztlich der Satan. Zustimmend M. Hengel, *Die Zeloten, Untersuchungen zur jüdischen Freiheitsbewegung in der Zeit von Herodes I. bis 70 n.Chr.* (Leiden/Köln: Brill 1961; [2]1976), 345. Das Problem dieser Deutung ist die Datierung "seit den Tagen des Johannes": Dämonen waren schon vor dem Auftreten des Täufers aktiv. Man muß die Zusatzannahme machen, daß sie seitdem erst gegen die Gottesherrschaft aktiv werden konnten.

| Anhänger Jesu mit falscher Einstellung | antimessianische Deutung: Sie wollen Jesus als irdischen König (Joh 6,15)[16]. | gegen Antinomisten: Sie sind gesetzesfreie Anhänger Jesu[17]. |

Interessant ist, daß sich bei einer Interpretation in bonam partem der Deutungsspielraum sofort einengt. Sieht man von der Deutung auf Täufer und Jesus selbst ab[18], so wären immer Anhänger Jesu gemeint. Unterschiede ergeben sich dadurch, daß verschiedene Verhaltenszüge bei ihnen im Blick sein können: so können Zöllner und Sünder gemeint sein, deren unrechtmäßiges Eindringen in die Gottesherrschaft verteidigt

---

14 Die antizelotische Deutung wurde von A. Schweizer 1836 begründet (vgl. P. S. Cameron, *Violence*, 77-86). Er sah die Schwierigkeit, daß der zelotische Widerstand gegen die Gottesherrschaft nicht mit dem Täufer begann, sondern mit Judas Galilaeus. Er nahm daher an, Jesus habe die zelotische Partei nicht zu weiteren Gewalttaten provozieren wollen, daher habe er verhüllt gesprochen. Die antizelotische Deutung wurde von J. Weiß, *Predigt*, 192-197 erneuert und wird in der Gegenwart vor allem von P. Hoffmann, *Logienquelle*, 66-79 im Zusammenhang mit einer antizelotischen Deutung der ganzen Logienquelle vertreten. – Auch hier paßt die Datierung "seit den Tagen des Johannes" nicht. Nur mit Hilfe von Zusatzannahmen läßt sich diese Deutung durchführen.

15 P. S. Cameron, *Violence*, 70f. nennt als ersten Vertreter dieser antipharisäischen Deutung M. Schneckenburger (1832), der in Mt 23,13 den Typos des "Gewalttäters" von Mt 11,12f. vorgebildet sieht. Ein prominenter Vertreter dieser Deutung war nach P. S. Cameron, *Violence*, 97, ferner A. Hilgenfeld (1854). – Wenn die Schriftgelehrten den Zugang zur Gottesherrschaft versperren, so sind freilich nicht sie die "Gewalttäter", sondern diejenigen, die sich gegen ihren Widerstand den Weg zur Gottesherrschaft bahnen.

16 Auch diese "antimessianische" Deutung hat eine lange Vorgeschichte. P. S. Cameron, *Violence*, 69f. nennt als ersten Vertreter J. C. R. Eckermann (1806), der Joh 6,15 als Hintergrund von Mt 11,12f. auffaßt. Es ist die erste Deutung, die eine bewußte "Beschleunigung" des Kommens der Gottesherrschaft annimmt und nicht an Feinde, sondern fehlgeleitete Anhänger Jesu denkt. Auch A. Schweizer (1836) und B. Weiß (1883) verweisen in diesem Sinne auf Joh 6,15 (vgl. P. S. Cameron, *Violence*, 83, 112f.). In der Gegenwart wird diese Deutung vor allem von P. W. Barnett, "Who were the 'biastai' (Matthew 11,12-13)", in: *RTR* 36 (1977), 65-70 vertreten. – Schwierig bleibt: Die 'Vergewaltigung' bezieht sich auf die Gottesherrschaft, nicht auf Jesus; und sie erstreckt sich über eine längere Zeit und nicht auf die situativ begrenzte Konfrontation Jesu mit Messiaserwartungen.

17 Die Deutung gegen "Antinomisten" wurde im letzten Jahrhundert von F. F. Zyro, "Erklärung von Matth. 11,12", in: *ThStKr* 33 (1860), 398-410 und "Neue Auslegung der Stelle Matth. 11,12", in: *ThStKr* 46 (1873), 663-704 (dazu P. S. Cameron, *Violence*, 99-106) vertreten. Sie ist vom lk Kontext von Lk 16,16 inspiriert und wurde erst sekundär auf Mt 11,12f. ausgedehnt: Die Gewalttäter wollen ohne Gesetz und Buße ins Gottesreich gelangen und mit Mose nichts zu tun haben!

wird[19]; oder die Schar der Jesusanhänger, die durch ihre Umkehr das Gottesreich herbeizwingen will[20]; oder Asketen, die durch Selbstüberwindung in die Gottesherrschaft eindringen[21]. Extensional, d.h. dem Umfang nach, umfaßt der Begriff βιασταί hier immer in etwa dieselbe Gruppe, intensional jedoch verschiedene Aspekte.

Die Fülle möglicher Deutungen läßt sich m.E. eingrenzen, wenn man einige Kriterien berücksichtigt: (1.) Die Interpretation des Stürmerspruchs muß die Aussage verständlich machen, daß die Gewalttäter die Gottesherrschaft tatsächlich "erbeuten"; sein Verständnis im Sinne eines Versuchs, sie zu erbeuten, basiert dagegen auf einer zusätzlichen Annahme. (2.) Die Interpretation muß plausibel machen, daß die Tätigkeit der βιασταί erst mit dem Auftreten des Täufers datiert wird. Nimmt man für die Zeit vorher wohl ihre Existenz, für die Zeit seit seinem Auftreten aber erst ihre Wirksamkeit an, so führt man eine rechtfertigungsbedürftige Zusatzannahme ein. (3.) Die Interpretation muß berücksichtigen, daß es sich um einen metaphorischen Ausdruck handelt. Die Verknüpfung von Gottesherrschaft und βιασταί verbindet semantisch inkongruente Wörter. Wie jede Metapher muß sie im Rahmen des gan-

---

18 J. P. Lange, *Das Evangelium nach Matthäus* (Bielefeld/Leipzig: Velhagen & Klasing 1857; [4]1878) z.St. denkt an Johannes und Jesus selbst als "Gewalttäter", die das Himmelreich erobern: "Christus der Bringer des Himmelreichs von dem Jenseits aus ist zugleich der Eroberer des Himmelreichs von dem Diesseits aus" (zit. n. P. S. Cameron, *Violence*, 98).

19 F. Danker, "Lk 16,16 – An Opposition Logion", in: *JBL* 77 (1958), 231-243, vertritt die These, Jesus zitiere in Lk 16,16 seine Gegner mit dem Vorwurf, daß Zöllner und Sünder die Gottesherrschaft vergewaltigen: Bei Jesus steht sie für alle offen. W. Stenger, Art. βιάζομαι (*EWNT* I), 518-521 und J. Schlosser, *Le règne de Dieu dans les dits de Jésus* (EtB, Paris: Gabalda 1980), 509-539 halten das für ein mögliches Verständnis des Wortes im Munde Jesu.

20 Diese 'heilsaktivistische' Deutung des Stürmerspruchs führt P. S. Cameron, *Violence*, 92f., auf Ch. H. Weisse zurück: Jesus spreche von dem durch ihn geschehenen Herabziehen des Himmelreichs auf die Erde als einer Gewalttat, die er und seine Jünger am Himmelreich verüben. A. Schweitzer, *Von Reimarus zu Wrede* (Tübingen: Mohr 1906), 354 = *Geschichte der Leben-Jesu-Forschung* (Tübingen: Mohr [7]1966), 415 hat diese Deutung nur geringfügig modifiziert: Nicht Jesus und der Täufer arbeiten am Kommen des Reiches, "sondern die Schar der Büßenden ringt es Gott ab." (vgl. dazu P. S. Cameron, *Violence*, 120-122). Zu den rabbinischen Parallelen, die eine Einflußnahme des Menschen auf das Kommen der Endzeit bezeugen, vgl. D. Daube, "Violence to the Kingdom", in: ders., *The New Testament and Rabbinic Judaism* (Jordan Lectures in Comparative Religion 2, London: The Athlone Press 1956), 285-300.

21 Das war die gängige Auslegung bei den griechischen Kirchenvätern, vgl. P. S. Cameron, *Violence*, 4-16.

zen Bildfeldes gedeutet werden, d.h. im Zusammenhang anderer rebellischer Metaphern in der Jesusbewegung.

ad 1) Der Stürmerspruch sagt, daß die "Gewalttäter" die Gottesherrschaft erbeuten. Sie haben Erfolg. Ihr Handeln wird mit ἁρπάζειν beschrieben und nicht mit μέλλουσιν ... ἁρπάζειν (wie in Joh 6,15). "Erbeuten" ist effektiv gemeint. Ein konatives Verständnis ist zwar nicht ausgeschlossen, bedarf aber zusätzlicher Argumente, um als notwendig zu erscheinen[22]. Bei einem effektiven "Erbeuten" würden alle Interpretationen in malam partem entfallen. Denn diese behaupten, daß Feinde, Konkurrenten oder Anhänger die Gottesherrschaft tatsächlich überwältigen, obwohl sie deren Intentionen entgegenarbeiten. Der Stürmerspruch würde von einer Niederlage Gottes sprechen. Das ist unwahrscheinlich[23]. Anders steht es mit dem Verständnis von βιάζειν. Dies Wort läßt sich auch konativ als Versuch eines gewaltsamen Zwingens oder Drängens deuten. Das zeigen einige Belege bei Josephus (Ant 16,37; Bell 3,423; 5,60)[24]. So verstanden würden die beiden Hälften des Stürmerspruchs nicht in einer Tautologie bestehen: Die Gottesherrschaft wird vielmehr zunächst mit Gewalt bekämpft (ohne daß dies notwendigerweise schon den Erfolg dieser Gewalttat einschließt); Gewalttäter erbeuten sie dann (und haben dabei Erfolg). Es handelt sich um einen

---

22 Die Schwierigkeiten einer konativen Bedeutung des "Erbeutens" betont mit Recht G. Häfner, *Gewalt*, 41ff.

23 Am unwahrscheinlichsten ist die Deutung, nach der die Gottesherrschaft bei ihrer gewaltsamen Selbstdurchsetzung (βιάζεται = Medium) auf gewaltsamen Widerstand stoße (βιασταί = in malam partem). Genau diese "antithetische" Deutung vertritt D. Kosch, *Gottesherrschaft*, 23-27. Entweder gelangt man dabei in einen Widerspruch: Beide Seiten des Konflikts scheinen sich durchzusetzen. Oder man muß das "Gewaltausüben" der Gottesherrschaft als mißglückten Versuch, ihren "Raub" durch die Gewalttäter aber als erfolgreiches Handeln, bzw. umgekehrt das Rauben als mißglückten Versuch, das Sich-durchsetzen der Gottesherrschaft aber als effektiv auffassen. Alle drei Auffassungen machen Schwierigkeiten. Hinzu kommt, daß man bei einem antithetischen Verhältnis der beiden "gewalttätigen" Vorgänge ein adversatives δέ oder ἀλλά anstelle eines καί erwarten würde. D. Kosch, *Gottesherrschaft*, 26 Anm. 62 verweist zwar (wie schon andere vor ihm) auf einen adversativen Gebrauch des καί. Da aber die beiden Gliedsätze ohnehin durch βιάζεται und βιασταί verbunden sind, wäre im Stürmerspruch eine eindeutig adversative Konjunktion am Platz. Vgl. ferner die Einwände von G. Häfner, *Gewalt*, 43ff. gegen ein antithetisches Verständnis des Stürmerspruchs.

24 E. Moore, "BIAZO, APΠAZO and Cognates in Josephus", in: *NTS* 21 (1975), 519-543 betont S. 534 den konativen Sinn von βιάζω: "The context of the two words often shows that an attempt is being made to force people or things against their will or nature."

typischen synthetischen Parallelismus, der im zweiten Glied weiterführt, was im ersten gesagt ist[25].

ad 2) Die meisten Deutungen der "Gewalttäter" sind mit der ausdrücklichen Datierung ihres Wirkens "von den Tagen des Täufers an" nicht vereinbar[26]. Machthaber regierten nicht erst seit Johannes dem Täufer über Palästina. Dämonen gab es seit eh und je. Die Widerstandsbewegung gegen die Römer formte sich schon im Jahre 6 n.Chr. und hat Wurzeln, die bis in die Makkabäerzeit zurückreichen. Der Spruch läßt sich am unbefangensten deuten, wenn man ihn auf eine Bewegung bezieht, die erst seit den Tagen des Täufers wirksam war – also auf die Täufer- und Jesusbewegung selbst. Bei jedem anderen Verständnis muß man die Zusatzannahme machen, daß die Gewalttäter zwar vor dem Täufer existierten, aber erst seit den Tagen des Täufers die Gottesherrschaft bekämpfen konnten. Das ist nicht unmöglich. Andere Worte der Jesusüberlieferung rechnen jedoch mit einer bis auf die Schöpfung zurückgehenden Feindschaft der Menschen gegen Gott: Von Abel bis zum letzten umgebrachten Propheten wird ein großer Unheilszusammenhang gesehen (Lk 11,49-52). Schon die alten Propheten wurden verfolgt (Lk 11,47f.). Ein Geschichtsbild, nach dem die Feindschaft gegen Gott erst

---

25 Gegen ein passivisches Verständnis von βιάζεται wird immer wieder eingewandt, es entstünde eine Tautologie (z.B. bei D. Kosch, *Gottesherrschaft*, 23-27). Es entsteht jedoch ein für unsere Überlieferung charakteristischer Parallelismus membrorum, der entweder als synonymer oder synthetischer Parallelismus aufgefaßt werden kann. So mit Recht R. Schnackenburg, *Gottes Herrschaft und Reich* (Freiburg: Herder 1959; ²1961), 89. Das Nazaräerevangelium hat später diesen Parallelismus als synonymen verstanden. In ihm steht: "Das Himmelreich" wird geraubt (διαρπάζεται). Vgl. W. Schneemelcher, *Neutestamentliche Apokryphen I* (Tübingen: Mohr 1987), 134; K. Aland, *Synopsis Quattuor Evangeliorum* (Stuttgart: Württembergische Bibelanstalt 1964), 152.
26 Die Datierung ist selbst nicht eindeutig: ἀπό in der Wendung "seit den Tagen des Johannes" (Mt 11,12) und "seit dann" (Lk 16,16) kann exklusiv und inklusiv verstanden werden, d.h. so, daß Johannes selbst noch eingeschlossen wird oder ausgeschlossen ist. W. G. Kümmel, "Das Gesetz und die Propheten gehen bis Johannes" – Lukas 16,16 im Zusammenhang der heilsgeschichtlichen Theologie der Lukasschriften, in: O. Böcher/K. Haacker (eds.), *Verborum Veritas, FS G. Stählin* (Wuppertal: Brockhaus 1970), 89-102, hat wohl recht, wenn er vom Sprachgebrauch her keine Möglichkeit sieht, Johannes aus- oder einzuschließen. Johannes ist auf jeden Fall ein Wendepunkt in der Geschichte. Die verschiedene Anordnung der Sätze führt bei Mt dazu, daß er eher als Ausgangspunkt einer neuen Bewegung erscheint, bei Lk eher als Endpunkt einer Epoche. Vielleicht wird in Mt 11,12f. sogar eine Dreiteilung anvisiert: 1. die Zeit bis Johannes, 2. die Zeit der "Gewalttäter" bis jetzt und 3. eine neue Zeit – nach der vorhergehenden Krise.

seit dem Täufer in ein von der vorhergehenden Epoche klar unterschiedenes Stadium getreten sei, wird durch andere Aussagen nicht bestätigt. Wohl aber ein Geschichtsbild, nach dem in der Gegenwart eine alles Vorherige überbietende Heilszeit begonnen hat (vgl. Mt 12,41f.; 13,16f).

K. Syreeni hat eine bestechende neue Deutung des Stürmerspruchs vorgeschlagen, die dem deuteronomistischen Geschichtsbild einer kontinuierlichen Feindschaft Israels gegen Gott entspricht[27]. Der Stürmerspruch lautet nach seiner Deutung sinngemäß: "Das Gesetz und die Propheten (wurden) bis Johannes (vergewaltigt), von jetzt ab wird (auch) der Gottesherrschaft Gewalt angetan ..." Aber darf man stillschweigend im ersten Satz dasselbe Verb wie im zweiten ergänzen, wenn dabei ein Tempus- und Numeruswechsel übersprungen wird? Müßte man vor ἡ βασιλεία nicht ein steigerndes καί erwarten, das deutlich macht, jetzt wird *auch* der Gottesherrschaft Gewalt angetan? Gegen diese Deutung spricht schließlich: Sowohl Mt als auch Lk setzen voraus, daß das Verb des zweiten Satzes etwas Neues bezeichnet. Es ist als βιάζεσθαι neu gegenüber dem προφητεύειν zur Zeit von Propheten und Gesetz (Mt 11,13). Es ist als εὐαγγελίζεσθαι der Gottesherrschaft neu gegenüber der Zeit vorher (Lk 16,16). Neu ist also nicht nur das Objekt des βιάζεσθαι, sondern auch der mit diesem Verb bezeichnete Vorgang selbst.

ad 3) Der Stürmerspruch hat eine metaphorische Struktur: Wenn "Gewalttäter" die Gottesherrschaft "vergewaltigen" und "erbeuten", dann werden semantisch inkongruente Vorstellungen verbunden: Die "Gottesherrschaft" ist (wörtlich verstanden) mächtiger als jede andere Herrschaft und kann daher nur in einem bildlichen Sinne "erbeutet" und "vergewaltigt" werden. Entsprechend ist zwischen Bildspender und Bildempfänger zu unterscheiden. So ist möglich, daß die Widerstandsbewegung als Bildspender Anschauungsmaterial für die Usurpation der Gottesherrschaft geliefert hat – aber eben als Bildspender, nicht als Bildempfänger, auf den sich die metaphorische Aussage bezieht[28]. Ferner ist die Variation des Bildes zu beachten: "Gewalt" zufügen setzt eine zweipolige Beziehung voraus – einen, der Gewalt ausübt, und einen, der sie erleidet. Die Fortführung des Bildes durch "erbeuten" führt eine dreipolige Beziehung ein: Ein Gewalttäter nimmt einer anderen Person etwas weg. Diese dreipolige Struktur ist im Bildwort vom Starken enthalten: "Niemand kann in das Haus des Starken hineingehen und ihm den Hausrat rauben (διαρπάσαι), wenn er nicht zuvor den Starken bindet; erst dann wird er sein Haus ausrauben (διαρπάσαι)" (Mk 3,27 vgl. Mt

---

27 K. Syreeni, *The Making of the Sermon on the Mount* (AASF 44), Helsinki: Suomalainen Tiedeakatemia 1987, 190: "...*as* the law was forsaken and the prophets were mistreated *then, so even now* the message of God's kingdom is facing the resistance and rejection of unrepentant Israel".

12,29/Lk 11,21). Das Bild vom Erbeuten und Rauben der Gottesherrschaft ist also für "Personen" und "Mächte" offen, denen die Gottesherrschaft gegen ihren Willen entrissen werden muß: Hier könnte an den Satan und die Dämonen gedacht sein, gegen die die Gottesherrschaft realisiert wird (Mt 12,28). Es könnten aber auch politische Machthaber gemeint sein oder Schriftgelehrte, die andere daran hindern, zur Gottesherrschaft zu gelangen (Mt 23,13)! Eben deswegen wäre bei den "Gewalttätern" nicht an feindliche Gegenspieler der Gottesherrschaft gedacht, sondern an Menschen, die gegen den Widerstand dieser Gegenspieler "gewaltsam" in die Gottesherrschaft eindringen. Daß man in der Jesusüberlieferung mit solchen kühnen Bildern rechnen muß, zeigen die Bildworte vom Starken (Mk 3,27 parr.), vom Attentäter (EvThom 98)[29], vom Krieg in den Familien (Mt 10,34-36 par.), von den "Menschenfischern" (Mk 1,17) und den "Eunuchen" (Mt 19,12). Wo selbst ein "Mord" (EvThom 98) zum Bild für positiv bewertetes Handeln der Jünger werden konnte, dürfte eine "Rebellion" als positives Bild nicht undenkbar sein.

Der Stürmerspruch ist also mit großer Wahrscheinlichkeit zunächst einmal positiv zu verstehen: Die "Gewalttäter" sind Anhänger Jesu (und des Täufers), die in einem übertragenen Sinne eine "Rebellion" durchführen, welche sie in den Besitz der Gottesherrschaft versetzt[30]. Seine in der Exegese vorherrschende negative Deutung enthält aber ein Wahrheitselement. Denn hier werden zweifellos negativ konnotierte Begriffe auf die Jesusbewegung übertragen. Diese bezeichnet sich selbst als Gruppe von "Gewalttätern" und "Rebellen", die sich in illegitimer Weise

---

28 Vgl. etwa die Beschreibung des Judas, Sohn des Hezekias, in Josephus *Ant* 17,272: Er ist durch ζηλώσει βασιλείου τιμῆς gekennzeichnet, will das Königtum aber nicht durch Praxis der Tugend, sondern durch Mißhandlung anderer (durch ὑβρίζειν) erlangen. Gerade weil die sogenannte "zelotische" Bewegung Anschauungshintergrund des Bildspenders ist, kann sie kaum gleichzeitig als Bildempfänger gemeint sein. Möglich ist jedoch, daß die Jesusbewegung von Sympathisanten der Widerstandsbewegung kritisiert wurde und der Stürmerspruch solche Kritik mit der Behauptung konterte: Wir sind die wahre Widerstandsbewegung, welche die Gottesherrschaft auch mit "außernormalen" Mitteln zugänglich macht. Aber das ist nur eine vage Möglichkeit, nicht mehr.

29 EvThom 98: "Jesus sprach: Das Reich des Vaters gleicht einem Mann, der vorhatte zu töten einen mächtigen Mann. Er zog aus der Scheide das Schwert in seinem Hause. Er durchbohrte die Wand, um zu wissen, ob seine Hand stark sein werde. Dann tötete er den Mächtigen". Zu diesem Gleichnis vgl. E. Haenchen, *Die Botschaft des Thomas-Evangeliums* (Berlin: de Gruyter 1961), 59f. Hier geht es wohl um eine Aufforderung zur Selbstprüfung angesichts der Forderung rückhaltloser Selbsthingabe.

in den Besitz der Herrschaft Gottes setzt. Es handelt sich um einen selbststigmatisierenden Zug im Selbstbild der Jesusbewegung. Durch bewußte Übernahme einer "negativen" Rolle wird Entstigmatisierung proklamiert: Die vermeintlichen Gewalttäter und Rebellen sind die wahren Besitzer der Herrschaft Gottes.

Die hier vorgetragene Deutung ist also weder ausschließlich eine Deutung in bonam partem noch in malam partem, sondern kombiniert beide Möglichkeiten: Ein negativ besetzter Begriff wird bewußt aufgegriffen und positiv umgeprägt. Eine solche Deutung wird dem ambivalenten sprachlichen Befund m.E. gerechter als einseitig positive oder negative Deutungen: βιάζεσθαι hat in der LXX einerseits negative Bedeutung – bezogen auf Vergewaltigung (Dtn 22,25.28; Est 7,8), das Durchbrechen eines Tores (II Makk 14,41) oder den Zwang, unreine Speisen zu essen (IV Makk 11,25). Andererseits ist eine positive Bedeutung häufig belegt, oft im Sinne eines eindringlichen Werbens angesichts von Widerstand. So dringt z.B. Jakob in Esau, um ihn mit sich zu versöhnen (Gen 33,11). Manoah versucht, den Engel zum Bleiben zu bewegen (Jdc 13,15.16 Alexandrinus). Dieser positive Sinn von βιάζεσθαι herrscht in der LXX sogar vor (vgl. u.a. Jdc 19,7; II Reg 13,25.27). Er ist in Gestalt des Kompositums παραβιάζεσθαι auch dem NT nicht fremd (vgl. Lk 24,29; Act 16,15)[31].

Eine Schwierigkeit bleibt: In Mt 11,12 par. wird von einem βιάζεσθαι gegenüber der Gottesherrschaft gesprochen. Ist eine solche kühne Aussage – ein "freundliches Überwinden göttlichen Willens" – in der Antike denkbar? Zwei Belege seien dafür angeführt. Clemens von Alexandrien

---

30 Diese Deutung setzt die von Ch. H. Weisse (1838) begonnene Auslegung fort, die vor allem durch Albert Schweitzer verbreitet wurde (vgl. Anm. 20). Entscheidend ist die positive Auffassung der "Gewalttäter", sekundär wichtig ist, ob βιάζεται medial oder passivisch verstanden wird. Das passivische Verständnis scheint mir ungezwungener zu sein. Jedoch ist auch das Verständnis des Stürmerspruchs mit medialem βιάζεται bei Th. Zahn, A. v. Harnack, R. Otto, J. Schmid (vgl. jeweils die Besprechung bei P. S. Cameron, *Violence*, 122ff., 160ff.) mit dem oben entfalteten Gedanken verträglich.

31 Vgl. die ausführliche Untersuchung von G. Häfner, *Gewalt*, 26-37, der als Ergebnis formuliert: "In welchem Sinn Mt 11,12 zu deuten ist, ob in bonam oder in malam partem, kann nicht durch die immer wieder behauptete Eindeutigkeit der die Aussage tragenden Vokabeln entschieden werden. Auch wenn man von einem überwiegend negativen Sprachgebrauch von βία, βιάζομαι und ἁρπάζω in der griechischen Literatur ausgehen kann, so hat sich doch gezeigt, daß dies nicht die einzig mögliche Verwendungsweise der fraglichen Wörter ist. Im Falle von βιάζομαι konnte in der LXX der Sinn einer Gewalthandlung nicht einmal als vorherrschend belegt werden..." (S. 37).

interpretiert Mt 11,12 in folgender Weise: "Dies ist die einzige gute Gewalt (βία), Gott Gewalt anzutun (βιάζεσθαι) und von Gott das Leben an sich zu reißen (ἁρπάσαι). Er, der die kennt, die gewaltsam oder besser: die beharrlich aushalten, weicht. Denn Gott freut sich, in dieser Weise überwunden zu werden" (*Quis div salv.* 21,2f.). Nun ist Clemens vom neutestamentlichen Sprachgebrauch beeinflußt. Jedoch geht er über ihn hinaus: Nicht nur die Gottesherrschaft, sondern Gott selbst wird quasi "bekämpft". Aber auch ein heidnischer Schriftsteller, Eunapius, kann von einem ἐκβιάζεσθαι der Götter sprechen[32]. Er berichtet von der These des neuplatonischen Philosophen Maximus, man müsse die Götter nötigen (ἐκβιάζεσθαι), einem ein wohlwollendes Orakel zu geben (*vitae sophistarum* 477). Beide Belege zeigen: Es ist in der Antike nicht undenkbar, auch gegenüber den Göttern oder Gott von einem βιάζεσθαι zu sprechen.

Dennoch bleibt ein βιάζεσθαι Gottes oder der Gottesherrschaft eine kühne Aussage. Die negativen Konnotationen der Begriffe βιάζεσθαι, βιασταί und ἁρπάζειν können ja nicht geleugnet werden, am wenigsten dort, wo sie kombiniert begegnen[33]. Nur so viel soll behauptet werden: Eine paradoxe Umwertung solch eines gewalttätigen Vorgehens gegen die Gottesherrschaft ist von der Wortbedeutung her möglich. Sie läßt sowohl eine negative wie eine positive Tönung von βιάζεσθαι zu.

Wie aber ist eine solche Aussage historisch möglich? Hier liegt das große Problem: Die im Stürmerspruch angesprochene "Gewalt" richtet sich gegen die Gottesherrschaft. Es wird zwar nicht direkt gesagt, daß sie sich damit auch gegen Gesetz und Propheten richtet. Aber da deren Wirksamkeit durch die einbrechende Gottesherrschaft begrenzt wird, kann man den Gedanken nicht fernhalten, daß auch Gesetz und Propheten von diesen "Gewalttätern" nicht respektiert werden. Auch die Wortwahl legt das nahe. Die Wendung βιάζεσθαι τοὺς νόμους kann bei Josephus die Verletzung des mosaischen Gesetzes bedeuten (*Ant* 4,143)[34]. Wenn Julius Cäsar vorgeworfen wird, er habe die republikanische Verfassung zerstört, so wird er charakterisiert als ein διαβιασάμενος τὸν κόσμον τῶν νόμων als einer, der Recht und Ordnung vergewaltigte (*Ant* 19,173). Auch im Stürmerspruch liegen solche Assoziationen nahe:

---

32 Ich verdanke den Hinweis auf diesen Beleg dem jungen griechischen Patristiker Konstantinos Bosinis.
33 Vgl. Plut. *Mor.* 203 C (Reg. et Imp. Apophthegmata): τοὺς στρατιώτας ... βιάζεσται καὶ ἁρπάζειν.
34 Vgl. dieselbe Wendung bei Thukydides 8,53.

Gesetz und Propheten[35] gelten in der Zeit der hereinbrechenden Gottesherrschaft nicht mehr so, wie sie früher gegolten haben – zumindest nicht für einige "Gewalttäter", die das Gottesreich an sich reißen[36]. Die Schwierigkeit, solch einen Spruch historisch verständlich zu machen, liegt darin, daß wir ihn aus jüdischen Voraussetzungen heraus erklären müssen – und nicht aus den Voraussetzungen des späteren Heidenchristentums, das sich von der Thora gelöst hatte. Ist der Spruch ein Indiz dafür, daß schon in der frühen Jesusbewegung, ja, bei Jesus selbst, ein Exodus aus dem Judentum begonnen hatte? Denn die Thora ist die Grundlage jüdischer Identität. Wer sie verläßt, verläßt das Judentum. Spricht aber nicht alles dafür, daß Jesus im Rahmen des Judentums gewirkt hat? Nicht das Gesetz selbst, nur das Gesetzesverständnis war zu seiner Zeit umstritten!

Nun muß man bedenken, daß der Vorwurf der "Gesetzlosigkeit" ein innerjüdischer Vorwurf sein kann. Auch die Jesusbewegung wirft Pharisäern und Schriftgelehrten ἀνομία vor (vgl. Mt 23,28). Der Vorwurf meint nicht, daß sie das Gesetz ablehnen; er setzt nur ein anderes Gesetzesverständnis und eine andere Gesetzespraxis bei den Kritisierten voraus. Es ist möglich, daß man einen solchen Vorwurf auch gegen Jesus und seine Bewegung erhoben hat. Dabei sind zwei Aspekte zu unterscheiden. Einerseits der Interpretationshorizont, innerhalb dessen man mögliche "Verletzungen" des Gesetzes bei der Jesusbewegung wahrgenommen hat. Andererseits die konkreten Verhaltensweisen, die Anlaß zu diesem Vorwurf gegeben haben. Zwischen beiden kann eine große Diskrepanz bestehen: Was für die einen eine liberale Handhabung des Gesetzes ist,

---

35 "Gesetz und Propheten" bezeichnen hier nicht zwei Teile des Schriftkanon, sondern die Gesamtheit des Willens Gottes; vgl. Jos. *Ant* 9,281; Lk 16,31; *Nazaräer Ev* frg.16: feci legem et prophetas. Weitere Belege bei K. Berger, *Die Gesetzesauslegung Jesu I* (WMANT, Neukirchen: Neukirchener Verlag 1972), Exkurs: "Der Ausdruck 'Gesetz und Propheten'", 209-227.

36 E. P. Sanders, *The Historical Figure of Jesus* (London/New York: Penguin Press 1993), 206f. unterscheidet sieben Möglichkeiten, von einem Gesetz abzuweichen: (1.) Ein Gesetz gilt als falsch und wird nicht eingehalten werden. (2.) Es gilt als falsch, wird aber bis zu seiner Aufhebung eingehalten. (3.) Es gilt grundsätzlich, aber wird unter bestimmten Bedingungen übertreten. (4.) Es wird so interpretiert, daß es de facto geändert wird. (5.) Man entzieht sich ihm, ohne es direkt zu brechen. (6.) Man hält es für nicht weitreichend genug und plädiert für seine Verschärfung. (7.) Einige praktizieren es und beachten dabei verschärfende Normen. Die Kategorie von Gesetzesübertretung, die in der Jesusbewegung bezeugt ist, fällt m.E. unter Nr. 3: In einer Interims-Situation angesichts des Endes und in Gegenwart des Repräsentanten der Gottesherrschaft werden einige Normen nicht praktiziert, ohne deswegen grundsätzlich aufgehoben zu werden.

ist für die anderen dessen Auflösung oder wird polemisch als dessen Auflösung gebrandmarkt.

Was den Interpretationshorizont angeht, so werden die "Gesetzesverletzungen" im Stürmerspruch in einem eschatologischen Rahmen gesehen. Es sind nicht irgendwelche Verstöße, sondern Verstöße in der Endzeit – angesichts der hereinbrechenden Gottesherrschaft. Entsprechende Befürchtungen für die Endzeit sind im Judentum gut belegt: In der Endzeit wird es zum großen Abfall vom Gesetz kommen. So sieht es etwa Jub 23,16f.[37]:

> Und in diesem Geschlecht werden die Kinder ihre Väter und ihre Alten schelten wegen der Sünde und wegen der Ungerechtigkeit und wegen der Rede ihres Mundes und wegen der großen Bosheiten, die sie tun werden, und wegen des Aufgebens der Ordnung, die der Herr zwischen ihnen und sich festgesetzt hat, daß sie bewahrten und täten all sein Gebot und seine Ordnung und seine Satzung und daß sie nicht abwichen nach links und nach rechts, so daß alle böse handeln. Und jeder Mund pflegt Sünde zu reden, und all ihr Werk ist Unreinheit und Abscheulichkeit, und all ihre Wege sind Befleckung und Unreinheit und Verdorbenheit.

Vergleichbare Warnungen vor Irrlehrern und Verführern in der Endzeit begegnen auch in AssMos 7; ApkBar(syr) 48,38; Sib III,68ff.; ApkEl 21,13ff. Solche Warnungen können sich gelegentlich auf Menschen beziehen, die Gesetz und Propheten verachten. So heißt es in TestLev 16,1: "Und das Gesetz werdet ihr entstellen und die Worte der Propheten verachten. Ihr werdet die gerechten Männer verfolgen und die Frommen hassen ...". Das alles wird für eine Zeit von 70 Wochen geweissagt, also für eine längere Zeit; aber es kann im Kontext auf die Endzeit bezogen werden (vgl. TestLev 14,1: "Ich, meine Kinder, erkannte, daß ihr am Ende gegen den Herrn sündigen werdet ...")[38]. In den Qumranschriften begegnen uns Irrlehrer der Endzeit sogar als "Gewalttätige" (als עָרִיצִים). Zu Hab 1,5 heißt es: "Und ebenso bezieht sich die Deutung des Wortes (auf alle Ab)trünnigen am Ende der Tage. Sie sind die Gewalt(tätigen am

---

[37] Die Weissagung ist (für uns erkennbar) ein vaticinium ex eventu auf die Apostasie der radikalen hellenistischen Reformer in Jerusalem Anfang des 2. Jhdts. v. Chr.; vgl. K. Berger, *Das Buch der Jubiläen* (JSHRZ II,3, Gütersloh: Mohn 1981), 443. Im 1. Jhdt. vor und nach der Zeitenwende aber wurde dergleichen natürlich als echte Weissagung gelesen.

[38] In der Textfamilie β wird die Beziehung zwischen TestLev 14,1ff. und 16,1ff. noch deutlicher. An beiden Stellen wird hier als Quellenangabe der Abfallsschilderung eine Schrift Henochs genannt; vgl. J. Becker, *Die Testamente der zwölf Patriarchen*, (JSHRZ II,1, Gütersloh: Mohn 1980), 56, 58.

B)unde, die nicht glauben, wenn sie alles hören, das kom(men wird über) das letzte Geschlecht ..." (1QpHab II,5ff.). Auch an anderen Stellen werden Gegner der Gemeinde als "Gewalttätige" angegriffen (vgl. 4QpPs 37 II,12-14; IV,13-14)[39]. Man kann daher sagen: Es ist ein verbreiteter Topos, daß sich in der Krisenzeit vor dem endgültigen Eintreten des Heils die Ordnung auflösen wird. Das kann u.a. auch so dargestellt werden, daß Gesetz und Propheten nicht mehr gelten und Menschen mit abweichender Gesetzesauffassung als "Gewalttäter" diffamiert werden.

Unsere nächste Frage ist: Konnte das Verhalten der Jesusbewegung solche Befürchtungen und Diffamierungen aktivieren? Unbestreitbar ist: Jesus hat nirgendwo grundsätzlich die Thora aufgehoben. Aber ebenso deutlich ist: In ungrundsätzlicher Weise werden in der auf ihn zurückgehenden Überlieferung Thoragebote mißachtet – ungrundsätzlich deshalb, weil diese Suspendierung von Thoragebote an seine Gegenwart und Sendung gebunden war und nur für seine Nachfolger galt. Die Aufforderung an einen Nachfolger, sich um das Begräbnis des Vaters nicht zu kümmern, ist ein Verstoß gegen das Elterngebot (vgl. Mt 8,21/Lk 9,60). Der Spruch über innere und äußere Reinheit (Mk 7,15) ist mit den Reinheitsgeboten unvereinbar (vgl. Lev 11ff.). Die Sabbatkonflikte Jesu lassen sich zwar als eine liberale Interpretation des Sabbatgebots interpretieren; aber wahrscheinlich haben die Zeitgenossen der Jesusbewegung sie als dessen Bruch erlebt (vgl. Mk 2,23ff.; 3,1ff.). Die Ablehnung des Fastens in Gegenwart Jesu (Mk 2,18f.) widerspricht dem Fastengebot am Versöhnungstag (Lev 16,29ff.), darüber hinaus aber der jüdischen Lebensform mit ihren vielen Fastentagen, wie sie sich aufgrund der mündlichen Thora entwickelt hat. In der Jesusbewegung wird diese liberale Gesetzespraxis durch ein eschatologisches Erfüllungsbewußtsein motiviert. Weil jetzt Freudenzeit ist, ist Fasten unmöglich (Mk 2,18f.). Weil der Blick auf das Reich Gottes gerichtet ist, kann man radikal mit der Vergangenheit – und auch mit seiner Familie – brechen (so in einem nur bei Lk überlieferten Logion, Lk 9,61f., das die vorhergehenden Nachfolgeworte sachlich richtig interpretiert). Bei der liberalen Sabbatpraxis und der neuen Reinheitsvorstellung könnte der Gedanke einer Wiederherstellung der Schöpfung eine Rolle spielen. Mk 2,28 bezieht sich auf die Schöpfung von Mensch und Sabbat zurück: Der Mensch ist vor dem Sabbat geschaffen und ihm übergeordnet. Wenn Gott bei der Schöpfung

---

39 Vgl. B. E. Thiering, "Are the 'Violent Men' False Teachers?", in: *NT* 21 (1979), 294-297. Gegen einen direkten Rückschluß von diesen Qumranbelegen auf Mt 11,12f. par. spricht, daß das Verb βιάζεσθαι in der LXX nirgendwo ein Verb mit dem Stamm ערץ wiedergibt.

alles für "gut" erklärt hat, so kann die Unterscheidung von rein und unrein in Lev 11 nur sekundär sein. Dies Erfüllungsbewußtsein führt im Stürmerspruch dazu, daß eine von Gesetz und Propheten bestimmte Zeit von der neuen Zeit der Gottesherrschaft unterschieden wird. Solche Periodisierungen sind im Judentum denkbar. Im babylonischen Talmud finden wir sie in bSan 97a/b; bAZ 9a: "In der Schule des Elia wird gelehrt: 6000 Jahre wird die Welt bestehen, (nämlich) 2000 Jahre Chaos, 2000 Jahre Torah, 2000 Jahre messianische Zeit; doch wegen unserer vielen Sünden sind schon manche von diesen verstrichen". Hier wird nicht die Aufhebung der Torah in der messianischen Zeit gelehrt[40]. Voraussetzung für deren Kommen ist vielmehr torahgemäßes Handeln: Wegen der Sünden Israels ist der Messias noch nicht gekommen, obwohl er eigentlich hätte kommen müssen. Wenn sein Kommen aber an die Erfüllung des Gesetzes gebunden ist, so kann der Messias nicht im Gegensatz zum Gesetz stehen. Er kann nur als Erfüllung des Gesetzes verstanden sein – als sein wahrer Interpret oder als seine endzeitliche Verwirklichung. Ähnlich hat wohl auch die Jesusbewegung im Stürmerspruch die Zeit der *basileia* gedeutet: In der liberalen Gesetzespraxis Jesu und seiner Anhänger kommen Gesetz und Propheten zur Erfüllung.

Andere aber haben das ganz anders erlebt. Wenn eine eschatologische Bewegung mit intensiver Naherwartung in Palästina mit "liberalen" Verhaltensweisen auftritt, muß sie fast notwendig die Befürchtung auslösen, jetzt sei die Endzeit da, in der sich die traditionellen Normen und Sitten auflösen; nicht Gott, sondern "Söhne der Gesetzlosigkeit" seien hier am Werk[41]. Dagegen könnte der Stürmerspruch gerichtet sein. Er sagt: Wer im Verhalten der Jesusbewegung nur "Gesetzlosigkeit" sieht, ist im Unrecht. Denn die vermeintlich "Gesetzlosen" erobern die Gottesherrschaft. Wenn demonstrativ behauptet wird, Menschen, die das Gesetz verletzen, erobern die *basileia*, so wird damit die These verfochten: Das "liberale" Gesetzesverständnis dieser Menschen ist das wahre Gesetzesverständnis, ihre Praxis die wahre Gesetzespraxis – nicht aber das Gesetzesverständnis und die Gesetzespraxis ihrer Gegner. Denn nur Vertreter des wahren Gesetzesverständnisses können die Gottesherrschaft erobern. Nur wer den Willen Gottes in Gesetz und Propheten erfüllt, kann sie besitzen. Das ist die unausgesprochene Prämisse des Stürmerspruchs.

---

40 Vgl. dazu grundlegend P. Schäfer, "Die Torah der messianischen Zeit", in: ZNW 65 (1974), 27-42.
41 Man erwartete in der Tat in der Endzeit einen "Sohn der Gesetzlosigkeit", den Antichristen (vgl. ApkEl 31,15ff.; 2Thess 2,3).

Der Stürmerspruch greift einen Vorwurf auf (oder antizipiert ihn), der Jesus und seine Anhänger als "Gewalttäter" gegen den Willen Gottes brandmarkt. Innerhalb des Judentums ist dieser Vorwurf ein Stigmatisierungsversuch. Der Stürmerspruch übernimmt diese Stigmatisierung und wertet sie um. Er sagt: In der Tat sind jetzt Menschen am Werk, die in den Augen ihrer Gegner gesetzlos handeln – gewalttätig und mit Raub. Aber ihr Handeln ist in Wirklichkeit positiv zu werten. Sie erobern mit Gewalt die Gottesherrschaft. Ihr Stigma ist ihr Charisma, ihr Defizit ihr Vorzug, ihre vermeintliche Gesetzlosigkeit ihre Heilsnähe. Eine diskriminierte Minorität bekennt sich demonstrativ zu ihrer Außenseiterrolle und erschüttert damit das Wertgefüge der Majorität nachhaltiger als durch direkte Kritik. Sie bedient sich derselben paradoxen Strategie, wie wenn sie sich demonstrativ den "Menschenfischern" (Mk 1,17)[42] oder den "Eunuchen" (Mt 19,12) zuordnet. Mit selbststigmatisierenden Etiketten provoziert sie die geltende Wertordnung und ihre Interpretation.

In diesem Zusammenhang könnte zum ersten Mal der Gedanke geäußert worden sein, daß die von der Thora bestimmte Epoche durch eine andere abgelöst wird, die sie überbietet: durch die Zeit der Gottesherrschaft. Wahrscheinlich gehen dieser Gedanke und der Stürmerspruch auf Jesus selbst zurück[43]. Aber erst später entfaltete er – nicht ohne tragische Auswirkungen – eine Dynamik, durch die Juden und Christen immer mehr voneinander getrennt wurden. Der Gedanke einer Erfüllung und Überbietung der Thora in der Gottesherrschaft wurde dabei in die Vorstellung verwandelt, die Thora sei überholt. Aus dem Streit um das wahre Gesetzesverständnis wurde ein Streit um das Gesetz selbst.

---

42 Vgl. H. Mödritzer: *Stigma und Charisma*, (s.o. Anm. 1), 102ff.; M. Hengel: *Nachfolge und Charisma* (BZNW 34, Berlin/New York: de Gruyter 1968), 86f.

43 Das Logion wird meist für authentisch gehalten: Das nachösterliche Urchristentum hätte die entscheidende Wende kaum mit Johannes dem Täufer, sondern mit Jesus selbst datiert. Das Logion ist auch sonst voll von Tendenzwidrigkeit: Die militant wirkenden Metaphern, nach denen die Jesusbewegung als Rebellion mißverstanden werden konnten, passen nicht zur apologetischen Tendenz, Jesus und seine Anhänger als politisch harmlos darzustellen. Umgekehrt paßt das Logion gut in einen jüdischen Kontext und zeigt in ihm als individuellen Akzent eine präsentische Auffassung der Gottesherrschaft – also ein Proprium der Jesusüberlieferung im Rahmen der jüdischen Eschatologie.

The Apostate Minority

Stephen Wilson

The process of joining an early Christian community has attracted considerable attention from those interested in the phenomenon of conversion or in the reasons why Christianity appealed to certain groups in ancient society. By contrast, the phenomenon of apostasy or defection has only occasionally been discussed. When it has, the focus has usually been on the New Testament evidence and not infrequently on the theological problem, raised largely by Calvinists, of the ultimate security of salvation for Christian believers, both of which restrict the way we might view an interesting, if limited, group of early Christians.[1]

This is not entirely surprising. Allusions to apostasy in early Christian sources are relatively infrequent, and some have concluded from this that the phenomenon itself was rare.[2] In addition it might be thought that since Christian communities in the ancient world were more cohesive than they are in our day, the boundaries were more tightly drawn and crossing them a more obvious, public, and therefore less common, occurrence. But this conclusion may be premature. Christian writers, then and now, have understandably not been predisposed to dwell on the incidence of defection, and certainly not to the degree

---

1   See, for example, H. Marshall, "The Problem of Apostasy in the New Testament," *Perspectives in Religious Studies* 14 (1987), 65-80, and the works he quotes. A. E. Harvey, "Forty Strokes Save One: Social Aspects of Judaizing and Apostasy," in A. E. Harvey (ed.), *Alternative Approaches to New Testament Study* (London: SPCK, 1985), 79-96, as his title indicates, takes a broader look at the phenomenon but confines himself to the New Testament.

2   The same has been said of early Judaism. There too, I suspect, apostasy was more frequent than is often recognised—but that is a subject for another paper. See, for example, V. Tcherikover, *Corpus Papyrorum Judicarum* (Cambridge, MA: Harvard University Press, 1957), Vol.1, 37; M. Hengel, *Judaism and Hellenism: Studies in their Encounter in Palestine during the Early Hellenistic Period* (Philadelphia, PA: Fortress, 1974), Vol.1, 31, Vol.2, 25 n.224; M. Williams, "Domitian, the Jews and the 'Judaizers'—A Simple Matter of Cupiditas and Maiestas?" *Historia* 39 (1990), 196-211, here 200 n. 22; L. Grabbe, *Judaism from Cyrus to Hadrian* (Minneapolis, MN: Fortress, 1992), Vol. 2, 536-37.

that they have on examples of conversion, for as much as the latter serve to enhance their self-image and promote their cause the former clearly undermine them. It is probable, too, that apostates themselves would normally have preferred not to draw attention to themselves. Moreover, there is no reason in principle to suppose that the boundaries of early Christian communities were always precisely demarcated. Insofar as we accept that there were different levels of adherence and commitment among those who attached themselves to Christian communities, so we should expect a similar penumbra as they became detached.[3]

It is of some interest that sociologists have begun to turn their attention to the phenomenon of apostasy in the modern world. While there has been a long-established interest in conversion, the problem of apostasy (otherwise described as defection, disaffiliation, disengagement, disidentification, dropping-out, leavetaking, etc.) has only recently begun to receive some attention. Here "apostasy" can cover anything from the gradual, barely noticeable, drifting away from a long-established religious community to the extraction and deprogramming of those who have been drawn into new religious cults. The evidence used can be as broad as national census data, as focused as the intensive study of particular religious groups, or as personal as the autobiographical accounts of those leaving a religious order. Much of this, while interesting in itself, is of limited use in considering ancient evidence because it is profoundly defined by the circumstances and values of the modern world.[4] One of its more interesting features, however, is the attempt to discover not only what has happened but why. This encourages us to approach the ancient evidence in the same fashion, that is, to consider

---

3 The analogy I have in mind is the study by S. J. D. Cohen, "Crossing the Boundary and Becoming a Jew," HTR 82 (1989), 13-33, who has shown that the evidence for the traffic of Gentiles towards Judaism presents us with a fairly broad spectrum of responses, ranging from simple admiration to full conversion. I would assume that for Judaism, as for Christianity, the reverse would be true too.

4 A useful recent discussion is found in D. G. Bromily (ed.), *Falling from the Faith: Consequences and Causes of Religious Apostasy* (Newbury Park, CA.: Sage Publications, 1988). See also T. Endelman, *Jewish Apostasy in the Modern World* (New York: Holmes and Meir, 1987). The sort of difficulty we have in passing from the modern to the ancient world is illustrated in C. K. Hadaway's article, "Identifying American Apostates: A Cluster Analysis," JSSR 28 (1989), 210-15, whose typology of apostates includes Successful Swinging Singles, Sidetracked Singles, Young Settled Liberals, Young Libertarians and Irreligious Traditionalists! Similarly, in 20th century America—often the field where such data have been collected—forced apostasy, common in the ancient world, is not mentioned.

where possible not only the incidence, but also the causes, of defection.

This has an added advantage, for by looking carefully at the reasons why people defected it may be possible, with a little imagination, to see apostasy from the point of view of the apostate. For although, as we have seen, references to apostasy in ancient sources are infrequent, they are invariably hostile. It is natural for modern readers to be affected by this, to take the side of early Christian writers and to view defectors with an equal lack of sympathy. Yet while the negative and peremptory treatment of apostates in ancient sources may be understandable, we need not let it govern our own perspective. Apostasy can be viewed more broadly as an interesting religious phenomenon worthy of sympathetic attention in its own right.

The definition of an apostate, like that of a heretic, is somewhat arbitrary and indeterminate. One person's radical, for example, might be another's apostate, and those designated apostates by one group in a community might not see themselves as such. Since it is difficult to define the taxonomic indicators, the possession of one or more of which signifies inclusion in a Christian community, it is equally difficult to know which ones have to be absent for an individual to be excluded.[5] I shall use the term apostate somewhat loosely to describe those who considered themselves, or were considered by others, to have abandoned the main practices and/or beliefs of their religious community, in extreme cases even turning against it. They are thus unlike heretics, who typically are seen as wayward members of the community, but members nonetheless. And, while various degrees of assimilation to the world outside may be possible without defection, apostates can be considered to be those whose assimilationist tendencies finally took them beyond the limits of their community.

In the New Testament the evidence for apostates is slight. To some degree this is a reflection of the nature of the documents, many of which deal with conflicting opinions within nascent Christian communities

---

5 The analogy I have in mind is the discussion of early Judaism by J. Z. Smith, "Fences and Neighbours: Some Contours of Early Judaism," in *Imagining Religion. From Babylon to Jonestown* (Chicago, IL: Chicago University Press, 1982), 1-18. Much of what he says could be applied to the enormously variegated phenomenon we call early Christianity. L. H. Schiffman, *Who was a Jew? Rabbinic and Halakhic Perspectives on the Jewish-Christian Schism* (New York: KTAV, 1985), 41, suggests the following distinction for Jews: heretics diverge from the established religion in their beliefs, apostates in their actions. This definition would not work so well in the more belief-centred Christian tradition.

who had little collective sense of what defined their movement as a whole. In the absence of accepted orthodoxies and established boundaries, defection was difficult to define. Thus, a great deal of energy is expended on attacking opponents who, whatever the authors thought of them, saw themselves as equally legitimate representatives of the Christian movement. Thus when 2 Peter warns its readers against falling into error (3:17) and suggests that those who do so revert to a state worse than their pre-Christian past (2:17-22), it is clearly implied that such Christians have put themselves beyond the bounds of the community. Similarly, 1 Timothy suggests that "some will renounce the faith" (ἀποστήσονταί τινες τῆς πίστεως, 4:1) by following a form of demonically inspired teaching which involved abstaining from food and marriage. Yet in both of these fairly late New Testament writings it is clear that we are dealing with conflicting visions of what Christian belief and practice involved. We do not need to define the precise shape of the opponents' views to know that they would not have accepted the judgement that they had defected or placed themselves beyond the community limits, for they presumably had a different definition of what those limits were.

There are one or two dramatic examples of behaviour which led individuals to be considered beyond the pale. Ananias and Sapphira were punished with death for their dishonesty (Acts 5:1-11) and Paul recommends that an immoral man in Corinth be "handed over to Satan for the destruction of the flesh," whatever that may mean. Yet it is clear that the Corinthians, prior to Paul's intervention, had taken a more relaxed view of the situation, and even Paul hopes that in the end "his spirit may be saved" (1 Cor 5:1-5). The man is thus perhaps not to be seen as a full apostate.

Despite these examples, it is generally true that Christian allegiance was defined more in terms of belief than of practice, so that defection would have been a less obvious and public affair than it was, for example, for Jews. Apart from attendance at Christian gatherings there may, in some instances, have been little overt distinction between Christians and other members of society. In the absence of public recantation, which was probably rare (though cf. 1 Cor 12:3), it would have been relatively easy to slip away inconspicuously from a Christian community. For those Jewish Christians who followed a Jewish lifestyle and continued their association with the synagogue, the situation would have been even less clear, since often the only thing which distinguished them from their fellow Jews were their christological beliefs. In some instances they may have been reluctant to confess their allegiance publicly—as with the secret believers whom some think can be identified in the Gospel of John (8:30-31; 12:42-43)—but whether they did so or not, a decision to sever their ties with Christianity could have been done discreetly and without fuss.[6]

As time went by, however, relations between synagogue and church began to shake down and they became more clearly distinguished entities. One effect of this may be found in the oblique comments of the author of Hebrews to his readers. Clearly there had been a problem with Christians who, in the eyes of the author, had reneged on their Christian commitment. They had already tasted the benefits of membership in the Christian community: knowledge of the truth, heavenly gifts, experience of the Spirit and the goodness of God's word. Yet now they had fallen away (παραπεσόντας, 6:6) and had—to use the unusually strong language of the author—spurned or re-crucified the Son of God. Repentance for such renegades is out of the question and their punishment will be severe (6:4-8; 10:26-31). These defections appear to lie in the past at the time of writing but, although the author expresses confidence in his readers (6:9), the issue is presumably raised because the possibility of a recurrence was not out of the question. What led to the defections is not clear, but the allusion to past experience of public harassment, confiscation and imprisonment may be the best clue (10:32-34). A number of other things remain unclear. The persecution may have been instigated by Jews, but is perhaps more likely a reference to state harassment during the reign of Nero or Domitian.[7] The readers are commonly thought to have been Jewish Christians. The deep concern to establish the supersession of Jewish traditions, especially those related to the cult, together with the exhortation to "go to him [Jesus] outside the camp and bear the abuse he endured" (13:13), certainly suggest that the author is trying to wean his readers from a hankering after Jewish thought and practice. It is also possible that they were Gentiles who had previously formed an attachment to Judaism and were now wondering if they had left too much behind when they allied themselves with the Christians.

---

6 Some might include Judas among the Christian apostates, though in fact he becomes the symbol of Jewish treason in later Christian tradition. But at most he "betrayed" Jesus, not Christianity. See further H. Maccoby, *Judas Iscariot and the Myth of Jewish Evil* (London: Peter Habban Publishers, 1992).
7 Harvey, "Forty," 89, thinks in terms of synagogue discipline. But did Jewish courts have the right to confiscate and imprison? The date (whether before or after 70 CE) and setting of Hebrews have been much discussed, but for our purposes they are not critical.

Whether Jewish Christians or Gentile judaizers, the defectors probably, but not certainly, headed back to the Jewish community. If this reconstruction is correct we may surmise that those who defected from the Christian community did so under the dual pressures of persecution and an unsatisfied longing for aspects of the Judaism they had left. Whether they thought this involved abandonment of their Christian beliefs is not clear, though the author of Hebrews is in no doubt that it did.

A somewhat similar situation may have arisen in Asia Minor towards the end of the century. Revelation speaks of "those who say they are Jews and are not" (2:9, cf. 3:9). Who these people were is not clear. Many think they were the Jews of Smyrna and Philadelphia, but then why the author should say they are not Jews remains obscure.[8] It is more likely that they were Jewish Christians or Gentile judaizers who had decided to associate themselves with the synagogue communities. If so, they were from one perspective defectors. Again, the reason for their defection remains unclear. But if we extrapolate from the general situation implied by the book—a beleaguered Christian community facing what was perceived to be a hostile Roman state—it was not unlike that implied by the epistle to the Hebrews.[9] Pressure from outside, which had led to at least one martyrdom (2:13), forced some Christians to defect to the synagogue. If they had previously been Jews or Gentile judaizers, no doubt an instinctive attachment to the synagogue and its way of life played its part as well.

A somewhat similar situation may be implied by *1 Clement*. It has been suggested that the double-minded who doubt God's power (11:1-2) are the same as the dissenters mentioned in 47:7, and that they may have been former converts from Judaism who had returned to the synagogue and turned against the Christians.[10] It must be said, however, that the

---

8   For further discussion see S. G. Wilson, "Gentile Judaizers," *NTS* 38 (1992), 605-16, here 613-14.

9   Revelation has commonly been associated with persecution of Christians during the reign of Domitian. Recently it has been noted that the crisis may have been as much a matter of perception as of reality, and there has been a concerted attempt to rehabilitate the reputation of Domitian, including his policies towards the Christians and Jews. So L. L. Thompson, *The Book of Revelation. Apocalypse and Empire* (Oxford: Oxford University Press, 1990), 95-115, who, I think, swings the pendulum too far in the other direction. A more balanced assessment is given by B. W. Jones, *The Emperor Domitian* (London: Routledge, 1992), 114-25; and by J. T. Sanders, *Schismatics, Sectarians, Dissidents, Deviants. The First One Hundred Years of Jewish-Christian Relations* (Valley Forge, PA: Trinity, 1993), 166-69.

10 So J. S. Jeffers, *Conflict at Rome. Social Order and Hierarchy in Early Christianity* (Minneapolis, MN: Fortress, 1991), 173.

allusions are fleeting and obscure. The same is true of *Barnabas* 5:4, which may refer to defectors when it speaks of the man who "deserves to perish if, having knowledge of the way of righteousness, he ensnares himself in the way of darkness". If so, we might surmise that since the author elsewhere expresses considerable alarm about the presence of Gentile judaizers in his community (3:6; 4:6), any defectors are likely to have moved in the direction of the synagogue. The attractions of Judaism rather than pressure from the state would seem to be the main impulse here.

That pressure from Roman authorities could lead to defection from the Christian community is implied by Pliny the Younger's much scrutinised letter to Trajan about the treatment of Christians in Bithynia (*Ep*.10:96-97). Pliny mentions three groups accused of Christian allegiance: those who unequivocally confirmed it, who were summarily executed; those who flatly denied it, who were released; and those who admitted association in the past but not the present. The last of these Pliny was inclined to release if they paid honour to the gods and the emperor and cursed Christ—a policy of which Trajan, in his reply, approved. This third group, Pliny says, claimed that they had withdrawn from the Christian movement three, five or even twenty-five years before. This would place some of them in the reign of Domitian, when they may have defected in circumstances similar to those in the time of Pliny. Or it may be that these people had quietly ceased their association in the past and were now forced for the first time into a public recantation. This evidence provides us with a fascinating glimpse of what happened in one corner of the empire and, although we are not told how many defectors Pliny saw, they made up a sufficiently distinctive group for him to be exercised about their fate. At a somewhat later date we are told, in connection with the martyrdom of Polycarp, that one Quintus from Phrygia publicly abandoned his Christian beliefs and honoured the emperor to avoid sharing Polycarp's fate. As such, according to Eusebius, he illustrated foolhardy and irreligious behaviour (*Mart.Pol.* 4; Eus. *H.E.* 4.15.7-8).

Whether any of the Christians caught up in such circumstances thought they could secretly retain their beliefs despite their public recantation—and it should be noted that most Christians were not subject to such trials and lived relatively undisturbed—is not known. Some Christian leaders, like Pionius, viewed those who succumbed during times of persecution sympathetically and tried to comfort and correct them (Eus. *H.E.* 4.15.47).

The *Shepherd of Hermas* twice mentions apostates and considers their fate. They are called apostates and traitors who "blasphemed the Lord, and in addition were ashamed of the Lord's name by which they were called," or "apostates and blasphemers against the Lord and betrayers of God's servants." For such there is no repentance, unlike the "hypocrites and false teachers" or "teachers of evil" for whom repentance is possible. Asked why, considering the similarity of their deeds, the author answers that the latter "have not blasphemed their Lord nor become betrayers of God's people" (*Sim.* 8:6.4-5; 9:19.1-3). In addition one individual, Maximus, is singled out as someone who had denied his faith in the past and might do so again in the future (*Vis.* 2:3.4). The severe judgement passed on apostates matches that of the author of Hebrews, and it may have something to do with the fact that they had not only apostasized and blasphemed but had also betrayed their fellow Christians. 'Betrayal' could mean simply that they had abandoned the community, a mere synonym for defection, but it might more precisely mean that they had become informers.[11]

The circumstances in which this occurred are not given. *Hermas* is usually thought to have been written in Rome some time in the second century, though recently a good case has been made for an earlier date.[12] In the text two things come to light which may shed light on these apostates. First, there are references to persecution, either past or yet to come (*Vis.* 2:2.7; 4:1.6-9; *Sim.* 8:6.4; 8:8.2). This could relate to the time of Domitian, Pliny or any similar second-century situation in which Christians were publicly arraigned and required to confirm or deny their faith. Second, apostasy and blasphemy are often associated with the problem of riches, a recurrent theme of the book (*Vis.* 1:4.2; 2:2.6-8; 3:6.5; *Sim.* 1:4-6; 6:2.3-4; 8:8.2; 8:9.1-3; 9:19.3). It seems that wealthy Christians, many of whom may have been benefactors and/or leaders of one of the house churches, found themselves prised from the Christian community by their social and financial connections with the outside world (*Sim.* 8:8.1; 8:9.1-3; 9:20.2; *Man.* 10:1.4-5).[13] The problems of the wealthy seem to have been a constant concern of the author, but they may have been exacerbated in times of intense pressure. For while the Romans did not

---

11 Jeffers, *Rome*, 129.
12 H. O. Maier, *The Social Setting of the Ministry as Reflected in the Writings of Hermas, Clement and Ignatius* (Waterloo: Wilfrid Laurier University Press, 1991), 55-58, summarizes the options and argues for a date towards the end of the first century.
13 So Maier, *Social*, 66-67. Jeffers, *Rome*, 171-72, separates the problems of apostasy and wealth.

authorise any official or widespread persecution, when Christians were brought to their attention by informers or by their own activities they were faced with a stark option: either confess and die or deny and live. For some of the wealthy and well-connected, it seems, allegiance was too great a price to pay. And, when they defected, they may have placed others in the same dilemma by betraying them.

Our final snippet of evidence comes from Justin's discussion of the relationships of various Jewish Christian groups with Gentile Christians and the synagogue communities (*Dial.* 46-47). At the end of his discussion he alludes to erstwhile Christians who had defected to the synagogue and who openly denied their previous Christian beliefs (*Dial.* 47:4). These may have been Jewish Christians, but the statement that they "switched over to" (μεταβαίνω) rather than "returned to" the synagogue perhaps suggests that they were Gentiles. We are not told what motivated them, only that they defected "for some reason or the other," but the general context suggests that a significant role was played by Jewish persuasion.[14] If so, we gain a glimpse of yet another element in the process of defection—active enticement from another quarter, in this case Judaism.

Conclusions

The scattered allusions to apostates could be classified in a number of ways. The most interesting for our purposes is to cluster them in terms of cause or motivation, the former of which is often more transparent than the latter. At least four categories suggest themselves.

The first were forced apostates, those who buckled when severe oppression left them, as often as not, with a choice between life and death. Several of the examples we have looked at include an element of external force, making it the most frequently documented context for apostasy. The oppressors were usually representatives of an unsympathetic state. It is probable most of those who defected in such circumstances did so against their will and would not otherwise have considered such a move. Yet for others the situation was more complicated. During the reign of Trajan some Christians, though ideally perhaps preferring anonymity, were eager enough to make public their earlier defection when named by informers to the state authorities. It is not implausible to suppose that some of those forced to apostasize in such circumstances thought they could remain secret believers, as has

---

14 For further discussion see Wilson, "Gentile Judaizers," 609-10.

often happened since, but this we are not told. In some cases—as in *Hermas*—apostasy was compounded by betrayal of others and evoked the harshest of condemnations.

A second type, well-documented in the modern world and doubtless having ancient counterparts, we might describe as gradual apostates, those who slowly but inexorably drifted apart from their religious community over a period of time. Their decision was neither precipitate nor a response to an immediate crisis; it was rather a cumulative response to the routine business of finding their place in the world. Many different things could have motivated them—disaffection with aspects of Christian belief or lifestyle, social and family pressure, political ambition, or simply a hankering to live like those outside their community. For many of those involved the process may initially have been imperceptible, a matter of making minor compromises rather than a conscious decision to change allegiance. Yet the cumulative effect of small compromises could eventually lead them to be viewed as apostates by others, if not by themselves. Unfortunately the ancient evidence rarely provides the sort of detail about such cases as we might wish for. Yet the evidence of *Hermas* suggests that some wealthy Roman Christians were (from the author's viewpoint) routinely compromised by their social and political ties, and that this was a constant source of tension even though it came to a head most dramatically in times of persecution. Pliny's evidence also implies that people could drift away from the Christian community without any public fanfare over a long period of time until they were forced into the open by local opponents.

We also found a few examples of what we might call atavistic apostates, those whose commitment to Christianity was undercut by the pull of their former allegiance. The epistle to the Hebrews is probably addressed to Jewish Christians feeling (and sometimes succumbing to) the pull of Judaism. Revelation may allude to Jewish or Gentile Christians in the same position, as may *1 Clement* and *Barnabas*. In these instances the urge to revert was in all likelihood heightened by external threats which made their more recent allegiance all the less attractive.

Finally, we may have one example of intellectual apostates, those who were led to doubt their position and abandon their community as a result of critical scrutiny of their own tradition and the consideration of rival claims. Thus the Christians who, according to Justin's account, defected to the synagogue may well have been persuaded to do so by Jews who convinced them of the weakness of Christian claims.

Of course, these categories are somewhat artificial. They clearly overlap and other groupings could be devised. Yet they do serve to point us to some of the major motives for defection. The last three can be readily paralleled in the modern world: gradual drifters, attracted to and then enticed away by aspects of life frowned on within their community; erstwhile converts who cannot resist the pull of their former life; and the intellectually disaffected, troubled by doubts about their own tradition and attracted to the claims of a rival. Many of these motives for apostasy are honourable, and in some cases they may speak directly to our own experience. We can at any rate attempt to weigh and understand them with sympathy.

In the ancient evidence apostates rarely speak for themselves. They are mostly so labelled by others, which may be an accident of the extant evidence. It may also be that it was a label which people did not often or publicly attach to themselves. This is in line with some modern research, which suggests that apostates, even when they recognise their position (which, in some of the examples we have considered, they may not have), tend not to advertise their defection.[15]

We may finally turn to the question of numbers. It could be argued that, spread over a period of approximately one hundred and fifty years, the incidence of Christian apostasy was rare. This however, as we have noted, may be partly because apostasy was not a happy topic to dwell on. One piece of evidence suggests that apostasy may have been more common than we have tended to think: the allusion in Pliny to Christian apostates in Bithynia. The allusion is fleeting, but may be the more telling for that, and it may suggest that apostasy was not so rare as some have supposed.

---

15 Bromily, *Apostasy*, 25, 178.

Bibliography of Jacob Jervell's Scholarly Publications

Svein Helge Birkeflet

1953

"Han kom til sitt eget". En bemerkning til Joh. 1,11. ["He Came to that which was His Own." A Remark on John 1:11]. *Norsk Teologisk Tidsskrift* 54 (1953) 129-43. [German transl. in Studia Theologica, 1956]

1954

Visdom og dårskap. Fra en universitetstale. [Wisdom and Folly. From a University Speech]. *Kirke og Kultur* 59 (1954) 233-41.

Skapertroen i forkynnelsen. [The Belief in the Creator in Preaching]. *Norsk Kirkeblad* 49 (1954) 35-40.

Trekk fra tysk teologi idag. [Trends in German Theology Today]. *Norsk Kirkeblad* 49 (1954) 241-46.

1955

Kristus – det himmelske bilde. Genesis 1 – Poimandres – Fil. 2. [Christ – the Heavenly Image]. *Norsk Teologisk Tidsskrift* 56 (1955) 202-19.

1956

"Er kam in sein Eigentum". Zum Joh. 1,11. *Studia Theologica* 10 (1956) 14-27. [First published in Norsk Teologisk Tidsskrift, 1953.]

Ny oversettelse av Apostlenes gjerninger. [A New Translation of Acts]. *Norsk Kirkeblad* 51 (1956) 84-89.

[Rev.] Om kerygmaets enhet. Eduard Schweitzer: Erniedrigung und Erhöhung bei Jesus und seinen Nachfolgern. Zürich, 1955. *Norsk Teologisk Tidsskrift* 57 (1956) 123-28.

[Rev.] Olaf Moe: Paulus' brev til efeserne. Oslo, 1956. *Norsk Kirkeblad* 51 (1956) 311-12.

1958

Avmytologisering på prekestolen. [Demythologization in the Pulpit]. *Kirkebladet* 1 (1958) 166-67.

Hva skal vi gjøre med helliggjørelsen?. [What Shall we Do with Sanctification?]. *Kirkebladet* 1 (1958) 193-95.

1959

Om tolkning av bibeltolkning og litt til. [On Interpretation of Bible Interpretation]. *Kirkebladet* 2 (1959) 266-67. [Reply to Carl Fr. Wisløff]

Saken gjelder Lazarus. [It is Lazarus we are talking about] . *Kirkebladet* 2 (1959) 266-67. [Reply to Carl Fr. Wisløff]

1960

Imago Dei. Gen. 1,26f im Spätjudentum, in der Gnosis und in den paulinischen Briefen. (Forschungen zur Religion und Literatur des Alten und Neuen Testaments 76). Göttingen: Vandenhoeck & Ruprecht, 1960. 379 pp. [Doctoral Dissertation]

Herodes Antipas og hans plass i evangelieoverleveringen. [Herodes Antipas and His Place in the Gospel Transmission]. *Norsk Teologisk Tidsskrift* 61 (1960) 28-40.

Til spørsmålet om tradisjonsgrunnlaget for Apostlenes gjerninger. *Norsk Teologisk Tidsskrift* 61 (1960) 160-75. [German transl. in Studia Theologica, 1962; English transl. in Luke and the People of God, 1972]

[Rev.] A. Adam: Die Psalmen des Thomas und das Perlenlied als Zeugnisse vorchristlicher Gnosis. Berlin, 1959. *Norsk Teologisk Tidsskrift* 61 (1960) 177-78.

1961

Evangelium, apostolat og kirkeordning. [Gospel, Apostelship and Church Order]. *Norsk Teologisk Tidsskrift* 62 (1961) 1-27.

Skilsmisse og gjengifte etter Det nye testamente. [Divorce and Remarriage according to the New Testament]. *Norsk Teologisk Tidsskrift* 62 (1961) 195-210.

Kirkens grunn og kirkens orden. Duplikk til biskop Skard. [Foundation and Order of the Church]. *Kirke og Kultur* 66 (1961) 219-26.

Lydighetens tjeneste. Det nye testamente om lydigheten. [In Service of Obedience. Obedience in the New Testament]. *Prismet* 12 (1961) 118-23.

Generell prekenbetraktning om påsketiden. *Kirkebladet* 4 (1961) 110-12.

[Rev.] Evangeliets evige vilje. Bjarne Skard: Contra kvinnelige prester. Oslo, 1960. *Kirke og Kultur* 66 (1961) 40-46.

[Rev.] Ja hvorfor ikke? Leif Aalen (red): Kvinnelige prester – hvorfor ikke? Oslo, 1961. *Kirke og Kultur* 66 (1961) 614-22.

1962

Den historiske Jesus. Oslo: Land og Kirke, 1962. 106 pp. [2nd enl. ed. 1969; 3rd enl. ed. 1978; English transl. 1965]

Zur Frage der Traditionsgrundlage der Apostelgeschichte. *Studia Theologica* 16 (1962) 25-41. [First published in Norsk Teologisk Tidsskrift, 1960]

Hva hovedfaget angår. *Kirkebladet* 5 (1962) 159-60.

God's Faithfulness to the Faithless People. Trends in Interpretation of Luke-Acts. *Word and World* 12 (1962) 29-36.

[Rev.] Per Lønning: Hva er kristendom? Oslo, 1962. *Kirkebladet* 5 (1962) 182-84.

[Rev.] Andreas Edwin: Sannhet eller usannhet? Oslo, 1962. *Kirkebladet* 5 (1962) 221-22.

1963

Agape og menighetsordning. Omkring 1. Kor. 12-14. [Agape and Congregation Order. On 1 Cor 12-14]. *Svensk Teologisk Kvartalskrift* 39 (1963) 227-45.

Kirkens rett til Jesus fra Nasaret. Omkring "Den historiske Jesus". [The Church's Right to Jesus of Nazareth. On "The Historical Jesus"]. *Minervas kvartalsskrift* 7 (1963) 502-11.

[Rev.] B. Gärtner: Et nytt evangelium? Stockholm, 1960. *Norsk Teologisk Tidsskrift* 64 (1963) 243-45.

[Rev.] E. Haenchen: Die Botschaft des Thomasevangeliums. Berlin, 1961. *Norsk Teologisk Tidsskrift* 64 (1963) 243-45.

[Rev.] H. Conzelmann: Die Mitte der Zeit. *Norsk Teologisk Tidsskrift* 64 (1963) 245-46.

[Rev.] Judentum, Urchristentum, Kirche. Festschrift für J. Jeremias. Berlin, 1960. *Norsk Teologisk Tidsskrift* 64 (1963) 246-48.

[Rev.] Om den såkalte bibelkrisen. Carl Fr. Wisløff: Vår tillit til Bibelen. Oslo, 1963. *Kirke og Kultur* 68 (1963) 478-85.

1964

Bibelsynskrisen nok en gang. Svar til Ole Modalsli. *Kirke og Kultur* 69 (1964) 50-52.

"Det er rett slik". *Kirkebladet* 7 (1964) 134. [Reply to Einar Stray]

Om den onde vilje. *Kirkebladet* 7 (1964) 234-35. [Reply to Einar Stray]

Historisk vitenskap og trostenkning. Forsøk på svar til J. Borgenvik. [Historical Science and Belief. Reply to J. Borgenvik]. *Luthersk Kirketidende* 99 (1964) 58-63.

Om Nils Johanssons kultiske embedstale. *Svensk Teologisk Kvartalskrift* 40 (1964) 285-89. [Reply to Nils Johansson]

1965

The Continuing Search for the Historical Jesus. Minneapolis: Augsburg, 1965. pp. [English transl. of Den historiske Jesus, 1962]

Das gespaltene Israel und die Heidenvölker. Zur Motivierung der Heidenmission in der Apostelgeschichte. *Studia Theologica* 19 (1965) 68-96. [First published in Norsk Teologisk Tidsskrift, 1965]

Det splittede Israel og folkeslagene. Til motiveringen av hedningemisjonen i Apostlenes gjerninger. *Norsk Teologisk Tidsskrift* 66 (1965) 232-59. [German transl. in Studia Theologica, 1965; English transl. in Luke and the People of God, 1972]

1966

Recht und Grenze der exegetischen Bemühung im Blick auf den Verkündigungsauftrag der Kirche. *Lutherische Rundschau* 16 (1966) 181-96. [English transl. in Lutheran World, 1966]

Legitimacy and Limitations of Exegesis in Relation to the Church's Task of Preaching. *Lutheran World* 13 (1966) 137-49. [German transl. in Lutherische Rundschau, 1966]

Johannes Munck. *Norsk Teologisk Tidsskrift* 67 (1966) 47-48. [Obituary]

Bread from Heaven. Opposisjonsinnlegg ved Peder Borgens disputas for den teologiske doktorgrad 11. juni 1966. [Bread from Heaven. Opposition at Peder Borgen's doctoral disputation]. *Norsk Teologisk Tidsskrift* 67 (1966) 227-43.

[Rev.] R. Repo: Der "Weg" als Selbstbezeichnung des Urchristentums. Helsinki, 1964. *Norsk Teologisk Tidsskrift* 67 (1966) 171.

[Rev.] H. J. Gabathuler: Jesus Christus. Haupt der Kirche – Haupt der Welt. Zürich, 1965. *Norsk Teologisk Tidsskrift* 67 (1966) 172.

[Rev.] W. Schrage: Das Verhältnis des Thomas–Evangeliums zur synoptischen Tradition und zu den koptischen Evangelienübersetzungen. Berlin, 1964. *Norsk Teologisk Tidsskrift* 67 (1966) 172-73.

[Rev.] J. C. Hurd: The Origins of 1 Corinthians. London, 1965. *Norsk Teologisk Tidsskrift* 67 (1966) 173-75.

[Rev.] Gads danske bibelleksikon. Red. av E. Nielsen og B. Noack. København, 1966. *Norsk Teologisk Tidsskrift* 67 (1966) 175-76.

[Rev.] Philip Houm i Den norske Kirke [Philip Houm : Mannen fra Nazareth og Den norske Kirke. Oslo, 1966]. *Kirke og Kultur* 71 (1966) 49-59.

1967

Da fremtiden begynte. Om urkristendommens tro og tenkning. [When the Future Began. Belief and Thought in Primitive Christianity]. Oslo: Land og kirke, 1967. 174 pp. [2nd enl. ed. 1976]

Ikke bare ruiner. [Not only Ruins]. Oslo: Land og kirke, 1967. 143 pp.

"Dersom jeg altså ikke kjenner sprogets betydning...". Om forkynnelsen. [On Preaching]. *Minervas kvartalsskrift* 11 (1967) 431-38.

1968

Paulus – der Lehrer Israels. Zu den apologetischen Paulusreden in der Apostelgeschichte. *Novum Testamentum* 10 (1968) 164-90. [English transl. in Luke and the People of God, 1972]

"Granskeren" 80 år. *Norsk Teologisk Tidsskrift* 69 (1968) 129.

Midt i Israels historie. [In the Middle of Israel's History]. *Norsk Teologisk Tidsskrift* 69 (1968) 130-38.

Jesu blods aker. [The field of Jesus' Blood]. *Norsk Teologisk Tidsskrift* 69 (1968) 158-62. [On Matt. 27,3-10]

1969

Den historiske Jesus. Oslo: Land og Kirke, 1969. 116 pp. [2nd enl. ed.; 1st ed. 1962]

Ein Interpolar interpretiert. Zu der christlichen Bearbeitung der Testamente der Zwölf Patriarchen. In *Studien zu den Testamenten der Zwölf Patriarchen. Drei Aufsätze herausgegeben von Walter Eltester* (Beiheft zur Zeitschrift für die neutestamentliche Wissenschaft 36). Berlin: Töpelmann, 1969. pp. 30-61.

"Se, jeg gjør alle ting nye". Om troen på oppstandelsen. ["Lo, I Make all Things New". On the Belief in the Resurrection]. *Den Norske kirkes presteforening. 30. generalforsamling* (1969) 84-93.

[Rev.] Bibelkommentar: Innledning og noter til "Jerusalembibelen" oversatt til dansk. København, 1968. *Norsk Teologisk Tidsskrift* 70 (1969) 63-64.

[Rev.] Nye muligheter for Det nye testamentes budskap. Det nye testamente oversatt fra gresk av Erik Gunnes. Oslo, 1968. *Lumen* 12 (1969) 176-86.

1970

Brevet til Jerusalem. Om Romerbrevets forandledning og adresse. [The Letter to Jerusalem. On Background and Address of Paul's Letter to the Romans]. In *Skrift og skole : Festskrift til Oddmund Hjelde på 60-årsdagen 15. mars 1970*. Oslo: Land og kirke, 1970. pp. 85-99. [German transl. in Studia Theologica 1971; English transl. in The Romans Debate 1977, 2nd ed. 1991]

Kvalbeins ubesvarte spørsmål. *Luthersk Kirketidende* 105 (1970) 266-71. [Reply to Hans Kvalbein]

1971

The Law in Luke-Acts. *Harvard Theological Review* 64 (1971) 21-36. [Reprinted in Luke and the People of God, 1972]

Der Brief nach Jerusalem. Über Veranlassung und Adresse des Römerbriefs. *Studia Theologica* 25 (1971) 61-73. [Norwegian original 1970; English transl. in The Romans Debate, 1977; 2nd ed. 1991]

Die offenbarte und die verborgene Tora. Zur Vorstellung über die neue Tora im Rabbinismus. *Studia Theologica* 25 (1971) 90-108.

Jesus og Paulus. *Kirke og Kultur* 76 (1971) 577-84.

1972

Den omskårne Messias. [The Circumcised Messiah]. *Svensk Exegetisk Årsbok* 37/38 (1972/73) 145-55. [German transl. in Theologie aus dem Norden, 1976; English transl. in The Unknown Paul, 1984]

Luke and the People of God. A New Look at Luke-Acts. Minneapolis: Augsburg, 1972. 207 pp.

Et politisk evangelium?. [A Political Gospel?]. *Kirke og Kultur* 77 (1972) 2-10.

Kristen praksis. [Christian Practice]. *Kirke og Kultur* 77 (1972) 588-96.

1973

Gud og hans fiender. Forsøk på å tolke Romerbrevet. [God and His Enemies. A Commentary on Paul's Letter to the Romans]. Oslo: Universitetsforlaget, 1973. 283 pp. [Reprinted 1989]

Barnetro – overtro – voksentro. [Childlike Faith – Superstition – Grown-up Belief]. *Kirke og Kultur* 78 (1973) 156-61.

1974

Imagines und Imago Dei. Aus der Genesis-Exegese des Josephus. In *Josephus-Studien. Untersuchungen zu Josephus, dem antiken Judentum und dem Neuen Testament. Otto Michel zum 70. Geburtstag gewidmet.* Göttingen: Vandenhoeck & Ruprecht, 1974. pp. 197-204.

Teologien og kirken i Lukasskriftene. [Theology and Church in the Lukan Writings]. *Præsteforeningens Blad* 64 (1974) 341-50, 365-68.

1975

...bare all makt. [*...only all Power*]. Oslo: Gyldendal, 1975. 154 pp. [A Collection of Sermons]

En allmektig Gud i en verden som er vår?. [An Almighty God in a World like Ours?]. *Kirke og Kultur* 80 (1975) 2-8.

Om Jesus og Paulus i kvinneåret. [On Jesus and Paul in the The Women's Year]. *Kirke og Kultur* 80 (1975) 555-69.

Prekenvennlige kommentarer. [Commentaries for Preaching]. *Teologi for Menigheten* 1, nr. 2 (1975) 15.

1976

Da fremtiden begynte. Om urkristendommens tro og tenkning. Oslo: Land og Kirke, 1976. 164 pp. [2nd enl. ed.; 1st ed. 1967]

Der schwache Charismatiker. In *Rechtfertigung. Festschrift für Ernst Käsemann zum 70. Geburtstag.* Hg. von Johannes Friedrich et al. Tübingen: Mohr, 1976. pp. 185-98.

Die Beschneidung des Messias. In *Theologie aus dem Norden.* Hg. von *Albert Fuchs* (Studien zum Neuen Testament und seiner Umwelt, Serie A 2). Linz: Fuchs, 1976. pp. 68-78. [Norwegian original 1972]

Forord til den norske utgave. [Foreword to the Norwegian Edition]. In *Hans von Campenhausen: Den kristne Bibel blir til.* Oslo: Land og kirke, 1976. pp. 9-10.

Den oppstandnes Ånd. Talen om Den hellige Ånd i Det nye testamente. [The Spirit of the Risen One. The Holy Spirit in The New Testament]. *Norsk Teologisk Tidsskrift* 77 (1976) 19-32.

1977

God's Christ and his People. Studies in Honour of Nils Alstrup Dahl. Ed. by *Jacob Jervell and Wayne Meeks.* Oslo: Universitetsforlaget, 1977. 295 pp.

Das Volk des Geistes. In *God's Christ and his People. Studies in Honour of Nils Alstrup Dahl. Ed. by Jacob Jervell and Wayne Meeks.* Oslo: Universitetsforlaget, 1977. pp. 87-106.

The Letter to Jerusalem. In *The Romans Debate.* Ed. by K. P. Donfried. Minneapolis: Augsburg, 1977. pp. 61-74. [Norwegian original 1970; German transl. 1971]

Guds siste fiende. Paulus' forståelse av døden. [God's Last Enemy. Paul's View of Death]. *Norsk Teologisk Tidsskrift* 78 (1977) 23-32.

Den karismatiske vekkelse. Om nåden og nådegavene i urkirken. [The Charismatic Revival. Grace and the Gifts of Grace in Primitive Christianity]. *Kirke og Kultur* 82 (1977) 578-91.

Menneske i morgendagens samfunn. [The Human Being in Tomorrow's Society]. *Kirke og Kultur* 82 (1977) 515-23.

[Rev.] G. Lohfink: Die Sammlung Israels. München, 1975. *Theologische Literaturzeitung* 102 (1977) 584-85.

[Rev.] W. Schmithals: Der Römerbrief als historisches Problem. Güthersloh, 1975. *Theologische Literaturzeitung* 102 (1977) 729-31.

1978

Ingen har større kjærlighet... Fra Johannesevangeliets Jesusbilde. [Jesus in the Gospel of John]. (Tankekors 2). Oslo: Universitetsforlaget, 1978. 94 pp. [English transl. 1984]

Historiens Jesus. Oslo: Land og Kirke, 1978. 146 pp. [3rd enl. ed. of Den historiske Jesus; 1st ed. 1962]

Via Dolorosa – Guds egen vei. [Via Dolorosa – the Way of God]. In *Størst av alt. Festskrift til Stephan Tschudi på 70-års dagen 2. januar 1978.* Ed. by Sverre Inge Apenes et al. Oslo: Land og kirke, 1978. pp. 77-84.

Matteusevangeliet?. [The Gospel of Matthew?]. *Norsk Teologisk Tidsskrift* 79 (1978) 241-48. [Reconstruction of Opposition at Helge Hognestad's Doctoral Disputation]

Maktkirken. [The Power Church]. *Kirke og Kultur* 83 (1978) 578-86.

1979

Paul in the Acts of the Apostles. In *Les Actes des Apôtres. Traditions, rédaction, théologie.* Ed. par J. Kremer et al. (Bibliotheca Ephemeridum Theologicarum Lovaniensium 48). Paris: J. Duculot, 1979. pp. 297-306. [Reprinted in The Unknown Paul, 1984]

Die Zeichen des Apostels. Die Wunder beim lukanischen und paulinischen Paulus. In*Studien zum Neuen Testament und seiner Umwelt,* Ser. A 4; Linz: Fuchs, 1979. pp. 54-75. [English transl. in The Unknown Paul, 1984]

1980

Bild Gottes. I. Biblische, frühjüdische und gnostische Auffassungen. In *Theologische Realenzyklopädie, Vol. 6.* Berlin: de Gruyther, 1980. pp. 491-98.

Der unbekannte Paulus. In *Die paulinische Literatur und Theologie. The Pauline Literature and Theology.* Ed. by Sigfred Pedersen. Århus: Aros / Göttingen: Vandenhoeck & Ruprecht, 1980. pp. 29-49. [English transl. in The Unknown Paul, 1984]

Guds Sønn – født av jomfru Maria. [Son of God – Born of Virgin Mary]. In *Frihet til tro. En bok om Bibel og bekjennelse.* Ed. by Inge Lønning. Oslo: Land og Kirke, 1980. pp. 49-71.

Forord. [Foreword]. In *Pagels, Elaine: De gnostiske evangelier. Evangeliene Kirken ikke ville bruke.* Oslo: Cappelen, 1980. pp. 9-10 [Foreword to the Norwegian ed. of E. Pagels: The Gnostic Gospels]

The Mighty Minority. *Studia Theologica* 34 (1980) 13-38. [Reprinted in The Unknown Paul, 1984]

Om menneskeverd. [On Human Dignity]. *Forskningsnytt* 25 (1980) 29-30.

Men mennesket da?. [What about the Human Person?]. *Norsk Hydros jubileumsskrift* 6 (1980) 31-35.

1981

Etiske problemer vedrørende genetisk forskning. [Ethical Problems Concerning Genetic Research]. Oslo: Rådet for medisinsk forskning, NAVF, 1981. 8 pp. [Co-author]

Skolen og kirken i 80-årene. [School and Church in the 80's]. *Kirke og Kultur* 86 (1981) 13-21.

For fortid og fremtid. [For Past and Future]. *Romsdalsmuseet. Årbok* (1981) 9-12.

1982

Hvorfor akkurat Gud?. [Why Exactly God?]. In *Dette tror jeg på.* Ed. by Kjell Bækkelund. Oslo: Cappelen, 1982. pp. 82-97.

En etisk vurdering. [An Ethical Evaluation]. *Kirke og Kultur* 87 (1982) 271-79. [Concerning Genetic Instruction and Prenetal Diagnosis]

1983

Etiske retningslinjer ved kunstig befruktning (AID) og in vitro fertilisering (IVF). [Ethical Directions about Artificial Fertilization and In Vitro Fertilization]. Oslo: Rådet for medisinsk forskningsutvalg for forskningsetikk, 1983. 20 pp. [Co-author]

Pedriatrisk forskningsetikk. Etiske retningslinjer ved biomedisinsk forskning på barn. [Ethics for Pedriatic Research. Ethical Directions for Biomedical Research on Children]. Oslo: Rådet for medisinsk forskningsutvalg for forskningsetikk, 1983. 8 pp. [Co-author]

Die Töchter Abrahams. Die Frau in der Apostelgeschichte. In *Glaube und Gerechtigkeit. In memoriam Rafael Gyllenberg*. Ed. by Jarmo Kilunen et al. (Schriften der Finnischen Exegetischen Gesellschaft 38). Helsinki: Finnische Exegetische Gesellschaft, 1983. pp. 77-93. [English transl. in The Unknown Paul, 1984]

Die Mitte der Schrift. Zum lukanischen Verständnis des Alten Testaments. In *Die Mitte des Neuen Testaments. Einheit und Vielfalt neutestamentlicher Theologie. Festschrift für Eduard Schweizer zum siebzigsten Geburtstag*. Ed. by Ulrich Luz and Hans Weder. Göttingen: Vandenhoeck & Ruprecht, 1983. pp. 79-96. [English transl. in The Unknown Paul, 1984]

The Acts of the Apostles and the History of Early Christianity. *Studia Theologica* 37 (1983) 17-32.

Etiske aspekter ved AID og IVF. [Ethical Aspects of AID and IVF]. *Tidsskrift for Den norske Lægeforening* 103 (1983) 347-49.

1984

The unknown Paul. Essays on Luke-Acts and Early Christian History. Minneapolis: Augsburg, 1984. 190 pp.

Jesus in the Gospel of John. Minneapolis: Augsburg, 1984. 96 pp. [English transl. of Ingen har større kjærlighet, 1978]

Livet i våre hender. [Life in Our Hands]. In *Det står om livet. Artikkelsamling om menneskesynet redigert av Gisle Hollekim*. Oslo: Vårt Land forlag, 1984. pp. 106-08.

Kristendommens politiske betydning og ansvar. [The Political Meaning and Responsibility of Christianity]. *Idea* 6 (1984) 13-29.

"Profetenes barn". Om Den hellige Ånd i Apostlenes Gjerninger. In *Spiritualitet. Teologiske studier og brugstekster. Festskrift til Anna Marie Aagaard 14. januar 1985*. Ed. by Hans Raun Iversen et al. Århus: Anis, 1985. pp. 41-50. [Part of an article published in The unknown Paul, 1984]

1985

Dåpen til døden. [Baptism to Death]. *Præsteforeningens Blad* 75 (1985) 525-29. [On Rom. 6]

1986

Diasporajødedommen og Jerusalems fall. [Diaspora Judaism and the Fall of Jerusalem]. In *Judendom och kristendom under de första århundradena*.

Nordiskt patristikerprojekt 1982-85. Vol. 2. Oslo: Universitetsforlaget, 1986. pp. 36-48.

Paulus in der Apostelgeschichte und die Geschichte des Urchristentums. *New Testament Studies* 32 (1986) 378-92.

Adam. In *Evangelisches Kirchenlexikon. Internationale theologische Enzyklopädie.* Ed. by Erwin Fahlbusch et al. Vol. 1. Göttingen: Vandenhoeck & Ruprecht, 1986. pp. 40-41.

Apostelgeschichte. In *Evangelisches Kirchenlexikon. Internationale theologische Enzyklopädie.* Ed. by Erwin Fahlbusch et al. Vol. 1. Göttingen: Vandenhoeck & Ruprecht, 1986. pp. 225-29.

Menneskebildet i år 2000. [The View of the Human Person in the Year 2000]. *Skoleforum* 85 (1986) 28-33.

Mennesket som åndsvesen. Foredrag under Ordførende Mesteres Møte 16. mars 1986. [The Human Person as Spiritual Being]. *Frimurerbladet* 38 (1986) 37-45.

1987

Menneskebildet i år 2000. [The View of the Human Person in the Year 2000]. In *Rapport fra rektorkonferanse på Klækken 17.-19. september 1986.* (RVO-rapporter 2). Oslo: Rådet for videregående opplæring, 1987. pp. 81-88.

Evangeliet om AIDS. [The Gospel on AIDS]. *Prismet* 38 (1987) 190-91.

Observasjoner fra tribunen. [Observations from the Tribune]. *Norges barnevern* 64 (1987) 5-8.

Gene-Ethics. *Laboratoriet* (1987) 1:5-11,19; 2:2,4-8.

1988

The Church of Jews and Godfearers. In *Luke-Acts and the Jewish People. Eight Critical Perspectives.* Ed. by Joseph B. Tyson. Minneapolis: Augsburg, 1988. pp. 11-20.

AIDS-epidemien – vår tids medisinske, politiske og etiske utfordring?. [The AIDS Epidemic – the Medical, Political and Ethical Challenge of Our Time?]. In *AIDS. Frykt og fakta. Utfordring til handling og omsorg.* Ed. by Torleiv O. Rognum et al. Oslo: Ansgar forlag, 1988. pp. 31-41.

En etikk for vårt forhold til naturen. [An Environmental Ethics]. *Samtiden* 97 (1988) 5-9.

1989

Gud og hans fiender. Forsøk på å tolke Romerbrevet. Oslo: Universitetsforlaget, 1989. 283 pp. [2nd ed.; 1st ed. 1973]

Mennesket i sentrum. [The Human Person in the Center]. In *Ledelse i en skole i utvikling.* Ed. by Tom Tiller. Oslo: Tano, 1989. pp. 206-12.

[Rev.] Richard I. Pervo: Profit with Delight. The Literary Genre of the Acts of the Apostles. Philadelphia, 1987. *Journal of Theological Studies* 40 (1989) 569-71.

1991

Det moralske Norge. Om samfunnsmoral. [Moral Norway. On Social Ethics]. Brennpunkt; Oslo: Cappelen, 1991. 89 pp.

Retrospect and Prospect in Luke-Acts Interpretation. In *Society of Biblical Literature. 1991 Seminar Papers.* Atlanta: Scholars Press, 1991. pp. 383-404.

Gottes Treue zum untreuen Volk. In *Der Treue Gottes trauen. Beiträge zum Werk des Lukas. Für Gerhard Schneider.* Ed. by Claus Bussmann et al. Freiburg: Herder, 1991. pp. 15-27.

Der Sohn des Volkes. In *Anfänge der Christologie. Festschrift für Ferdinand Hahn zum 65. Geburtstag.* Ed. by Cilliers Breytenbach and Henning Paulsen. Göttingen: Vandenhoeck & Ruprecht, 1991. pp. 245-54.

The Letter to Jerusalem. In *The Romans Debate. Revised and Expanded Edition.* Ed. by K. P. Donfried. Peabody: Hendrickson, 1991. pp. 53-64. [Norwegian original 1970; German transl. 1971; English transl. 1st ed. 1977]

1992

Etikk mot AIDS. [Ethics against AIDS]. *AIDS-info* 6 (1992) 3.

1993

Om folkekirken. Fra urkirken til Hamar bispedømme. [On the Folk Church. From Primitive Christianity to the Diocese of Hamar]. In *Kirken i tiden. Troen i folket. Festskrift til biskop Georg Hille.* Oslo: Verbum, 1993. pp. 61-68.

1994

The Lucan Interpretation of Jesus as Biblical Theology. In *New Directions in Biblical Theology. Papers of the Aarhus Conference, 16-19 September 1992.*

Ed. by Sigfred Pedersen. (Supplements to Novum Testamentum 76). Leiden: Brill, 1994. pp. 77-92.

Historisk kritisk metode – det ene nødvendige. [Historical Critical Method – the One thing necessary]. In *Prekenen, et kunsthåndverk? Det teologiske fakultet, Det praktisk-teologiske seminar, Etterutdanningskurs 1993.* Etterutdanning for prester; 1. Oslo: Etterdanningskomitéen ved Det teologiske fakultet, 1994. pp. 1-14.

Må kristendomsundervisning være kjedelig?. [Does Instruction in Christian Education Have to Be Boring?]. *Schola* 2 (1994) 27-29.

1995

The Theology of the Acts of the Apostles. (New Testament Theology). Cambridge: Cambridge University Press, 1995. Forthcoming.

Die Apostelgeschichte. (Kritisch-exegetischer Kommentar über das Neue Testament 3). Göttingen: Vandenhoeck & Ruprecht, 1995. Forthcoming.

Fremtid fra fortiden. Frelseshistorie og Lukas som historiker. [The Future of the Past. Luke's Vision of Salvation History and its Bearing on His Writing of History]. In *Ad Acta. Studier til Apostlenes gjerninger og urkristendommens historie. Festskrift til Edvin Larsson.* Ed. by Reidar Hvalvik and Hans Kvalbein. Oslo: Verbum, 1995. pp. 157-73.

Das Aposteldekret in der lukanischen Theologie. In *Texts and Contexts. Biblical Texts in Their Textual and Situational Contexts. Essays in Honor of Lars Hartman.* Ed. by Tord Fornberg and David Hellholm. Oslo – Copenhagen – Stockholm – Boston: Scandinavian University Press, 1995. pp. 227-43.

The Future of the Past. Lukes's Vision of Salvation History and Its Bearing on His Writing of History. In *The Acts and the Historians. Acts and Ancient Historiography.* Cambridge: Cambridge University Press, 1995. Forthcoming.

Grunnforskning, samfunn og etikk. [Research, Society and Ethics]. In *Festskrift til Bjarne Waaler.* Oslo: 1995. Forthcoming.

Abbreviations

For the abbreviations of names for Biblical Books with the Apocrypha, Pseudepigraphical and Early Patristic Books, Dead Sea Scrolls and related texts, Other Jewish texts, and Nag Hammadi texts the following two systems have been used:

(a) The system of the *Journal of Biblical Literature (JBL): Instructions for Contributors*;

(b) The system of the *Theologische Realenzyklopädie (TRE): Abkürzungsverzeichnis*, ed. S. Schwertner, 2nd edition, Berlin/New York: de Gruyter 1994.

Index of Passages

Old Testament

Genesis
2:24	171
33:11	194
39:12	20
41:40-43	20

Exodus
4:21	14
9:34-35	14

Leviticus
11ff.	198
16:29ff.	198
17-18	4
19:18	137

Numbers
12:7f.	103

Deuteronomy
6:5	137
18:20	146
18:21-22	164
22:25	194
22:28	194
33:2	103

Joshua
19:49	28

Judges
13:15-16 (Alex.)	194
19:7	194

1 Samuel
15:22   139

2 Kings
13:25   194
13:27   194

Psalms
26:4-5   143
57:18 (LXX)   103
110:1   19, 147
118:26   145

Job
34:30   142-143
36:13   143

Isaiah
6:9-10   13
42:1-4   139-140
54:13   140
55:1   86
56:7   71, 75, 145

Jeremiah
2:13   86
2:34   146
5:21   15
5:22-24   15
7:6   146
7:11   145
11:21-23   145
14:14-16   145
22:3   146
23:9-40   145
23:39   143
26:7-19   145
29:8-9   145
31:33-34   140
44:16-18   145

Ezekiel
33:31   143
47   86

Esther
7:8   194

Daniel
7   164
7:9   18
8:15-16   18
8:18   22
9:21   18
10:5   18
10:9-12   22

Hosea
6:6   139-140

Amos
2:12-16   17

Nahum
3:4   142

Habakkuk
1:5   197

Apocrypha, Pseudepigrapha and Other Early Jewish Texts

Apocalypse of Elijah
21:13ff.   197
31:15ff.   199

Assumptio Mosis
7   197

Index of Passages

2 (syr) Baruch
14:8	158
48:38	197

4 Ezra
10:29-36	22

Jesus Sirah (Ben Sira)
1:25-30	142
32:14-24	142
33:1-3	142

Josephus (Flavius)
Antiquitates
4.143	195
5.277	18
9.281	196
13.376-383	142
15.5.3	103
16.37	190
17.41-45	142
17.272	193
19.173	195
20.200f.	9, 142

De bello Judaico
1.92-97	142
1.108	142
1.110	142
2.162	142
2.254-56	95
3.423	190
5.60	190

Vita Josephi
191	142

Jubilees
23:16f.	197

2 Maccabees
3:26	18
3:33	18
6:21-26	142
11:8-10	18
14:41	194

4 Maccabees
6:15-19	142
11:25	194

Oracula Sibyllina
(incl. Christian Oracles)
III. 68ff.	197
III. 604	85
III. 550	85
V. 328	85
VI	85

Philo
De decalogo
158-61	30

De migratione
9	37

De posteritate
26	37

De somniis
1.140-41	30
1.141ff.	103

Psalms of Solomon
12:1-4	143

Testament XII Patriarchs
Testament of Levi
14:1ff.	197
16:1ff.	197

Testament of Dan
5-6   134

Testament of Zebulon
9:5-9   134

Wisdom of Solomon
14:22-28   155

Qumran and Related Texts

CD
1:3-4   143
1:13-21   142
4:19   142
8:12   142
19:24-33   142

CAVE 1
1QS
4:9-14   155
11:19   158

1QH
4:11   143
4:13   143
7:34   143

1QpHab
2:5ff.   198

CAVE 4
4QpNah
1:2   142
1:7   142
2:1-10   143
3:1-8   143
4:1-6   143

4QpPs 37
2:12-14   198
4:13-14   198

Rabbinic Texts

1. Mishna, Tosephta, Talmudtract.
bʿAvoda Zara
9a   199

bSanhedrin
97a/b   199

mSanhedrin
10:1   143

bSota
22b   143

bYoma
86b   143

tYoma
5:12   143

2. Midrashim, Targumim et. al.
ʾAbot
3:15   143

Mekilta de Rabbi Ishmael
Exodus 19:8   143

New Testament

Matthew
1:19   148
2:17-18   145
3:2   184

Index of Passages

3:8	149	12:1-8	139
3:17	184	12:9-14	139
4:17	149	12:15-21	140
4:23-5:2	135	12:18-21	139
5-7	4, 135	12:28	193
5-6	141	12:29	192
5:3	184	12:35	58
5:5	184	12:41f.	192
5:13-16	148	13:16f.	192
5:17-48	135	14:33	14
5:17ff.	185	15:1-28	140
5:18	4	16:13-23	147
5:20	135, 149	16:14	145
5:43-48	135, 140-141	19:12	193, 200
5:47	149	19:19	140
5:48	149	20:20-28	140
6:2	141	20:24-28	141
6:4	149	21-25	135
6:5	141	21:11	145
6:6	149	21:36	145
6:16	141	21:43	149
6:18	149	22:6-7	145
7	141	22:34-40	137-138, 140
7:1-23	138	22:41-46	147-148
7:3-5	141	22:41-45	137-138, 146
7:15-20	141	23-25	135, 148
7:16-18	58	23	133-149
7:18	58	23:1-12	136-141
7:23	138	23:2-3	141
7:24-27	119	23:13-23	141-144
8:10-13	139	23:13	143, 187-188, 193
8:21	198	23:23	148
10:5f.	4	23:28	138, 196
10:16-42	144	23:34-39	144
10:34-36	193	23:35-36	146
11:2-6	184	23:38	143
11:11	184	23:39	146
11:12f.	183-200	24-25	135-136
11:13	192	24	164
12	139		

24:4-5	148	4:12	15
24:9-11	148	4:71	12
24:12	140	6:51-52	14
24:15	147	7	70
24:23	148	7:3-4	73
24:36	149	7:3	74
24:40-41	149	7:6	70
24:42-44	149	7:15	198
25:31-46	147	7:26	71
25:32	149	7:31-37	15
25:34-40	149	8	15
25:37	148	8:17	14-15
25:44-45	149	9:6	22
25:46	148	10:33	71
26:31-58	146	10:34	17
26:60-66	146	10:42	71
26:69-75	146	11-13	135
27:3-5	146	11:17	71, 75, 145
27:8	147	11:32	70
27:9	145	12	74
27:24-26	146	12:24-27	74
27:25	144, 146	12:29	70, 140
28:15	147	12:35-37	74
28:19	4, 149	12:36	19
		12:37b-40	136
Mark		12:41-44	136
1:14-15	11	13	18
1:17	193, 200	13:10	71, 75
1:47	70	13:20	23
2:18-22	72	13:27	23
2:18f.	198	14:2	70
2:18	73	14:15	80
2:23-28	72	14:51-52	16-17, 20
2:23ff.	198	14:62	19
2:28	198	15:34	60
3:1ff.	198	15:46	18
3:23	12	16:5	18, 20
3:27	192-193	16:6	22
4	12-13	16:8	21-22
4:11-12	11		

Index of Passages 233

Luke		10:37-41	185
6:47-49	119	11:17	139
9:60	198	11:20	9
9:61f.	198	12:10	125
11:37-52	142	13:5	124
11:42	139	13:14	124
12:11	29	14:1	124
16:15b-18	187	14:6-23	125-126
16:16	183-200	14:13	124-125
16:31	196	14:19	125-126
20:20	29	15:9	139
24:29	194	15:21	124
		15:28	156
John		15:29	3, 123
4:14	87	15:40	7
6:15	188, 190	16:11-40	126-128
8:30-31	205	16:12	125
11:47-48	129, 191	16:15	124, 194
11:49-52	191	16:19	124
12:42-43	205	16:23-40	124
16:25-29	12	16:34	124
18:34-35	16	17:1-9	125
		17:1	124
Acts		17:7	124
1:10	18	17:10	124
2:34-36	146	17:16	107-131
2:41	1	17:17	124
3:2	125	17:22-23	121
3:10	125	17:22	120
4:4	1	17:23	120-122
5:1-11	204	18:1-17	125
6:1	9	18:2-3	125
6:5	159	18:4-6	125
6:7	1	18:4	124
7:38	103	18:7-11	125
7:41	123	18:7	124
7:53	103	18:12-17	124
9:24	125	18:19	124
9:29	9	18:26	124
10-11	4	19:8	124

234 *Mighty Minorities*

19:23-41	128-130	8	102, 160
19:27	124	8:5f.	36
19:29-41	124	10	160
20	118	10:4	86
20:7-12	124	10:14-22	160
21:8	160	10:19ff.	102
21:20ff.	94	10:25-26	160
21:21-24	4	10:27-11:1	160
21:30	125	11:3	178
22:20	9	12	180
23:3	141-142	12:3	204
26:5	142	13	140
		15:20-28	147
Romans		15:24	29
3:19	76		
5:12-19	144	2 Corinthians	
8:28-39	149	11:22ff.	94
8:38f.	30	11:22-23	8
9-11	2, 94	12:2	28
9	13		
9:4f.	105	Galatians	
9:17-18	13	2:3-4	9
11	152	2:4	8
11:7-8	13	2:7-8	8
11:18	105	2:11-18	8
11:25	158	2:11-16	141
11:33	158	2:11-14	9
14:4	160	2:14	10
14:14	160	3:1	60
14:17	160	3:19	103
14:20	160	4:3	35
15:30ff.	94	4:9	35
		6:15	4
1 Corinthians			
1:23	60	Ephesians	
2:2	60	1:14	179
2:10	158	1:22	179
5:1-5	204	2:13	96
5:9-10	161	2:14	175
7:1	35	5	167-181

5:18	174	2:11	28, 35
5:19	175	2:13	28, 35
5:20	175	2:14	29, 38
5:(21)22-6:9	167, 170, 173	2:15	29, 34
5:21	174-175, 177	2:16	26, 28-29, 33, 38
5:22	178	2:17	33, 38
5:23	178	2:18	28-29, 33, 35, 38
5:25-33	179	2:19	33
5:26-27	179	2:20	34, 38
5:30	180	2:21	26, 28, 35
6:12	29	2:22	29
		2:23	27-28, 36, 38
Philippians		3:12	28
3:2ff.	94	3:18-4:1	173
3:5	8	3:18	178
		3:19	175
Colossians		4:15	26
1:5	38-39		
1:6	38	1 Thessalonians	
1:9f.	39	1:9	123
1:12	39	2:14-16	94
1:13	39	4:9-10	141
1:16	29, 38-39		
1:18	33	2 Thessalonians	
1:19f.	38	2	164
1:19	33, 39	2:3	199
1:20	37, 39		
1:22	37, 39	1 Timothy	
1:23	38-39	1:7-10	6
1:24	33	4:1	204
1:26f.	35	4:3	35
1:27	39		
2:1	26	Titus	
2:2	35, 39	1:10	6
2:4	26-27, 38	1:14	6
2:8	25-27, 29, 34, 38	3:9	6
2:9f.	33		
2:9	38-39	Hebrews	
2:10	29, 33	1-2	103
2:11-15	39	1:1-4	102

1:5-14	102	3 John	43
2:2	103		
2:14	98, 102	Revelation	
3:1ff.	103-104	1:17-20	22
3:2ff.	103	2-3	153, 161
3:12	97	2:6	152, 154
5:11	99	2:9	206
5:12	99	2:13	162, 206
6:1f.	97	2:14	9, 152, 154, 156
6:2ff.	99	2:15	152
6:4-8	205	2:19-23	154
6:6	205	2:19	154, 157
6:9	205	2:20-21	156
6:10	99	2:20	9, 152, 156-157
7-10	103	2:22	156
8:4-8	99	2:23	157
10:25	99	2:24	152, 156, 158
10:26-31	99, 205	2:26	165
10:32ff.	98, 205	3:1-6	3
10:35	99	3:9	206
11:6	97	4:1f.	28
12:1-11	99	6:9-11	164
12:15-17	99	6:10	165
12:29	101	6:15	165
13:13	205	7:4-8	151
13:22	102	7:9-10	151
		7:17	87
James		8:13	165
	43	9:4ff.	165
3:11-12	58	11:10	165
		13:8	165
1 Peter		13:10	161
2:13-3:7	171, 173	13:14	157
		13:16-17	161
2 Peter		14:1-5	151
2:17-22	204	14:6-7	151
3:17	204	16:15	18
		17-19	157
2 John		17:2	157
	43	17:7	165

18:3	157	82.1	85
18:4	161		
21:6	87	*Protreptikos*	
		2.12	84

Apostolic Fathers and Other Early Christian Texts

Quis dives salvetur?
21.2f.   195

Athanasius
Contra Sabellianos
PG 28.97.30ff.   87

Stromata
1.11   34
3.1.1   83

Epistula ad Afros episcopos
PG 26.1033.12-13   87

Didache
7   20
11-13   43

Barnabas
3:6   207
4:6   207
5:4   207
11.2   86

Epiphanios
Panarion (Haereses)
157.22-23   87

Epistle to Diognetos
11:2   12

1 Clement
11:1-2   206
40:1   158
47:7   206

Eusebios
Historia ecclesiastica
2.23.4-18   9
3.31.3-4   160
3.39.9   160
4.15.7-8   207
4.15.47   207
5.24.2   160

Clement of Alexandria
Adumbrationes ad 1 Pet 5:13   69

Excerpta ex Theodoto
1.6-7   86
4.78   83
36.2   83
63.2   83
64   83
65.1   83
78   62
78.2   84

Praeparatio evangelica
13.12.13   30

5 Ezra
1:35   135
1:37-38   135

Hermas
Visiones
1:4.2	208
2:2.6-8	208
2:2.7	208
2:3.4	208
3:6.5	208
4:1.6-9	208

Mandata
10:1.4-5	208

Similitudines
1:4-6	208
6:2.3-4	208
8:6.4-5	208
8:8.1	208
8:8.2	208
8:9.1-3	208
9:19.1-3	208
9:20.2	208

Hippolytus
Refutatio omnium haeresium
6.37.6-8	87
7	145

Traditio Apostolica
21	20

Irenaeus
Adversus haereses
1.7.1,5	83
1.13.2	85
1.13.3,6	83
1.21.3-4	83
1.21.3	84
3.5.1-2	144
3.17.4	87

Justinus
Apologiae
I. 61	88
I. 61.3	83
I. 65	83, 88

Dialogus cum Tryphone
10.1	84
13.1	87
14.1	87
19.2	86-87
35.5-6	91
46-47	209
47:4	209
51:3	185

Lactantius
Divinae institutiones
4.13.21	85
4.15.3,25	85
4.18.20	85

Martyrium Polycarpi
4	207

Mileto
Homilia in passionem Christi   3

Musei Capitolini
Fragments   79-92

Gospel of Nazareans
Fragment 16   196

Origenes
Commentarii in Joann.
10.19	83
13.11	83

Pseudo-Clementines
Homiliae
2.17   5

Pseudo-Origenes
Fragmenta in Psalmos
58.17,18   87

Tertullianus
Adversus Valentin.
1   84, 87
30-32   83

Nag Hammadi Texts

CODEX I
Tripartite Tractate (I, 5)
122:12ff.   83

CODEX II
Gospel of Thomas (II, 2)

22	42
23	43
46	42
49	42
50	42
73	43
74	42-43
75	42-43
98	193

Gospel of Philip (II, 3)

16	87
47	87
66-67	87
68	83-85
73	87
76	83-84
82	86
87	83-84
102	83-84
122	83-84
123-125	87
124	83
126-127	83
127	84, 87

CODEX VII
Apocalypse of Peter (VII, 3)

70:13-84:14	46-50
70:13	51
70:14-72:4	51
70:20-32	61
70:21-25	59, 62
70:22	59
70:23-25	61, 62
71:4	62
71:9-15	59
71:14f.	63
71:21	62
71:25-27	62
72:4-84:11	51
72:5-73:14	51-52, 60
72:5-9	52
72:9-73:14	52
72:10-15	55
72:23-27	55-56
73:12-14	55
73:14-84:11	51
73:14-80:23	51-52, 57, 63
73:14-75:5	57
73:14-23	53, 58
73:23-75:7	53, 58
73:23-28	64
73:23f.	64
73:23	44
73:27	59
74:13f.	63
74:16-22	64

74:22	63	80:15f.	65
75:5-76:23	67	80:23-83:15	51, 53, 60
75:7-76:23	53, 61	80:23-82:3	53
75:7-76:4	60	80:25	55, 59
75:7-11	58	80:31	65
75:11-12	61	81:2	59
75:13	61	81:15-21	55
75:14	61	81:18	56
75:16	61	81:30-32	55
75:19-26	61	82:4-83:15	53
75:24-26	58	82:4-14	55
75:24	62	82:15-16	56
75:25	63	82:17-20	56
75:26f.	61	82:19-20	66
75:31f.	61	82:21-83:15	60
76:4-23	60	82:21-26	64
76:4-8	58	82:28f.	56
76:13	61	83:3	56-57
76:14-17	59	83:6-8	56
76:15-17	58, 63	83:8-10	56
76:15f.	61	83:13-15	56
76:21-23	57, 63	83:15-84:11	51, 61
76:24-80:23	57	83:15-84:4	53
76:24-79:31	53, 58	83:15-22	65
76:27-77:22	65	83:15-18	53
77:4-8	59	83:15	52
77:10	65	83:17	61
77:22	44	83:18	61
78:17	63	83:19-84:6	53
78:22	43	83:23	61, 63
78:31	65	83:30f.	61
79:19	43	84:7-11	53
79:21-31	64	84:12-13	51-52
79:21	65	84:12	51
79:32-80:23	53, 58	84:14	51
79:32-80:7	65		
80:2-4	64	CODEX XI	
80:3f.	44, 64	Valentinian Exposition (XI, 2)	
80:9-17	65	2:22-25	86
80:11-12	43	2:28	86

2:36-37	86
2:40	86
2:43	86

Classical Texts: Greek and Latin

Augustus
Lex Julia
18 SD	170

Lex Papia
9 SC	170

Catullus
Carmina
61-62	86
61.2	86
61.36-40	82
61.114	83
62	82
62.3	83

Cicero
Epistuae ad Quintum fratrem
II. 3.7	83

Claudianus
Fescennina
13	85

Cleomedes
De mutu
II. 1.86-87	32

Corpus Hermeticum
XI. 20	60

Dio Chrysostomos
Orationes
12	123
44.1-2	115

Epictetos
Dissertationes
2.9.19-21	144

Fragmenta
668	32

Eunapius
Vitae sophistarum
477	195

Firmicus Maternus
Libri Matheseos
II. 30,1	33
	34

Herodas
4.56	88

Homeros
Ilias
5.300	81

Odysseia
4.400	88
8.292	82

Juvenalis
6.202	83

(Pseudo-)Manilius
Astronomica
I. 25-32	31
II. 115-23	31-32
IV. 407	33-34

Pausanias
Graeciae descriptio
1.1-19   120
1.1.4   121
1.3.5   121
1.8.5   121
1.14.1   121
1.17.1   121
1.24.3   121
1.39.3   121
10.4.1   124

Pindaros
Pythia (scholion)
4.313   86

Pittacus
Epigrams in Anthologia Graeca, ed. Beckby
11.440   88

Plato
Theaetetos
162E   27

Plautus
Casina
1.1.30   82

Pliny (the Younger)
Epistulae
10.96-97   207

Plutarchos
De fato
572F-574C   30

Moralia
203 C   195

Ptolemeus
Ant. Palatina
IX. 577   31

Seneca
Suasoriae
4.1   31

Themistius
Orationes
5:71a   80, 84

Thukydides
8.53   195

Timon
Epigrams in Anthologia Graeca, ed. Beckby
11.296   88

Vettius Valens
Anthologiae
VI. 1.8f.   33
VI. 1.16   32